tea with
WINNICOTT

 INTERVIEWS WITH ICONS SERIES

tea with WINNICOTT

Brett Kahr

With illustrations by
Alison Bechdel

Routledge
Taylor & Francis Group

LONDON AND NEW YORK

First published 2016 by
Karnac Books.

Published 2018 by Routledge
2 Park Square, Milton Park, Abingdon, Oxon OX14 4RN
711 Third Avenue, New York, NY 10017, USA

Routledge is an imprint of the Taylor & Francis Group, an informa business

British Library Cataloguing in Publication Data

A C.I.P. for this book is available from the British Library

ISBN: 9781782203421 (pbk)

Edited, designed, and produced by Communication Crafts

Printed by CPI Group (UK) Ltd, Croydon CR0 4YY

To Lisa and Marcel,
Two of my most favourite pre-posthumous dramatis personae,
With deep love and affection

"... a highly satisfactory experience such as may be obtained
at a concert or at the theatre or in a friendship."

Dr Donald W. Winnicott, "The Capacity to Be Alone"
(*The International Journal of Psycho-Analysis*, 1958, p. 419)

In this new series of "posthumous interviews" we have resurrected the most famous psychoanalysts from the dead and have invited them for a frank and detailed conversation about their lives and their work.

DONALD WINNICOTT returns to his consulting room in London's Chester Square to reminisce about his childhood, his training, his work at Paddington Green Children's Hospital, his technical experiments with patients, and even the morning of his death and, also, provides readers with a comprehensive survey of his many contributions to developmental psychology and to clinical practice.

SIGMUND FREUD pays another visit to Vienna's renowned Café Landt-mann, where he had often enjoyed reading newspapers and sipping coffee. Freud explains how he came to invent psychoanalysis, speaks bluntly about his feelings of betrayal by Carl Gustav Jung, recounts his flight from the Nazis, and so much more, all the while explaining his theories of symptom formation and psychosexuality.

JOHN BOWLBY takes us on a grouse-shooting expedition – his favourite weekend passion – through the English countryside, while lambasting his colleagues for their failures to understand the true origins of mental illness.

MELANIE KLEIN teaches us some of her favourite kitchen recipes while discussing the art of talking with patients.

These posthumous interviews with icons – beautifully written, concisely composed, steeped in historical rigour, and full of hitherto unpublished archival gems – will provide students and qualified professionals alike with a master-class in psychological theory and practice, comfortably contained within one portable, affordable, and lavishly illustrated volume.

CONTENTS

ABOUT THE AUTHOR AND ILLUSTRATOR

Brett Kahr (Author) has worked in the mental health profession for over thirty-five years. He is Senior Fellow at the Tavistock Centre for Couple Relationships at the Tavistock Institute of Medical Psychology in London, and Consultant in Psychology to the Bowlby Centre. His first book on Winnicott won the Gradiva Award for Biography in 1997. His upcoming book is entitled *Winnicott's* Anni Horribiles*: The Creation of "Hate in the Counter-Transference"*, an historical study of Winnicott's famous paper. Co-Editor of the Karnac Books' "History of Psychoanalysis Series", he is also a Trustee of the Freud Museum, London. He maintains an independent practice for individuals and couples in Hampstead, North London.

Alison Bechdel (Illustrator) is an American cartoonist. Originally best known for the long-running comic strip *Dykes to Watch Out For*, she came to critical success in 2006 with her graphic memoir *Fun Home*, which was subsequently adapted as a musical and won the Tony Award for Best Musical in 2015. She is a 2014 recipient of the MacArthur "Genius" Award.

Books by Brett Kahr

D. W. Winnicott: A Biographical Portrait (1996)

Forensic Psychotherapy and Psychopathology:
Winnicottian Perspectives (Editor) (2001)

Exhibitionism (2001)

The Legacy of Winnicott:
Essays on Infant and Child Mental Health (Editor) (2002)

Sex and the Psyche (2007)

Who's Been Sleeping in Your Head?:
The Secret World of Sexual Fantasies (2008)

Life Lessons from Freud (2013)

tea with
WINNICOTT

INTRODUCTORY NOTE

Some forty-five years after Donald Winnicott's death, I had the deep privilege of meeting him for tea.

To my great delight, Dr Winnicott consented to an interview about his life and work. We talked for many hours.

I present herewith the unexpurgated transcript of our conversation, typed by his former secretary, Mrs Joyce Coles, in the hope that this might be of interest to students of psychology, psychotherapy, and psychoanalysis, and to others concerned with the care and development of babies, children, adolescents, and grown-ups.

DRAMATIS PERSONAE

DW: Dr Donald Woods Winnicott, physician, child psychiatrist, psychoanalyst, author, broadcaster, and theoretician. (Died on 25th January, 1971.)

JC: Mrs Joyce Coles, private secretary to Dr Donald Winnicott from 1948 until 1971. (Died on 1st January, 1997.)

BK: Professor Brett Kahr, interviewer. (Not yet deceased.)

Time: The Present.

Location: 87, Chester Square, Belgravia, London S.W.1.

THE INTERVIEW

"I shall never forget the cups of tea with the tea bags,
which added to the whole magic of the experience for me.
Magic, that is, when I started
but changing into something very real and unique."

Dr Colin James, Letter to Mrs Clare Winnicott, 26th January, 1971,
writing about his supervisions with Dr Donald Winnicott (James, 1971)

CUP 1

The resurrection of Dr Winnicott

BK: Mrs Coles, how can I ever thank you for arranging this meeting for me? As you know, I have always wanted to talk with Dr Winnicott.

JC: Well, I am so pleased that we could manage it.

BK: I suppose you must have gone to a great deal of trouble.

JC: No, not in the least.

BK: But surely ... a posthumous interview?

JC: It is true that these posthumous interviews are not entirely straightforward. One must arrange all these permissions with ... well, you know ...

BK: Yes, I understand.

JC: Dr Winnicott turns down most of the requests for posthumous interviews.

BK: You mean, other people have asked?

JC: Oh yes, we must receive two or three such invitations each week. Mostly from the Americans. But when I explained to Dr Winnicott that you had already written a biography about him, he told me that if I could make the arrangements, he would be willing to talk on record, just this once.

BK: Mrs Coles, you have my everlasting gratitude. I very much hope that this interview might be of use to the many students of Dr Winnicott's work who would appreciate this opportunity to hear him "live", especially those of us who never met him first time around.

JC: Between you and me, I think that Dr Winnicott agreed to this cup of tea ... oh, did I tell you that he has asked that we think of this not so much as an interview, but more as a chat over tea?

BK: That sounds absolutely fine.

JC: I think he agreed to this chat, in part, because he knows that his posthumous reputation has taken something of a bruising over that nasty business.

BK: You mean ... Masud Khan?

JC: Yes, precisely.

BK: Of course.

JC: And I think that he would like to set the record straight.

BK: Well I would hope that this posthumous interview – excuse me, this cup of tea – might give Dr Winnicott an opportunity to tell us anything that he might wish to do about his life, his work, his legacy. I had certainly planned to ask him about Masud Khan, among many, many other topics.

JC: I think that would be very satisfactory. And I am here to assist you gentlemen, I believe.

BK: You've already been such a great help.

JC: Dr Winnicott has asked me to type up the transcript. He trusts in my typing, you see. Some of these young girls from these so-called "agencies" ... Well, they can't type for toffee!

BK: We would be extremely honoured to have you prepare the

transcript of our talk. You are very generous. Tell me, is there anything in particular that I should know about Dr Winnicott – you know, his present condition – before we start? Will he get tired very easily? Does he still have cardiac pains?

JC: One of the advantages of being "posthumous" is that one does not feel the body in quite the same way, so Dr Winnicott should be just fine in that respect. But you know Dr Winnicott … he still works too hard. He continues to write, you know.

BK: Does he really?

JC: "Mrs Coles", he will say, "just because I am now the *late* Dr Donald Woods Winnicott does not mean that I haven't still got lots to say."

BK: What is he writing?

JC: A new book, I believe … endless drafts, as ever.

BK: About?

JC: Well, we've gone through so many titles, but his favourite thus far is, *How to Be Alive, Though Dead.*

BK: Good title. A reference to that wonderful *cri de coeur* from his unfinished autobiography, "Oh God! May I be alive when I die."

JC: Yes, that's the one. But frankly, I think it will be very hard to find a publisher.

BK: May I ask him about his recent writing?

JC: Yes, I don't see why not. Dr Winnicott loves to talk about his writing. He still meets with colleagues, you know, in private seminars. And they share case material, just like in the old days.

BK: Really?

JC: As I said, he still does too much. But he has so much knowledge to impart. We have mothers and babies aplenty upstairs, you know, and well …

BK: How remarkable!

JC: But look, I think I can hear him coming, perhaps I had best get the typewriter ready.

BK: Oh, but please stay to introduce us. I must confess, I'm a bit nervous, this being my first posthumous interview.

JC: Certainly. People do find these interviews a bit unsettling. But you'll soon forget that you're alive and we're deceased.

[*At this moment, Dr Donald Woods Winnicott appears, carrying a sheaf of handwritten papers.*]

DW: Good day, Mrs Coles.

JC: Good day, Dr Winnicott. Shall I take those papers from you?

DW: Yes, I don't know if these are any good, but it's a bit of scrawling. An old case history from Paddington Green – a little six-year-old boy – that I just remembered. I thought we might see if this would fit somewhere in Chapter Twenty-Nine.

JC: Very good, Dr Winnicott, I shall get straight onto this.

DW: Oh, and just in case you can't tell, this word here …

JC: You mean "incommunicado".

DW: Yes, "incommunicado".

JC: Your handwriting is still very clear to me, Dr Winnicott.

DW: Well, my pen slipped just at that moment, and I thought …

JC: Dr Winnicott, may I introduce …

DW: Ah, yes, you're the chap who's come for tea.

BK: I am so honoured to meet you Dr Winnicott.

DW: Nonsense, nonsense. A pleasure. I understand from Mrs Coles that you know a great deal about me already.

BK: Well, I have had the privilege of studying your life and your contributions for many years.

DW: Have you really? How fascinating. And Mrs Coles tells me that she gave you a whole stack of hand-painted Christmas cards that I had sent her.

JC: Well, I thought an historian would keep them safe.

DW: Splendid! I had great fun doing those every year. I love to paint.

JC: Will there be anything else, Dr Winnicott, or shall I go and see about tea?

DW: No, that will be all for now, Mrs Coles.

JC: Very good, Dr Winnicott.

[*Mrs Joyce Coles exits the consulting room.*]

BK: It feels strange to invite you to sit down in what used to be *your* old home.

DW: Good God, are we in Chester Square?

BK: Yes, Number 87.

DW: But I hardly recognise it. Someone has redecorated. But I can see, nevertheless, that this is indeed Number 87.

BK: You lived here for nearly twenty years, if I am not mistaken.

DW: Yes, and died here too, though that took rather less time. It happened very quickly, as I recall. I remember getting up in the middle of the night to use the loo, and next thing I know ... Well, mustn't grumble. It is so moving for me to be back here in this house.

BK: The new owners have very kindly allowed us to sit here in your old consulting room and have tea. They've gone out for the day, you see, and they've even given Mrs Coles full use of the kitchen.

DW: How very generous.

BK: Yes, when we told them that you would be returning for a posthumous interview, they became quite intrigued. Alas, there is still no blue plaque on the front of the house commemorating you, but the owners do like the fact that one of the world's greatest child psychologists used to live here, in their house.

DW: How very sweet.

BK: Well, shall we sit down?

DW: Over here, I suppose?

BK: Yes. If you would.

DW: This is very strange. I used to have the couch over there, against that wall, and then my chair, you see ... would have been just there by the door ... yes, this is very strange indeed.

BK: I imagine it must be. Before we begin, Dr Winnicott, would you mind if I were to tape-record our "cup of tea". I understand that Mrs Coles is on standby to prepare a transcription.

DW: Yes, she is the best person to decipher my garbled speech. That would be fine.

BK: Thank you. If you'll bear with me a moment, I'll just press this button … yes, that seems to be working.

DW: What an unusual-looking recording machine. We had much bigger, clunkier ones in my day, with lots of fussy tape that kept getting tangled.

BK: The technology has moved on somewhat.

DW: And much else too, no doubt. We do get to hear about the latest news, of course, but I don't always have time to keep up, you understand. I still see patients "upstairs", you know. It seems that there is still a great demand for what I have to offer. Being deceased is not as straightforward as one would expect – at least not from the psychological point of view. It creates its own very special anxieties.

BK: I can well imagine. So, perhaps we can begin.

DW: Shall I test the microphone to see if it is working, like we used to do at the BBC?

BK: A sound-check, yes, what a good idea.

DW: Winnicott speaking. This is Donald Winnicott speaking into the microphone.

BK: Excellent, that seems to be working just fine. Well … good day to you, Dr Winnicott. Thank you so much for agreeing to speak with me. I am most grateful.

DW: I must say that this reminds me of my days at Broadcasting House. Talking into a very large microphone. But yours is rather an unusual one. I am not used to that. But where are the sound technicians? You know, those funny little men, with headphones covering their ears, constantly checking wires.

BK: The technology has become rather more streamlined, so we do not need the technicians for this sort of informal interview.

DW: "Streamlined." Oh, I like that. But "streamlined" is not a word I remember hearing very often.

BK: Well, popular culture has moved on. If I should happen to use any words that might not make sense to you, please do stop me and let me know.

DW: Right-o! Most kind of you to think of that. Yes, I suspect that much has changed. I can see straight off the bat that your suit – it's a very nice suit – but it's not tailored in quite the same way as mine.

BK: You had a great reputation for always being very smartly dressed.

DW: Did I? Did I really?

BK: I believe that you had all of your suits handmade.

DW: How could one dress otherwise? Of course handmade.

BK: Well, shall we proceed?

DW: You know, it feels rather strange to be alive again, but I am glad of it. And how peculiar to be back in my old consulting room, here in Chester Square. I do like the new décor. It is growing on me. But my couch has gone, and so have all my toys. The toys I used in child analysis. I wonder what has happened to those. But at least there are fresh flowers. I had so many experiences in this room. I heard so many tales … so many tragic tales, you see.

BK: And helped to foster much relief as well, I suspect, for your patients.

DW: Yes, I certainly tried.

BK: Since your death, mental health professionals all around the world have become increasingly interested in your work – in all aspects of your work – and I thought it would be a great treat for us to hear you speak.

DW: How kind. Is my work really well known now, or have people forgotten me?

BK: I think it fair to say that you have become immortal, and that your name now sits beside those of Sigmund Freud and Carl Gustav Jung in the pantheon of great psychologists.

DW: I am a bit embarrassed … but only a bit. This is very gratifying to hear.

BK: Perhaps we could begin by discussing your personal history, if you have no objection. I know that shortly before your death in 1971, you had begun to write an autobiography …

DW: Oh, yes, that's right. Let me see … if I remember, I had planned to call it *Not Less Everything*. I made a good start of it, but never quite finished. What with my illness and all of that, I simply didn't have the time.

BK: Well, I hope that this interview might give you an opportunity to tell us about your remarkable life, and to share some of the highlights of what you might have written if you had completed your autobiography.

DW: Yes, what a good idea.

BK: Your autobiography came to my mind because I know from the fragments which did survive that you had begun the book with a wonderful phrase. If you recall, you wrote a prayer, "Oh God! May I be alive when I die."

DW: Yes, that could be my credo … perhaps everyone's credo. Being alive when one dies is very important. Of course, I didn't mean that *solely* as a primitive denial of death. We all wish to deny death. But I suppose I also wanted to celebrate the importance of aliveness when so many people feel themselves to be dead inside.

BK: Your whole body of work really celebrates the possibilities of human aliveness, of creativity, of playfulness.

DW: Yes, that's right. I like to play.

BK: And I gather from your secretary, Mrs Coles, that you are still writing? And that you are working on a book about *How to Be Alive, Though Dead*?

DW: Yes, that is the book. And that is the human challenge: *How to Be Alive, Though Dead*. Play helps, you know. Play, to me, is the ultimate expression of aliveness.

BK: You have become intimately linked in the minds of all psychological professionals with the concept of play and its importance.

DW: As I said, I like to play. We've already mentioned those hand-painted Christmas cards. I stayed up very late at night painting those. That was play, you see. Clare – my wife – used to chastise me for going to bed so late, but as I have already told you, I really enjoyed painting.

BK: Your Christmas cards are truly wonderful – so vibrant, so colourful.

DW: How remarkable that you should have all of Mrs Coles's Christmas cards. Remind me how you came to meet her? You knew her, I believe, before she became posthumous, like me?

BK: Yes, I met Mrs Coles back in 1994, a few years before her death on New Year's Day, 1997. A child psychoanalyst from the Anna Freud Centre – Miss Irmi Elkan …

DW: I remember Miss Elkan. Is she … you know?

BK: Yes, Miss Elkan passed away some years ago. She lived to a ripe old age … ninety years, in fact.

DW: I haven't seen her yet "upstairs" … so many people to meet, you understand … literally billions and billions.

BK: Yes, I can imagine.

DW: But Miss Elkan put you in touch with Mrs Coles? They would have known each other through me, I suppose.

BK: Yes, Miss Elkan had indeed put me in touch with Mrs Coles, and then I went to see Mrs Coles at her flat in Ealing, in West London, many times, and she kindly allowed me to conduct a very full series of interviews about her experience of working for you. I must confess, I rather fell in love with Mrs Coles – what a gracious lady. So kind, so generous, so observant. She really fired up my interest in you as a person as well as a thinker, and that set me on course to write your biography.

DW: How fascinating. We must talk about the biography that you wrote about me. What is it called?

BK: *D. W. Winnicott: A Biographical Portrait* – a rather straightforward title.

DW: Best not to be vague, I suppose.

BK: It appeared in 1996, on the occasion of your centenary. In retrospect, I think that I should have chosen a more whimsical title.

DW: I often wondered whether anyone would ever come to write my story. How fascinating. But back to Mrs Coles. She is ... or should I say *was* ... I never quite know the protocol. She was, at any rate, a wonderful woman.

BK: Indeed.

DW: She and I would infuriate each other, you know, but only a little. In over fifty years, I never had a better secretary. But getting back to the painting, you must know that I didn't paint particularly well, but I had so much fun doing it. Clare – as I said – used to give me quite a hard time about it. I was ill with heart disease. Forgive me, I'm repeating myself.

BK: Not at all, Dr Winnicott.

DW: Speaking of Mrs Coles, I wonder whether she has managed to sort out some tea yet? I wouldn't mind a cup? And perhaps a biscuit? And you, I presume?

BK: Yes, thank you.

DW: I'll just ring for Mrs Coles, shall I? You know, she and I worked side-by-side from 1948 until my death in 1971. Together we consumed more tea and more cigarettes than I could possibly recall. Do you smoke?

BK: No. No, I don't.

DW: In my time, it would be unthinkable to practise psychoanalysis without a cigarette. Back in the 1920s and 1930s, even into the 1950s and 1960s, we all smoked – doctors and patients alike. I used to keep extra cigarettes in my consulting room for patients, in case they had forgotten to bring their own. And I always ensured that the patient had a separate ashtray, perched on the edge of the couch, and that I had *my* own ashtray. Sharing an ashtray with a patient might be too intimate, don't you think?

BK: No one smokes in session nowadays. We have learned so much about the links between smoking and a whole variety of illnesses, not least cancer.

DW: That is something that I managed to avoid. No cancers, but plenty of coronaries. I did rather well to make it to seventy-four, in spite of having had quite a few of those nasty heart things.

BK: Indeed you did.

DW: But look, you don't want to hear about Christmas cards and heart attacks. What is it that you think you want to know?

BK: Well, I wonder if we could attempt to explore your life and your work – a vast undertaking, I realise – but I have so many questions. My colleagues would really enjoy coming to learn about you in a more personal, more direct way. And students need to come to know you too.

DW: How very lovely. Yes, certainly. I am at your disposal.

[*At this juncture, Mrs Coles enters the consulting room with a tray of tea cups, a tea pot, a jug of milk, several spoons, and a plate of biscuits.*]

DW: Mrs Coles, how simply splendid. Now we have tea. Thank you, Mrs Coles. Oh, and look, you've brought my favourite kind of tea cup, the really large ones. Mrs Coles has not forgotten that I love especially large tea cups. I always thought that one can have so much more tea that way. But I've not seen this particular cup before.

JC: No, Dr Winnicott. These large cups belong to the new owners.

DW: Of course they do. How silly of me.

BK: Dr Winnicott, one of your former clinical supervisees told me that he really struggled when you served him tea in one of these big cups during a supervision session, because he felt compelled to drink it all, and then he had to pee very badly, but he felt too intimidated to excuse himself mid-session!

DW: Oh dear, that is awkward. Poor chap. He should have said something.

JC: Will there be anything else, Dr Winnicott?

DW: Have you made a stab at Chapter Twenty-Nine? I don't suppose you've had much time yet.

JC: Oh yes, Dr Winnicott. I've typed up those pages already. With a carbon copy, just as you like, ready for you to revise. I managed to find some of those old typewriter ribbons – with the typeface that you prefer.

DW: Thank you Mrs Coles. Very decent of you. I suppose there are no letters needing my attention?

JC: No, Dr Winnicott.

DW: You know that after I died in 1971, I did continue to receive letters for many months, including quite a few requests to give lectures, mostly in America, of course. I suppose that not everyone – especially the Americans – had heard about my death straight away.

BK: You may not remember, Dr Winnicott, but you died in the midst of a very prolonged postal strike.

DW: Really? I am a bit hazy.

BK: Yes, the Royal Mail went on strike. So it took some time for foreigners to learn about your passing.

DW: But they've cottoned on by now, I should think.

JC: Yes, Dr Winnicott.

DW: And those letters from America inviting me to lecture … I believe Mrs Coles told them that I would not be available. Isn't that so, Mrs Coles?

JC: Yes, Dr Winnicott. You had many letters, even one from the American College of Neuropsychiatrists.

DW: How fascinating! I am not entirely certain that I know what a neuropsychiatrist is. But I know with certainty that I am *not* one of those. Well thank you, Mrs Coles. I'll give a shout when we need more tea. Oh, I couldn't ask you for a cigarette, could I?

JC: Dr Winnicott! Mrs Winnicott would be horrified if I gave you …

DW: Very well, then, Mrs Coles, that will be all for now.

[*Mrs Coles exits the consulting room.*]

BK: Mrs Coles had really looked after you.

DW: Still does, it would seem! Oh, yes, she is a prize. She had worked as a secretary for a lady physician before coming to me, so Mrs Coles had already acquired quite a bit of experience of looking after doctors. What a relief that I found her. She did so much for me: typing my letters, doing the invoices for my patients, typing my papers, even bringing my car into the garage for servicing. All sorts of lovely things.

CUP 2

The making of a maverick

BK: Are you enjoying the tea?

DW: Yes, it is ages since I've had a cup like this. Most pleasant, really. Most pleasant. So, shall we return to our interview ... our posthumous cup of tea?

BK: Perhaps we could start by discussing your early life.

DW: Well, I was born in 1896 ... during the very twilight of the old Queen's reign.

BK: Queen Victoria, of course.

DW: Yes, Queen Victoria. I was too young to *remember* her Diamond Jubilee in 1897 – I would have been a baby, and not yet able to read newspapers – but I suspect that there would have been quite a lot of excitement about it all, and I think I might have been aware of the excitement. But I do remember the huge fuss over her death, a few years later, in 1901. All the newspapers were published with a black border round the rim, as a mark of respect, honour, and mourning.

BK: A very different moment in British history.

DW: Oh, yes, we grew up in a period of great ignorance of anything psychological back then. We were not psychological, but we were reverent. We respected our elders.

BK: How would you describe parenting during the very late nineteenth century?

DW: Back then, parents did their best, I believe, but they knew nothing, absolutely nothing, about the mind of the child. Wealthy parents abandoned their children to governesses and nannies, whereas those without financial resources left their children to roam the streets. Most parents tried to do their best, but they did not understand that children could be *meaningful* and worth getting to know in *detail*.

BK: I like the idea that a good parent must come to know the child in a detailed way, as opposed to a generalised way.

DW: Absolutely so. Observing the most minute twists and turns of the baby, and listening to the tiniest gurgles and babblings – well, that is the art of motherhood, I think.

BK: Would it be fair to say that very few infants and children enjoyed the security of what you would later come to call the "holding environment" and the "facilitating environment"?

DW: I can see that you *have* read my work. Jolly good. Yes, that is absolutely right. A baby needs a mother or a father to be available – reliably so. Reliability is the very essence of good child-care, as well as the very heart of good psychoanalytic clinical practice. But returning to me, I suppose that as far as Victorian childhoods go, I had one of the better ones. I never suffered profound abandonment of any kind – no parental deaths, no unbearable bereavements. I had a lot of provision of continuity.

BK: You followed two older sisters.

DW: Yes, my parents – Frederick Winnicott and Elizabeth Woods Winnicott – had three children in all: my older sisters Violet and Kathleen – whom I always called "V" and "K" for short – followed by yours truly. You must understand that I had a great deal of looking-after in my childhood. As the baby of the family, I received quite a lot of attention from my mother, from my older sisters, and from all the other women who lived in our house: an aunt or two from time to time, and a whole gaggle of female servants – not unusual back then – including a cook, a governess for my sisters, a nanny for me – and some housemaids.

BK: You maintained a long-standing correspondence with your nanny, I believe?

DW: I loved my nanny, and I really did keep an interest in her all my life.

BK: I believe that you came to think of your nanny and all these other women – mother, sisters, aunts, servants – as your "multiple mothers".

DW: Yes, I often spoke of them that way. I had the benefit of not one mother, but maybe eleven! Not only did I get a lot of mothering from the women and girls at Rockville – that was the name of our house in Plymouth – but my aunt and uncle and all my cousins lived literally next door. Uncle Richard and his family … So I had an immense amount of caretaking from a literal village of Winnicotts. Of course, we all felt very much at home in Plymouth – very embedded in Plymouth – having been there quite a long time. My father devoted the whole of his life to public service for Plymouth. He became Mayor twice, as did my uncle Richard, and before that both had served as justices of the peace and as aldermen. They virtually ran Plymouth. So I would describe the family as very well settled. And Uncle Richard had lots of children, who became my playmates.

BK: It seems as though you had very little time to be alone. I know that in the late 1950s you wrote about aloneness and togetherness in your essay, "The Capacity to Be Alone", one of your most brilliant papers.

DW: Well, in spite of all of the attention, and all of the opportunity for relating, I did find quiet moments, which I came to relish. I played the piano a lot, you know, and that required concentration and solitude – especially when playing Beethoven. One really can lose oneself in Beethoven, don't you know? But of course, one can also find oneself in Beethoven. But alongside music, I liked to play outdoors and swim, what with Plymouth being on the coast and all that.

BK: Thinking about your "multiple mothers" and your search for solitude in order to play …

DW: Would you care for a spot more tea?

BK: How kind. Yes, thank you.

DW: And do you take milk in your tea?

BK: Yes, some milk would be lovely.

DW: I'm guessing no sugar for you. Everyone is so health-conscious, it would seem, what with all this no smoking business!

BK: No. No sugar for me, thank you. So … you had this very rich, very full, very well-observed childhood, with lots of caretakers and lots of playmates. Can you tell me about your parents as personalities? I have a much clearer picture of your father, as he lived a very long life, and he wrote you many letters, which I have read, but your mother died at a relatively young age, and consequently she remains a much more shadowy figure to historians.

DW: You know, I spent so many years in psychoanalysis – ten years with Mr Strachey, and then quite a few years more with Mrs Riviere – I wonder what else I can say about my parents … very difficult to sum them up, you see. You are quite right, my father is in many ways a much more straightforward figure. If you had known him, you would have found him delightful. He had endless energy, great generosity and huge warmth and, also, a certain benignity about him. Everyone loved him. They made him a knight, you know, and he became *Sir* Frederick Winnicott. We all rather enjoyed that. My mother accompanied him to the investiture at Buckingham Palace, and he met King George – King George V, you know, not his son, who was also King George. But of course, Father had met the King on other occasions. As Mayor of Plymouth, he hosted all the visiting dignitaries, including the young Prince of Wales, the one who later gave up the throne for Mrs Simpson.

BK: Yes, of course.

DW: I'm waffling, am I not? I often do. That is how my mind works. It meanders. I don't think in straight lines. I think in curves. But where were we? Oh, yes, my father. So I think I would describe my father as a rather good man, but also as a busy man. Sometimes, I would see him only at weekends, and sometimes only on the way to church of a Sunday. He had so many committees to look after … so many.

BK: You, too, became a very dedicated committee person during the peak of your professional years.

DW: Yes, I suppose I did. I served on the Training Committee, the Scientific Committee, the Publications Committee, and various others at our Institute of Psycho-Analysis. And I held the Presidency of the British Psycho-Analytical Society twice … and we mustn't forget the Presidency of the Paediatrics Section of the RSM.

BK: That would be the Royal Society of Medicine.

DW: Yes, the Royal Society of Medicine, on Wimpole Street. And oh, yes, I almost forgot, I had also been President of the Medical Section of the British Psychological Society. We mustn't leave that one out! Yes, I suppose that I rather followed my father's example, taking on all these leadership posts, and more besides. I think I made quite a hash out of some of those jobs. But I think I may have been … well, shall we say, if not a *good* President, then at least a *good-enough* President.

BK: Clearly, both you and Sir Frederick had a tremendous capacity for creative work.

DW: I would like to think so.

BK: And Lady Winnicott, your mother?

DW: Well, we had a more complicated relationship, and I am not sure that I can do it full justice today.

BK: You wrote a poem about her towards the end of your life – "The Tree".

DW: My goodness, how did you come to read "The Tree"? I sent that to my brother-in-law Jimmy … Jimmy Britton, Clare's brother. I can't quite remember why, but I do remember writing that poem, very clearly.

BK: After your death, your wife Clare and Mrs Coles spent a great deal of time organising your papers and your letters into a very impressive archive. I believe that Mrs Winnicott destroyed some of your more intimate papers and letters, but she and Mrs Coles lovingly preserved literally tens and tens of thousands of papers and notes and correspondence, including some of your poetry and your doggerel. And also, some of your drawings.

DW: How remarkable. And people can read these papers? My private papers? And my case notes? Those are very confidential, you know.

BK: Well, you will be relieved to know that most of your patient records remain under lock and key. Mrs Coles told me that she spent many, many hours going through the case notes with a black marker pen, covering up the names of your many patients.

DW: I suppose that took her ages. But she would be just the right person to do that. Joyce had so much discretion. She never, ever blabbed about any of my patients, and I did have some well-known people come to see me over the years … some quite well-known people, in fact.

BK: You had begun to tell me about your mother, and about your poem, "The Tree".

DW: Well, that's the poem in which I describe my mother as "weep-ing". I suppose you want to know if I found her depressed. Well, I think she was. Not clinically depressed, you understand … not psychiatrically depressed … but still, she was depressed. Three children, an often-absent or preoccupied husband, and a huge household to manage, as well as all her civic commitments. She also ran committees – the ladies' committees in Plymouth. She even started a group for impoverished mothers and their babies, don't you know? And she would sometimes cook, even though we had a cook at Rockville. My mother did love to make jam. Alice – I suspect you know that Alice is my first wife?

BK: Yes, I know of Alice.

DW: Well, Alice got on very well with my mother – extremely well, I would say – and they used to make jam together. Is this the sort of picture you want? Is this useful?

BK: Yes, very much so. Thank you.

DW: But my mother – in spite of all her ego-strength – and she had quite a lot of that – in spite of her ego-strength, she had this very private depression. I don't really know from whence it came, but she had it, and I sensed it.

BK: I know it must be rather difficult to speak about your parents in the context of an interview of this kind, especially as you have already spent so many years in psychoanalysis talking about your parents in a much more intimate way.

DW: That's right, of course. But the main point we should stress is that whatever their capacities, whatever their foibles, my mother and father managed to give me enough of what I needed. I mean, they held me, they handled me, and they introduced me to the world. They gave me a foundation so that I could just *be*. And so that I could carry on *being*. You know, when the beginning is good, then all the rest can follow.

BK: So you had a "good-enough" childhood, to use your phrase?

DW: Oh yes, I had a "good-enough" childhood … and then some. But one doesn't want to boast, especially as most of the children that I saw at The Green did not.

BK: That would be the Paddington Green Children's Hospital in West London, where you worked for forty years.

DW: We always called it "The Green". It catered to the most wretched and the most deprived families from Paddington and the surrounding areas. These children grew up in poverty, in violence. They came from very harsh backgrounds. Some had good-enough homes, it must be said, but many did not. So compared to them, I had a very easy time of it. But you are right to remind me about "The Tree", because in that poem … now do

I remember it properly? Oh, yes – "Mother below is weeping / weeping / weeping / Thus I knew her." My mother did have a sadness about her, and I think that as a little boy I had already become a psychoanalyst, a fledgling psychoanalyst of sorts, trying to find a way to be with her in her sadness.

BK: I suppose that some colleagues might wonder whether growing up surrounded by "multiple mothers" had not only advantages, but also its shadows.

DW: Well, you are right, I suppose. We all have complicated aspects of our biographies that we must navigate. But on the whole, my parents did give me the foundations.

BK: And did your parents have a huge impact on your ultimate choice of career?

DW: Yes, I suppose they did. Not directly, you understand. Of course, when my parents came of age, no one knew anything about psychiatry and certainly not anything at all about psychoanalysis. Even psychiatry at that time ... well, it was pretty rudimentary, pretty unimpressive. Psychiatrists – actually, we called them "alienists" – they hadn't a clue about babies or about the unconscious. We didn't have a proper profession of psychiatry in those days. And psychoanalysis ... well, that had only just got going in Vienna. Only *just*, you understand.

BK: So you became an honorary psychoanalyst, almost before the invention of psychoanalysis.

DW: Yes I did. By having to be attentive to my mother, and by having to be a good public servant like my father, I suppose it was only natural that I found my way to psychoanalysis, Freud's psychoanalysis. That profession gave me a chance to look after others, and also, with my own analysis, to have a chance to have myself looked after as well.

BK: The Winnicotts prided themselves, so I understand, on public service. Does this relate to your religious background, to your Wesleyan Methodism?

DW: Absolutely so. Do you know about Plymouth and its Methodists?

BK: Well, I have had to learn …

DW: All my family are Methodists … *were* Methodists, I should say … and it really gave us a platform, a base of belief, and a wish to do good work. John Wesley started it off, back in the eighteenth century. He was, as I suppose you must know, an itinerant preacher, a lecturer. And he went round and round all of England preaching about the importance of good works. In many ways, he anticipated modern social services. He also wrote about "physick", you know, medicine. So he was a kind of doctor of the soul and of the body. I think Wesley influenced me greatly. He wanted people to do good, to be Good Samaritans, I suspect. And all the Winnicotts took that as a duty – a sacred duty. We all found a way of doing good.

BK: Your father, I suppose, did "good" through his public works in Plymouth. He helped establish the library in Plymouth, and the museum, as well, if I am not mistaken.

DW: Yes, indeed, he did. And so much more. You know, if you visit Plymouth, you will see his name etched into the foundation stones of various buildings. I think one could call him not just a Good Samaritan but, rather, a *great* Samaritan.

BK: And your sisters did goodly works too.

DW: Oh yes, you couldn't stop V. and K. I think they had more energy than all of us. If they had been not born girls, they might have become doctors too. By which I mean girls *at that time* in history. Both very bright girls, V. and K. … they tended to the wounded soldiers during the Great War. They made bandages, they ran scout troops, they did everything, really. They did a lot of good work in the '39–'45 war too. Always helping. They learned first aid. Extraordinary sisters, really! Altogether, the Winnicotts made an impression on Plymouth, and that would be our Methodism … our commitment to goodly works. I did mine through children's medicine and through psychological work. I could just as easily have become a minister of some sort, but I needed psychoanalysis to cure me – I had my problems, you know, personal problems – and so I found my way to psycho-analysis.

BK: Methodism clearly had a huge impact. In fact, your parents sent you away to a Methodist boarding school at the age of fourteen.

DW: The Leys ... lovely Leys.

BK: The Leys School in Cambridge.

DW: Yes, that is where I had many very happy times. Although you wouldn't know it to look at my aged body, I used to be quite an athlete – running, footer, all the rest – I really inhabited my body as a young man, and so I played a lot of sport at school, and also made a lot of music. I loved the piano, and I played in the chapel whenever I could. I sometimes gave concerts. I played all sorts of music, Beethoven and such. I even learned more modern pieces, you know, like MacDowell.

BK: Edward MacDowell?

DW: Yes, he wrote such tender piano sketches, don't you think? I loved working on those. But yes, Methodism occupied us greatly at the Leys. The school certainly reinforced the tradition of Wesleyan Methodism.

BK: But I know that you regarded yourself not only as a Methodist, but also as a Lollard.

DW: You know about me and Lollardy? You seem to know a great deal about me.

BK: Well, I became interested in your work as a young student – passionately interested in fact – and then I began to study your writings, and that led me to interview many of your surviving colleagues about you and your contributions.

DW: I hope I haven't bored you.

BK: Quite the opposite. The more I have learned about you, Dr Winnicott, the more absorbed I have become in your work and in your world.

DW: You're very kind. But I know nothing about you. Do tell me something, please.

BK: Well, I am happy to tell you about my background, but perhaps in the first instance we can carry on with our conversation about you, because my colleagues will be very disappointed otherwise.

DW: Lollards, was it?

BK: Yes, the Lollards. You wrote a very revealing letter towards the end of your life in which you described yourself, quite bluntly, as a Lollard. I suppose not everyone will know about the Lollards.

DW: Well, the Lollards ... let me see ... they date back to the Middle Ages, I think – they were the first English dissenters. They objected to the Catholic Church and to all the pomp and ritual of popery. The Lollards absolutely loathed all the corruption in the Catholic Church, long before Henry VIII shut it down. Also, you see, they wanted to offer prayer in *English*, not in Latin, so that the real people – not just the monks and priests – could study religion. Lollards had their own minds. We don't appreciate how shocking it would have been to preach in English back in those days. Latin had completely dominated Catholicism. One couldn't find an English-language prayer book at all!

BK: Perhaps one could think of the Lollards as the medieval equivalent of the "Middle Group" or "Independent Group" of mental health professionals, the group to which you came to belong within the British Psycho-Analytical Society.

DW: Not only *belonged* to, but also helped to *found*, don't you know. Yes, I really started the "Middle Group". I hated the rigidities of my psychoanalytic colleagues. I hated their orthodoxies. Miss Freud – a real genius, like her father – thought that one could help children only in five-times-weekly analysis. She never had much time for my work doing brief therapeutic consultations. But I had no option. As a busy hospital doctor, I had *thousands* upon *thousands* of children to treat, and she didn't. She had a very small nursery – very small indeed. And Mrs Klein ... Melanie, dear Melanie ... she had her rigidities aplenty. She also saw only a *tiny* number of children. And she had her own way of working and of preaching, you understand. But perhaps we'll come to that. I wanted an arena where people could think psychoanalytically in a more independent way, not enslaved to the dogmatism and "popery" of Miss Freud and Mrs Klein, if you will. So in that respect, I am a natural Lollard.

BK: So, the Lollards and the Methodists helped to inculcate a love of dissent.

DW: Absolutely. I love dissent. I love to disagree. But I also love to be disagreed *with*. I never saw disagreement as an attack. I always saw it as a real opportunity to understand one's own position and that of one's adversaries … a real opportunity to know what one thinks. We need more dissent, I think, especially in psychoanalysis. Otherwise, we shall become too stodgy, too tame. And I fear we have become that already.

BK: I know that you really distinguished yourself in the profession for having a very open mind. I remember reading some unpublished documentation in the archives about whether the British Psycho-Analytical Society should offer training to *psychotherapists* as well as to *psychoanalysts*, and most of your colleagues voted against the idea. But you always advocated sharing knowledge with the widest possible number of people, and you really supported the fledgling psychotherapy movement in Great Britain, whereas many of your colleagues regarded the psychotherapists as a threat.

DW: Yes, we engaged in lots of wars, lots of fights about ownership. My colleagues often thought that only they had the anointed right to practise psychology. But because of my Methodism, because of my natural Lollardy, I always did absolutely everything that I could do in order to share my knowledge as widely as possible. We need more than just a few hundred psychoanalysts to change the mental health of the country.

BK: Perhaps we can return to your chronology, Dr Winnicott. What else can you remember from your time at the Leys School?

DW: I told you about sport. And I told you about music. But I haven't mentioned my academics, and you haven't asked. If truth be told, I was not a great scholar. Oh, I was smart enough to get through, but I did not have the sort of brain that could master knowledge in a tidy way. My mind wanders too much and strays too far afield. I think horizontally, not vertically, and I always had a devil of a time remembering endless lists of historical facts. But I did all right. Well enough to go to university afterwards.

BK: You encountered the works of Charles Darwin during your time at the Leys School, I believe?

DW: Yes, I used my pocket money to purchase some editions of Darwin from the Cambridge bookstalls. Cambridge had so many second-hand bookstalls in those days.

BK: What appealed to you, in particular, about Darwin?

DW: When I began to read his works, I felt that I had met someone I could really understand. Not in a bookish way – I couldn't tell you what he wrote on page such-and-such – but in an essential way. I engaged with quite a lot of Darwin. You know he wrote a great deal about hatred. About how we hate.

BK: That became a very important thematic for you throughout your writings.

DW: Yes, but not only that. I enjoyed Darwin for other reasons, too.

BK: Please tell us.

DW: Well, Darwin, you see, spoke about this inexorable unfolding of human development, about the development of the species. One didn't have to *do* anything special to humans ... shape them, stretch them, mould them ... nothing like that. They would simply evolve slowly, naturally, over time. And that is what I came to find with babies and with human physical development and human psychological development. One does not have to *do* anything to a baby. One can just *be* with a baby, and miraculously, the baby will grow.

BK: You disagreed harshly with child-care "experts", such as the New Zealander Truby King, who made all sorts of practical suggestions about what a mother should or should not "do".

DW: Did you ever meet Henry Dicks of the Tavistock Clinic? A younger colleague of mine.

BK: Sadly, no.

DW: Dicks once said that Truby King was single-handedly responsible for the development of Nazism, and I think he may have a point. Of course King did not cause National Socialism, you understand, but he did epitomise a certain cruel sort of parental paedagogy. All that bodily rigidity. And all those stiff salutes. Those postures come from harsh treatment of the infant's body. And neglect of the infant's body as well. Yes, I have a great hatred for Truby King and for his people. They would advise mothers to adopt very rigid routines of feeding, sleeping, and so forth, and they insisted that mothers must not touch their babies.

BK: It seems quite incredible from our perspective that physicians could have endorsed such a philosophy.

DW: Shocking, I know. But Truby King had mothers treat their babies as objects and not as persons back then. In fact, under his influence, parents came to relate to their babies not only as objects but as *detestable* objects, to boot.

BK: So, unlike Charles Darwin, who allowed development to unfold, Truby King tried to shape the infant's growth in a very artificial, very calculated way.

DW: Yes, Darwin helped me to see that one need not do much, and that development will proceed just fine on its own. Truby King should have read more Darwin.

BK: I really admire the creative and original way in which you allowed yourself to "use" Darwin and to derive inspiration from Darwin.

DW: Well, people are there to be "used", and this can be done in a good way as well as a bad way.

BK: You also made great friends – lifelong friends – at the Leys School.

DW: One friend in particular, Jim Ede. Of course back then we all called him Stanley. His full name was Harold Stanley Ede. He became "Jim" only in later years. That took some getting used to. But we were best friends … best friends throughout life. Yes, we had a very intimate friendship.

BK: You shared the same birthday, I believe?

DW: April the seventh. That's correct. Albeit one year apart. He was born in 1895, and I was born in 1896.

BK: And Ede became a noted art historian and art lecturer.

DW: He virtually discovered quite a number of the modern artists, you know – people such as Henri Gaudier-Brzeska, and Constantin Brâncuşi ... he discovered them for English audiences. A very fine art historian, Jim was. Worked at the Tate gallery for many years. He made the Tate purchase Brâncuşi pieces long before anyone knew how valuable those statues would become. Then Jim and his family moved to Tangier in Morocco, and Alice, my first wife, and I used to visit him ... must have been back in the 1930s. A very long time ago.

BK: And you became a godfather to his children?

DW: Elisabeth and Mary. Such lively, healthy girls. Elisabeth became a doctor, don't you know? Perhaps I had some influence there. And Mary became a mother, I believe. Jim and his wife Helen used to travel a great deal, and sometimes they left the girls with me and Alice, because we all lived near to one another.

BK: In Hampstead, in North London.

DW: Yes, that's right. You know, once I even asked whether I could adopt Elisabeth and Mary – beautiful, lovely girls – but Jim refused.

BK: You never had children of your own, yet you worked with more than 20,000 children.

DW: Yes, I would have welcomed fatherhood, but it never happened. This has been a great sadness to me. But I have had many, many children in my life, and some I have even helped. You know, thinking about Leys days, the other important fact about the Leys is that it gave me a great hankering to go university in Cambridge. Perhaps I could have gone to Oxford, perhaps not, but I really wanted to go to Cambridge. Having been a schoolboy at the Leys for four years – you know, it is right in the centre of Cambridge town – I fell in love with those majestic buildings, and with those little medieval streets, perfect for cycling, which I love too – and so I knew that I had to go to university in Cambridge. And so I did. I was not clever enough to get a scholarship, but I got a place all the same.

BK: You graduated from the Leys School in 1914, and after the summer holidays you matriculated to Jesus College, one of the oldest colleges in the University of Cambridge.

DW: Yes, Archbishop Cranmer – Henry VIII's archbishop – he went to Jesus College. Did you know that? He was a reformer, like me, I suppose. Anyway, it pleased me greatly to have got through my admissions interview with the Master, Arthur Gray, a strange duck who wrote ghost stories in his spare time. But I got a place at Jesus, and so I went.

BK: You had a somewhat unusual experience of university, because just prior to your matriculation, war had erupted throughout Europe.

DW: Yes, shortly before I arrived, the Serbs went mad, the Austrians went mad, and then the Germans went mad, and I suppose that we did too – the English – and then we declared war. So by the time I went up to Cambridge, most of my contemporaries – all those fine young men – had already enlisted.

BK: I believe that you did not enlist in the services.

DW: No, I was a medico, you see, by which I mean a medical student, and I had a long road ahead in order to become a physician. And we medics were given special exemption. The country knew that doctors would be needed, and so I took up my place at university. I could have enlisted, of course – many future doctors did – but I thought I might be more useful as a medic than as a sailor. If I were to have enlisted at that time, it would have been in the Royal Navy.

BK: Of course, you grew up in coastal Plymouth, with the Royal Navy right on your doorstep.

DW: It would have been unthinkable for a Plymouth man to do anything else. We knew the Royal Navy only too well, and various Winnicotts had served in the Royal Navy for many, many years. I had at least one ancestor who worked in the dockyards … probably quite a few more, I shouldn't wonder. So if I *had* joined up in 1914, it would have been the Navy. Of course, I did join up eventually, but not for another three years or so.

BK: You began your course in Natural Sciences – the pre-clinical requirement for medical training.

DW: Yes, at Cambridge we studied anatomy, physiology, botany, even zoology … all of the basic sciences, I suppose. I didn't enjoy it particularly much, and I just scraped through. I suppose that even then I wanted to relate to people – real people, with real personalities – not chemical elements and bones and teeth and skulls and body parts. Oh, it was interesting enough all right, but I wanted people with biographies, with histories behind them. I couldn't really get on with people at the cellular level, and I still can't. But I got through the course, albeit with only a third-class degree at the end of it all.

BK: But your course of study at Cambridge gave you the foundations for your ultimate work in children's medicine and then, years later, in psychoanalysis.

DW: Yes, the Cambridge medical course allowed me to become a doctor. But my training kept getting interrupted, you see, because we had to work at the field hospital in Cambridge for wounded soldiers, who had just returned from the front. Virtually the whole of the university became transformed into a hospital, with sick bays put up in the college quads and all of that. It was a mad time. But we got through.

BK: You spoke of the Serbs being mad, and the Germans being mad …

DW: Look, we all carry great hatred around with us. And most of us manage to turn our hatred into words. But back in 1914, the whole world went mad, with too much hatred, too much madness, and it all exploded. Perhaps we had felt so guilty at all the peace that we had had in the run-up to the war. Perhaps we in Great Britain felt guilty about all the lands that we had conquered and colonised. You know that we used to own fully one-fourth of the world with our great British Empire – Queen Victoria's empire. And then, when we saw the other countries, the Germans and the Russians, trying to gain control in the Balkans … well, we didn't like that. Whatever the reason – and here, you would need to speak to historians and politicians, as well as to psychologists – we all went mad.

BK: And you lost many friends.

DW: Virtually all of my schoolmates from the Leys died in combat or from disease. And virtually all of the young chaps who should have been my classmates at Jesus College died too. I often felt myself to be the sole survivor. And because of that, I pledged to devote myself even more wholeheartedly to public works, to medical practice, to the care of the ill and the dying. I felt as though I owed it to my friends, to my "lost generation". I resolved that I would do not only my own work, but also the work that they would have done, had they lived, these young men who lost their lives.

BK: You had to endure many painful bereavements. How did you manage? How did you find support for yourself?

DW: Well, I didn't. We just got on with it. We had to. I was too busy even to think while studying at Cambridge. Not only did I have to learn all about the natural sciences, but I also worked long hours in that makeshift hospital with the soldiers. Hundreds and hundreds of wounded soldiers poured into Cambridge, with very few doctors and very few nurses to care for them. Most of the medics and the nurses had gone off to the front to fight ... well, not to fight as such but rather to deal with those who did fight and who did get injured. So we young students, left behind in Cambridge, well, we had to do quite a lot of the basic looking-after.

BK: You must have seen horrific injuries.

DW: Dreadful injuries ... just dreadful ... and most of the time, we could do nothing for these men, at least not from a medical point of view. Many lost legs and arms and eyes. Many had their faces blown to bits. It was absolutely devastating. I would often just sit and talk to the men, and we would have ordinary conversations. Sometimes I would play the piano. They were so dead inside, these soldiers, and they needed enlivening. They rather liked me at the piano, and so I played. Do you know "Apple Dumplings?" ... a funny little song from that time. That became a real favourite with the men in Cambridge. "Apple Dumplings, Apple Dumplings, dee-dee-dee-dee-dah-dah-dah.

Apple Dumplings, Apple …" Oh dear, I've plain forgotten the words. I used to know all the choruses by heart. That song goes on for ages with chorus after chorus, but I can't remember it at all. It has been almost a hundred years since I last sang that one!

BK: It might amuse you to know, Dr Winnicott, that back in 1996, when I published the biography that I wrote about you, we had a launch party for the book at the Tavistock Clinic. And knowing of your love for the song "Apple Dumplings", we tracked down the music, and I got the Tavistock Clinic Choir to sing this song to all the guests.

DW: Oh, I do like the sound of that. I wish I could have heard it: "Apple Dumplings, Apple Dumplings, dee-dee-dah-dah-dee-dee-dee." How marvellous. Are you a musician too?

BK: Yes, I play piano. In fact, although your psychoanalytic work has long interested me, I became even more engaged with your writings when I discovered your great love of music.

DW: How did you know about my love of music?

BK: I must first have discovered this aspect of your life from a conversation with your psychoanalytic colleague Marion Milner.

DW: Dear Marion. Yes, of course, she would have known of my musical parts.

BK: But quite apart from the fact that you play the piano, I have always thought that your books and papers have a unique musicianship, a unique tone and cadence and rhythm, which, I believe, contributes greatly to their appeal … at least for me. I always thought that you used your musicianship quite pro-foundly to speak and to write at a pace that an audience could absorb. Unlike many other psychoanalytic writers who simply write – often not holding an audience in mind – you write like a performer. You know that an audience will be listening and responding.

DW: I had never quite thought of it that way before, but what you say makes sense. Yes, music does inhabit my very fibre. I would have been very happy to have been a musician, I think. Perhaps we can come back to that as well. I have many thoughts on music and babies, and on the rhythm of mother's speech. That is an area that really needs more thought and discussion, don't you think?

BK: Indeed it does.

DW: How did we get onto music? Oh, yes, playing the piano for the wounded soldiers in Cambridge, during the Great War. A dreadful, tragic period of history. With no time to think, as I said. But we did get through it.

BK: In 1916, the government introduced compulsory conscription for all British men.

DW: Yes, and I could well have joined up at this time, but I had already begun the second year of my Natural Sciences course, and I still had the exemption from being a medical student. But after I had completed my *third* year of Cambridge studies, I did join up with the RNVR.

BK: The Royal Naval Volunteer Reserve?

DW: That's right. It had to be the navy in some capacity. And I became a Surgeon Probationer, which is a very fancy title for a young, green medical student at sea. At sea in every sense of the word! And I really was on probation. Remember, I knew virtually nothing about medicine. We had studied only the *natural* sciences like anatomy and physiology by this time, not the *clinical* sciences like surgery or pharmacology. Apart from my encounters with the wounded soldiers, I had no practical experience of a real, proper hospital. So I became Surgeon Probationer Winnicott … at sea.

BK: You spent several months on *HMS Lucifer*, I believe.

DW: I did indeed. She was a great big destroyer.

BK: How did you pass your time on the *Lucifer*?

DW: Well, I would have to be in uniform – a lovely blue uniform, which matched the colour of my eyes. And I would have to do all that a sailor does, you know, saluting one's superiors and all of that. It is quite ritualised in the Royal Navy. But as a medic

I also had a great deal of freedom, at least in terms of my time on board ship. Most of the men were fairly fit, fairly healthy, and they didn't really need a doctor, although I suppose their mothers would have been content to know that they had a doctor on call. And so I got to spend a lot of time reading. But I did, also, have my time, on duty, in the Sick Bay.

BK: You saw action, I believe?

DW: Oh yes, the destroyers functioned as convoys, protecting merchant ships. And we did get rather close to enemy torpedoes … quite frightening, I must say. But we survived. I did have to tend to the odd injury, but mostly, I treated syphilis and gonorrhoea, well, as best I could. Some of the men had had sex in port, with ladies, and also, perhaps, with each other, I suspect, and so they contracted these sexual infections. One can only speculate. I had no idea about these conditions, having had rather a sheltered life before all this.

BK: And I suppose you had the opportunity to fraternise with men from very different backgrounds to your own.

DW: Very much so. I had a comfortable, gentrified life in Plymouth. And at the Leys, and at Cambridge, I met mostly well-to-do, highly educated people. My father, though only a merchant, was nonetheless a very prosperous merchant. He and my uncle Richard ran Winnicott Brothers, and they made a good deal of money at times, selling hardware and fancy goods and all that. So, apart from our household servants, I did not really "mix" with men from other classes. But on board *HMS Lucifer*, well, we had to share very tight quarters. And those men taught me all I needed to know about a very different sort of life. They had girls, you see, and they taught me much more about sex than I would have learned from other sources.

BK: Did the experience in the navy help you in your later work at The Green?

DW: Indeed it did. You see, Paddington Green catered to very poor children, very poor families. I also worked at the Queen's Hospital for Children in Hackney, in the East End of London.

So I saw the poor of West London *and* the poor of East London. These people had very different lives to those of my people in Plymouth. They had no governesses and nannies. They had alcoholic fathers, prostitute mothers, and such like. So the experience of meeting the lower ranks in the Royal Navy really did help me to learn how to talk to people from very different worlds to my own. I rather enjoyed it, of course. And, don't you know, they really did make fun of me. The sailors simply did not believe that a chap with a very plummy accent such as mine could have a merchant for a father!

BK: You spent a few months in the Navy?

DW: That is correct. Not quite until the end of the war, but for a few months, that's right. The country needed us to qualify as doctors, and so we returned to our studies, you see.

BK: In November, 1917, I believe, you entered St Bartholomew's Hospital Medical College in London.

DW: I did indeed. Goodness … 1917 … such a long time ago.

CUP 3

An undistinguished physician

BK: Well, perhaps we can now turn to your professional development as a physician.

DW: I went to London so that I could complete my medical training. Good to be back on dry land after all those months on the *Lucifer*. As you know, I'd already done the basic natural sciences at Cambridge, taking my third class degree, but I hadn't undertaken my formal clinical training as yet. And so now I did. And as Cambridge had no postgraduate clinical school in those days, one had to come to London in order to finish one's studies.

BK: How did you get on at Barts?

DW: I see you know the lingo. Everyone called the hospital Barts, never "St Bartholomew's". Only a tourist would say "St Bartholomew's". How did I get on? Well that's a difficult question. You see, at one level I got on just fine, and I learned a great deal about clinical medicine, but at another level I floundered. None of the traditional, respectable areas of formal medicine really gripped me in a passionate way. I had chums there who devoured every anatomy lecture, every surgical textbook, every pathology specimen. They spent all their time studying, and the clever ones even started writing medical papers of their own – proper medical papers – often before qualifying. But I never had that sense of mission or that aptitude. I was the more literary one, the more musical one. Not really a scientist at all, at least not in the traditional sense.

BK: Can you describe your work at Barts?

DW: Well, of course, I had attachments to the various firms, as one does. I worked as a dresser – you know, a surgical dresser – basically, the man who does the bandaging. And I spent time as a fledgling physician working under all sorts of brilliant senior doctors. But I never fell in love with clinical medicine. So I got through, but only just. I spent my spare time engaged in extracurricular activities. I wrote poems and reviews for the hospital magazine, and I really indulged my passion for theatre, especially musical events, in town. I went to as many musical shows and revues and operettas as I could afford. I had never lived in London before, and … well, London … what can one say? Distraction never failed to engage me! I had some money, from my father, so I could go out, but I often got seats in the "gods", you know, way up at the top of the theatres – the cheap seats.

BK: In view of your later concentration in the field of children's medicine, and then in psychiatry, I suppose you might have felt quite disappointed that Barts did not really offer proper instruction in these relatively underdeveloped disciplines.

DW: You are right. Children's medicine and psychiatry … well, you see … doctors regarded those disciplines as the two Cinderella subjects for physicians in my day. No one wanted to specialise in those areas. The real medical men practised surgery or general physical medicine (internal medicine, heart disease, lungs, etc.). I suppose that if I am to be completely honest, most senior medics would have thought a man a bit thick or a bit of a sorry 'un to have become a children's doctor or a mad-doctor.

BK: Physicians in Great Britain had not yet begun to use the term "pediatrician" in those days.

DW: God Lord, no. British doctors loathed that dreadful Americanism "pediatrician". We were called "physicians in children's medicine".

BK: I see.

DW: As you have indicated, these were still relatively primitive disciplines. In fact, children's medicine barely existed as a speciality at Barts ... or anywhere else, for that matter. Did you know that in my day we used to lump the child patients in with the adult patients on the general wards? People simply thought of children as smaller adults. And we knew very little about their special medical needs, and certainly nothing about their special psychological needs. And psychiatry was not much better. In fact, we didn't even use the term psychiatry by and large. We called the field "mental diseases".

BK: Did you turn to "children's medicine" and later, to "mental diseases", by default, as you had not distinguished yourself in surgery and internal medicine, or did you have a genuine interest in these more marginalised specialities?

DW: If truth be told, a bit of both. I knew that I would never, ever get a posting in surgery. That was quite clear. I simply did not have the necessary qualities that the other chaps had. All that cutting and slicing ... it simply did not appeal. But certainly, with children's medicine, I did find that interesting, and I got on well with children. I knew how to play with them, and the other chaps didn't.

BK: You had a disappointing experience studying "mental diseases" with Sir Robert Armstrong-Jones, I believe?

DW: A fool of a man, Armstrong-Jones. He taught us nothing that could really help one to *understand* madness.

BK: He held a very prominent position in British psychiatry at that time.

DW: Yes, but he knew absolutely nil about the unconscious. Did you know that Armstrong-Jones ultimately became the grandfather of Anthony Armstrong-Jones, the photographer, who later became Lord Snowdon after he married Princess Margaret? How about that? Sir Robert did have very regal aspirations. Sir Robert didn't live to see his grandson marry into the Royal Family, did he? But he would have enjoyed that.

BK: I discovered that Sir Robert actually came from a very modest Welsh family called Jones – simply Jones – and that he changed his name to Armstrong-Jones in later years.

DW: That hardly surprises me. Sir Robert had a great pomposity about him. He taught mental diseases, but he gave only a few lectures and demonstrations in the whole of our medical school studies. Not very helpful to have had so little contact with the mad. It takes *time* to learn to understand the mad, and Sir Robert really did not do anything to facilitate that process. He regarded the mad as mad ... pure and simple ... not as people, not as people struggling, or people with childhoods, or people with minds.

BK: And he hated psychoanalysis, I believe.

DW: With a passion! Freud had only just begun to develop a toehold in British medical circles at this time. We all read a smattering of articles and reviews about this new Viennese psychology in our magazines and journals, so we knew a tiny bit about Freudianism. But Sir Robert loathed Freud. He was also quite anti-Semitic, you see, as were many of his contemporaries, and he always used to say that "psycho-analysis" – which we then spelled with a hyphen ... we always spelled it with a hyphen in those days – that psycho-analysis might be suitable for Viennese Jews, but that it had nothing to offer English people.

BK: And he came from Wales!

DW: Yes, but he had upward aspirations, and he always ponced about like an Englishman, not like a proper Welshman whose people had worked the mines. I used to have a holiday cottage in Wales during the 1940s – in Cardigan Bay – and I certainly knew a great many proper Welshmen. Sir Robert avoided his lowly Welsh roots, and he became an English knight. You know, when my father earned his knighthood, he never put on airs and graces, and he never pretended to be anything other than a Plymothian.

BK: So you had the great challenge of finding your way to paediatrics and to psychiatry before these medical concentrations had even come to exist as full-fledged specialities. You really had to become a pioneer.

DW: Well, I would say that I was rather pig-headed and a bit desperate, more like. These were really the only fields of medicine that interested me, and they turned out to be not very medical at all. One really does not need to know much about physical medicine to help an enuretic child or a depressive grown-up. One needn't know much about the structure of the urethra, for instance, or about the positioning of the frontal lobes. But one does need to be a very good psychologist to treat children, and one needs to be a good psychologist to treat the mentally troubled. In fact, I eventually came to forget most of the physical medicine that I learned. But of course, the training is good in terms of developing a thick skin for dealing with disaster and death. But still, both paediatrics and psychiatry require little medical knowledge – at least that seems to have been the situation in my day.

BK: Paediatrics has changed greatly over the last eighty years or so, and like most branches of medicine, it has now become very technologised and pharmacologised, and often, quite effectively so.

DW: Is that the case? I suppose it must be. I try to keep abreast of the psychoanalytic literature from my little consulting room upstairs, but I must confess that I have rather neglected the new developments in paediatrics. But in my time, you know, we had no medicines to offer children, or none that really worked properly. Of course we used bromides. People prescribed bromides for *everything*. They might just as well have given the patient a brandy or a whisky. And so, you see, I turned to psychological approaches partly out of desperation, and partly because I sensed that children needed psychological understanding. Also, I came to realise that psychologically troubled grown-ups needed understanding too.

BK: You persevered in spite of your difficulties at Barts.

DW: Yes, I did. I stuck with it, you see. But physical medicine never fitted me in a deep way.

BK: Nowadays, most institutions of higher learning would have student counsellors or progress advisers to help trainees with their difficulties and dilemmas. Did anyone help guide you as a young physician-in-training?

DW: In my day, one simply got on with it. We had no career counselling or guidance counselling at medical school. The teachers certainly liked me well enough, but I did not have "star quality" medical potential, and so none of older men ever took me under wing. It soon became clear that I would never be a medical professor or a knight. Did you know that we had a very high percentage of knighted men on the staff, like Sir Robert? I suspect we had more knights at Barts than the other teaching hospitals had.

BK: You studied surgery, I believe, with Sir Anthony Bowlby, father of Dr John Bowlby who would eventually become one of your psychoanalytic colleagues.

DW: Yes, I didn't meet Bowlby – John, that is – until many, many years later, not until he had started to train as a psychoanalyst in the 1930s. In fact, we both had analysis from Mrs Riviere – Joan Riviere – who had had her analysis from Freud, and also from Ernest Jones previously, I believe. I had my second analysis from Mrs Riviere, but Bowlby had only one analysis, as far as I know … no, I don't think he ever had more analysis after Mrs Riviere. But, yes, of course, I knew Bowlby's father. I found Sir Anthony most impressive. He made huge contributions to the surgical treatment of war wounds, based on his time in the Great War, you see.

BK: And during the Boer War as well, I believe.

DW: Yes, he did go back quite a bit. He must have been born round about the same time as my own father.

BK: But you never found a senior physician to whom you could look up as a special figure?

DW: At that time … sadly, no. Well, maybe Sir Anthony a bit, and maybe Tommy Horder, a bit.

BK: Dr Horder …

DW: Later Lord Horder, you know.

BK: He had a huge private practice, I believe.

DW: Oh, quite enormous. He drove a very grand car to the hospital – one of the most expensive ones – and we young medics looked on with a certain amount of envy and disbelief.

BK: Did men like Bowlby and Horder – hugely successful men – make you feel inadequate, or did they perhaps inspire you and give you hope that you, too, could succeed and become a distinguished physician?

DW: Mostly the latter, I fear. I think that if I speak to you honestly, I had a very lousy time from the academic point of view.

BK: You took some time to find your *métier*, whereas your other mates … I am thinking of Christopher Andrewes and Geoffrey Bourne, for instance, both of whom became more traditional medical doctors and researchers.

DW: I have not heard these names for a very long time. I have many good memories of Andrewes and Bourne. But you are right, those chaps took to medicine in an uncomplicated way. They seemed not to have had to go on a journey. They simply started, got on with it, and finished. I had a more bumpy ride.

BK: You might have felt quite lonely at times.

DW: Well, I had a lot of friends. I always did. But it would have helped greatly if I had had someone who had really cradled me and really took me on as a protégé. A man needs another man to be his mentor, I think, like a father. My father, well, he behaved in quite a benign way … quite a loving way, I believe. So other men would have paled by comparison. I found so many of my teachers – my medical teachers, that is – rather disappointing in terms of their human abilities.

BK: But after qualification as a physician you had a happier experience, I believe. You did find something of a mentor in Professor Francis Fraser.

DW: Yes, I found Francis Fraser. He was a Barts man, and after our senior professor Sir Archibald Garrod went up to Oxford to become the Regius Professor, Francis Fraser took over his old post as the medical professor at Barts, and I went to work for him as a lowly House Physician. I had joined the Medical Register by this point – I did so in 1920 – and I became a proper doctor at last; however, I didn't *feel* like a proper doctor. But Fraser did give me excellent tutelage. He prepped me for my membership exams for the Royal College of Physicians of London, and also for my exams for the Royal College of Surgeons of England, and though I never took a medical degree, which one needn't have done in those days, I did receive my licentiateship and my membership, and those letters allowed me to practise medicine.

BK: Contemporary readers may not understand that in the early twentieth century, a physician did not need to have a degree in medicine in order to practise medicine. Nowadays, it would be unthinkable for a physician to practise medicine without a degree.

DW: Yes, the Americans would find that an outrage, I suppose. But we had a different system here, as you know. Only the really clever chaps took higher degrees in medicine in my day, the Bachelor of Medicine, the Bachelor of Surgery degree, and all that. Most of us got on just fine with our licentiateship, which meant that we had passed an exam, but did not take a university degree. I snagged my LRCP – the licentiateship of the Royal College of Physicians, and also, my MRCS – the membership of the Royal College of Surgeons – even though I never practised surgery. All of that got me onto the Medical Register. I did have my undergraduate degree from Cambridge, but not a medical degree.

BK: So you never became Dr Donald Winnicott, MD.

DW: That caused a great problem for me when I had my books published in America in later years. My American publishers wanted to put "D. W. Winnicott, M.D." on the front cover, since one could not be a real American doctor unless one had an "M.D.". I told them that I had no M.D., and that most British doctors had no M.D. But I think they still gave me one for publicity purposes, otherwise no one would have believed me to be a medical man, and, in those days, no one would have bought the books.

BK: Of course, nowadays the mental health field has become increasingly de-medicalised, and most British psychotherapists and psychoanalysts come from backgrounds other than medicine.

DW: That does not surprise me. One does not need to be a physician in order to have a conversation! But in my day, one did. And I could not have done it without Professor Fraser. Yes, I owe a lot to Francis Fraser. The King gave him a "gong" – you know, a knighthood – in his later years ... and he became Sir Francis. I kept in touch with him until just before he died. A lovely, lovely man, Sir Francis.

BK: So you had qualified in medicine, and then, after having earned your licentiateship, you also then acquired your full membership in the Royal College of Physicians of London?

DW: Yes, I had all that completed by 1922, and I became D. W. Winnicott, MRCS [Member of the Royal College of Surgeons of England], LRCP [Licentiate of the Royal College of Physicians of London], MRCP [Member of the Royal College of Physicians of London].

BK: And the following year – 1923 – proved to be rather a watershed for you in so many ways, I believe.

DW: 1923 changed my life in every respect. First of all, I had completed all of my house jobs in medicine, and I could now apply for a proper post, becoming an Assistant Physician at The Green ... Paddington Green, that is. I also had a similar post at the Queen's Hospital for Children in the East End, where I had done some work previously. Both of these hospitals specialised in treating children – quite unique for the time – and these appointments really consolidated my growing interest in children's medicine and in children's diseases. And I remained a children's doctor for the next forty-seven years.

BK: If I understand correctly, your new posts as Assistant Physician carried a great deal of gravitas – more so, perhaps, than the descriptor "Assistant" would imply.

DW: How true. Back in the 1920s, Assistant Physicians had real status – not as much status as the full-fledged Physicians, of course, but status nonetheless. I suppose it would be the equivalent of being a newly appointed Consultant in the National Health Service nowadays.

BK: But unlike contemporary Consultant Physicians, you received no salary.

DW: I think I had a modest stipend, but mostly, we received no full salary. In those days, one felt honoured to have a hospital position. It signified that one's colleagues regarded one as a man of substance. And as a result, one's reputation increased overnight. Although we had no salaries as such, the celebrity and renown which accrued from having a hospital post helped to provide us with private patients for our Harley Street practices, and that is how we were meant to pay our way.

BK: So you opened a private practice?

DW: One had to, really.

BK: But not quite in Harley Street, I think.

DW: Yes, shortly after joining the staff at The Green, I took rooms on Weymouth Street, just perpendicular to Harley Street, and thus right in the heart of London's wealthy, private medical community. The only problem is that, unlike the surgeons and the general physicians who had all the aristocracy flocking to them, I treated children, not adults. And back in those days, very few parents had the willingness or the foresight to bring their children to see a private physician. Those with money took their children to the old family doctor. So I had hardly any private patients at first. And I found that quite shaming, I must tell you.

BK: Would it be correct that you struggled financially in the early days, in spite of having two consultant-style hospital posts?

DW: My father helped me out. He did so for many years. And thank goodness for that!

BK: And I believe that you sometimes paid for your impecunious Paddington Green patients to come to Weymouth Street.

DW: I did give some of them tram fare to come into town from West London. In this way, I saved face with the porter at Weymouth Street, as I didn't want him to think me a rank amateur or a clod. But also, by seeing my Paddington patients in my private office, I could thus have more time with them, and this proved to be a very important experience for me. By spending a lot of time with my Paddington Green patients – which I couldn't do quite so easily at the hospital when we had a full waiting-room, but which I could do in private practice – this helped me to understand more about the nature of their problems. So I suppose you could say that I paid my private patients to come to see me. I paid them to teach me. And they certainly repaid me with knowledge.

BK: Of course, we all know the dedication that you wrote in one of your books: "To my patients who have paid to teach me."

DW: I meant that in a very heartfelt way. Even when I started to earn larger sums from my private consulting work, I still felt that my patients were my teachers. Although by the end of my life, *they* paid *me*, and I did not have to pay them. Though goodness knows, I saw a lot of people without fee, even in later years. One has to help the needy, you know.

BK: Would it be correct that at this point in time – during the early 1920s – you specialised very much in the physical side of children's medicine?

DW: Oh, yes, it would still be a little while before I actually began to bring psychoanalysis into my work with children, at least in a formal way. You may know that I did a lot of work with children suffering from juvenile rheumatism and heart problems and all of that. Of course, sometimes these cases had psychological origins, don't you know.

BK: So in 1923 you received your hospital posts, and you opened your private practice. But you also began to undergo psychoanalysis. You became a patient yourself. How did this come about?

DW: Well, as we have said, I got to know something about Freud and his thinking during my time as a young medic at Barts. Sir Robert Armstrong-Jones's frequent attacks on Freud only made me all the more curious. So I started reading. I began with Pfister's book. Do you know it?

BK: Oskar Pfister – Freud's Swiss colleague?

DW: That's the man. I knew very little about his relation to Freud, but I read his rather thick textbook called *The Psychoanalytic Method,* which I found very engrossing, very captivating. And then I realised that I probably ought to have psychoanalysis myself.

BK: Did you have the intention of working ultimately as a psychoanalyst?

DW: Oh no, I needed help … I was quite ill.

BK: "Ill" in the psychiatric sense, or "ill" in the Winnicottian sense?

DW: "Ill" in the Winnicottian sense, by which I mean I was not happy, not really myself. You see, I had also just got married for the first time … to Alice – Alice Taylor – a surgeon's daughter – and, well … let's just say that I thought it would be useful to have analysis. So I found my way to Ernest Jones. I can't remember precisely how I got to Jones, but everyone knew Jones to be Freud's key man in Britain. So I saw him at Harley Street, in his private office, just a stone's throw from mine.

BK: What happened during your consultation?

DW: Jones was undoubtedly a difficult man. Everyone struggled with him. Everyone fought with him. But somehow I never did. I cannot know why, but I really had got the best of him. We never got into a muddle or a spat, which – so I came to learn – was quite unusual.

BK: How do you understand this?

DW: Well, I went to Jones as a young children's doctor, and I think this gave us an immediate connection. You see, he too had worked in children's medicine as a young man, and he had published scads of papers about physical diseases in the young. So I think he wanted to know from me what had happened in the field over the intervening twenty years or so. He had left children's medicine to focus on psychoanalysis. I think we did talk about that. But we also talked about *me.* We talked mostly about me. And I found that tremendous. I think Jones knew more about me than I knew about myself.

BK: Did you want to have analysis with Jones?

DW: Perhaps I did. But he had no vacancies at that time. Everyone went to Jones in those days. And I had very little money, and I suppose he knew that. And he charged big, fat fees. And I think he spared me the embarrassment of asking to see him, knowing that I couldn't pay him properly. So he sent me to the "new boy", James Strachey, who had only recently returned from Vienna, where he'd been in analysis with Freud. And Strachey's wife, Mrs Strachey – Alix – had also been in analysis with Freud. So each of the Stracheys needed patients, and Jones sent me to Mr Strachey. Jones wanted to help out. He liked Strachey, and I think he enjoyed the fact that Strachey came from a well-connected literary family – you know, brother to Lytton Strachey and all that. And Jones was a Welshman, like Sir Robert Armstrong-Jones, and he, too, wanted to fit in with the English. And Strachey was very English. Very, *very* English, in fact. So he liked that about Strachey – the Englishness. And hence, I went to see Strachey in Gordon Square, and we started to work psychoanalytically together, on Jones's recommendation.

CUP 4

On Strachey's couch

BK: How would you describe the practice of psychoanalysis in the 1920s? Did it differ greatly from the psychoanalysis that you came to practise in the 1930s and 1940s, and beyond?

DW: Did you know that back in the early days, before I became an analyst myself, patients used to attend six days each week, rather than five? We all went on Saturdays, as well as Mondays to Fridays. I must say that I found that a bit exhausting, and that practice gradually disappeared. But Freud had always worked on Saturdays, and so, consequently, all of his disciples did as well. For very troubled people – for the more borderline or psychotic people with fears of being dropped – the Saturday session must have been indispensable, a godsend. But I lived in Surbiton, in Surrey, with Alice, and I found it a nuisance to train into Central London on Saturdays for my session, especially if I did not have consulting hours at Paddington Green (which I sometimes did have).

BK: You went to Mr Strachey's house in the heart of Bloomsbury? Did you know about Strachey's close ties with Virginia Woolf and John Maynard Keynes and the others?

DW: Mr Strachey – I always called him Mr Strachey – he wasn't a doctor, you see, but that didn't matter. He knew his Freud better than almost anyone in the British Psycho-Analytical Society. He may have known his Freud better than Jones, in fact. I am sure you know that James Strachey translated all of Freud into English, and that such a vast undertaking really made him a great Freud expert. Mr Strachey rarely talked about his private life, but I did know him to be the brother of Lytton Strachey. Everyone knew Lytton Strachey, because his books became best-sellers, like *Eminent Victorians*, you see. I think Lytton Strachey even came to dedicate one of his books to my analyst. So, yes, in answer to your question, I did know of the special relationship between psychoanalysis and the writers of Bloomsbury. I suspect I must have passed Virginia Woolf on the street many times without even knowing! I may well have seen Maynard Keynes, who shared a house with Strachey for a time – you know, John Maynard Keynes, the economist. And certainly I remember seeing his wife, Lydia Lopokova, the Russian ballerina, wearing her tutu!

BK: What about Mr Strachey's technique?

DW: Oh, he practised a very traditional, very classical technique. He used the couch, of course – unthinkable not to have used the couch – and I would lie down and just free-associate. He would make interpretations, mostly about my oedipal desires and about my resistances to recognising those oedipal desires. Very classical indeed.

BK: I presume that you discussed dreams quite a lot.

DW: Yes, of course, plenty of dream analysis. I loved to tell Mr Strachey my dreams … so very interesting … well, at least to me.

BK: So you had a very traditional Freudian analysis. But Mr Strachey's technique changed somewhat over time, I believe?

DW: Yes, as the years unfolded, I noticed that Strachey became more and more preoccupied by the transference. At first he talked only about me and my unconscious, but towards the end of the analysis he began to interpret more about my relationship to him and demonstrated that the analyst himself can become a mutative ingredient in the treatment relationship. This really signalled a transition within the field of psychoanalysis. We witnessed a transformation, you see, of psychoanalysis as a process whereby the analyst *treats* the patient to one whereby the analyst and the patient become *involved*, together, in a treatment process, in which both contribute to the dynamic of the interaction.

BK: A shift from a one-person psychology to a two-person psychology?

DW: Indeed, very much so.

BK: And did you find your analysis with James Strachey a helpful experience?

DW: I could not have had a better psychoanalyst at that time. There is much that Mr Strachey didn't know and didn't understand, but I can't hold that against him because nobody really understood very much at all about the more primitive parts of the personality then. Not really. But Strachey gave me a very helpful analysis of the neurotic parts of my mind. And he always treated me in a truly gentlemanly fashion. He had excellent manners and excellent "class". He also encouraged me to read Freud more fully, even though I rarely did. I was not a scholarly reader. But all that didn't matter, because Strachey gave me an opportunity to talk about what I could not talk about anywhere else. I don't know if he cottoned on to the more fearful parts – what I later described as the baby's fears of going to pieces, and the baby's fear of falling forever.

BK: Did this mean that Mr Strachey did not quite help you grapple with the more frightening elements of the mind?

DW: Well, he did and he didn't. I don't think he tackled them directly. He missed the more preoedipal components. But he did a great job on the oedipal aspects, helping me understand my rivalry with my father. In many ways, he gave me a voice, which allowed me to challenge authority and to become a potent man in my own right. At least in certain areas. I do think he managed to do that.

BK: In all of your writings, especially those from the 1930s and 1940s, you demonstrate immense bravery, speaking up against the errors of your fellow paediatricians and, later, against the sadism of the organic psychiatrists who practised electroconvulsive shock and leucotomy (which became better known as lobotomy).

DW: Well, we might just trace that to Mr Strachey and to the positive results of the analysis. He allowed me to become truly outspoken, without fearing retaliation unduly. As I said, he really allowed me to have a voice … to speak in my own voice.

BK: And did that experience also help you to become a broadcaster on the radio in later years?

DW: Absolutely so. As I said, Mr Strachey gave me permission to speak, and he made me feel that my words mattered. And although I have always talked softly and slowly, as you can hear, I think I do have a *big* voice nonetheless.

BK: Both big and soft at the same time.

DW: Yes, quite.

BK: In the obituary tribute that you wrote for Mr Strachey, published some two years after his death, you described him in very favourable terms, and I know that you maintained a warm and collegial correspondence with him until his death in 1967. But in spite of this, you still felt it necessary to have many more years of analysis with Joan Riviere.

DW: My word, I seem to be quite an open book.

BK: Well, I have wondered … indeed, several of my colleagues have also wondered … whether you felt that your time with Mr Strachey had really got to the bottom, as it were. Whether it had really reached the most primitive parts of you. You know, the very parts that you attempted to engage with in your own clinical work with some of your more regressed patients.

DW: This is a good question and an important question. Most certainly. In truth, I think that we could have gone deeper. One can always plumb deeper in any piece of analysis, don't you think?

BK: Oh, absolutely.

DW: But it may be that Strachey didn't know about those more primitive parts within himself. Or it may be that he didn't know about those parts of me.

BK: Might it also be the case that Mr Strachey had a sensitivity to timing. After all, we sometimes sense very fragile aspects of our patients, but we must respect the patient's defences, and not be too intrusive.

DW: You may be right. Being intrusive can be annihilatory for some of our patients. You may well be right. And I was a very defensive young man at the time. I had a great many unanalysed and rigid defences. Yes, you may well be right.

BK: You had quite a long analysis with James Strachey?

DW: I stayed in psychoanalysis with Mr Strachey for ten years. I can't think of any of my contemporaries who had had as much analysis as I had. Clifford Scott ... do you know Clifford Scott?

BK: Yes, he came from Canada to study psychoanalysis in England.

DW: That's right. He had his training analysis from Mrs Klein. He was in and out of that analysis with lightning speed. But then Scotty had always been very sane to start with. I don't think he needed ten years. But I did. I enjoyed the process, even though I found it painful. At the beginning, I used to cancel sessions here and there. I'd forget to sign my cheque on occasion – typical neurotic resistances, but based on a deeper fear of annihilation, I suppose.

BK: So throughout the early 1920s and the mid–1920s you had your analysis with James Strachey, and you embarked upon it as an ordinary private patient. But then, in 1927, you changed course, I believe, and you became an official "training" patient.

DW: Yes, I decided, with Mr Strachey's approval, to apply to become a psychoanalyst myself. To become a candidate. I didn't *need* to become a psychoanalyst from a professional point of view. In fact, I would have had a much easier time of it if I *hadn't* become a psychoanalyst. In those days, people thought analysts were no better than mumbo-jumbo witch doctors or trick-cyclists. Psychoanalysis had a terrible reputation, and poor Ernest Jones always had some sexual scandal hanging over his head, you know, being accused of sexual improprieties with patients. But I found psychoanalysis to be essential for my own sanity, and I had also begun to find it quite necessary for my work in hospital.

BK: You had already begun applying psychoanalysis to children's medicine?

DW: In a clumsy way, yes, I had.

BK: But quite pioneering!

DW: I can't claim credit to have been the first. Long before my time, Leonard Guthrie, the main man at Paddington Green during the very early years of the twentieth century, had done just that. He wrote a wonderful book on *Functional Nervous Disorders in Childhood,* which broke important ground by examining the impact of the child's emotional life on physical symptomatology. And we all knew that book at The Green and we read it too. But Guthrie didn't have personal knowledge of psychoanalysis apart from the odd paper or two by Freud, so although he got *somewhat* far, he didn't get *very* far. And I had this interest, you see, in developing that line of work.

BK: So you applied to the Institute of Psycho-Analysis, the training arm of the British Psycho-Analytical Society?

DW: Yes, Edward Glover put me through my paces. He was Jones's mandarin, his right-hand man. But for some reason they took me in and allowed me to train. I became one of the very first people to participate in the formal scheme of lectures – one of the very, very first to do a proper training in psychoanalysis in Great Britain. Before that, the older guard became psychoanalysts simply by chatting with Ernest Jones from time to time, and he took them in ... keen, I suppose, to have a Society.

BK: So your analysis became transformed from an ordinary analysis as a patient to a "training analysis" as a student.

DW: Indeed it did. I went from being a patient to becoming a candidate, though still a patient as well. Candidates are patients also, you see.

BK: Your sheer physical workload must have increased greatly at this time.

DW: Yes, of course. I had quite a lot more on my plate. I still had my clinical work with children and their families at my two hospitals, specialising in juvenile rheumatism at The Queen's, and in more general cases at The Green. And I still kept developing my Weymouth Street practice. And I had six sessions of psychoanalysis each week. But now I also had lectures at the Institute of Psycho-Analysis on Gloucester Place, in town, during the evenings. And I didn't even live in London. I spent a great deal of time on the train. You might say that I spent a lot of time on the *train* in order to *train*!

BK: Would you mind telling me about your domestic life at this time?

DW: I lived in Surbiton, in Surrey, as I believe I had mentioned, and so I had to travel in to Charing Cross station, and then I would set off from there, as everything happened in London. I worked very hard. But I can see in retrospect that I had been on something of an evangelical mission – hints of my Wesleyanism, I suppose. I saw lots of mental suffering everywhere. Horrible, horrible mental suffering in my child patients, as well as horrible, horrible physical suffering. And I wanted to make an impact. And I came to appreciate that with psychoanalytic understanding as part of my treatment repertoire, I would have many other ways – powerful ways – of alleviating children's illnesses.

BK: I would be very keen to learn more about your psychoanalytic training experience, and also about how you came to integrate psychoanalysis and children's medicine, and whether anyone helped you to do that.

DW: We did have one children's doctor in the British Psycho-Analytical Society, David Forsyth. He worked at the Evelina Hospital, so I had very little contact with him. He was very senior to me, and for some reason he didn't teach at the Institute of Psycho-Analysis, at least not by the time I had arrived, so I had very few exchanges with him. And we students weren't permitted to go to the Scientific Meetings of the British Society back in those days. So I kept missing Forsyth. He had analysis from Freud in Vienna, after the Great War, but I never really talked with him properly. But he did use psychoanalysis with children, though I couldn't quite tell you how. Not in the way that I did, I expect. So, in many ways, I felt on my own.

BK: But you soldiered through.

DW: Yes, and I kept myself engaged by trying to apply what I learned from lectures with Dr Jones and Dr Glover and the others, and from what I learned on the couch with Mr Strachey. And I brought all of this into my clinics with children. I started to see that when little babies had fits and convulsions, this did not always mean a problem in the brain. Children's physicians would have suspected a somatic disturbance. But I learned that sometimes babies and young children simply wanted to murder their mothers or their fathers, and so their whole bodies would shake with rage. And when I would say this to the parents, the shaking and the convulsions in the infants would stop. People thought me rather mad for believing in this.

BK: But you had direct clinical, observational experience to this effect.

DW: That's right. But it still sounded quite mad, quite potty. No one had language to discuss hateful feelings in the family at that time, you see. It violated every precept of Christianity and every precept of Victorianism. Is that a word, "Victorianism"? Yes, I suppose it must be. But in spite of all the propriety of the time, I came to realise that of course, we *all* hated our families. And that is what psychoanalysis allowed me to talk about.

BK: In many ways, you helped to pioneer psychosomatic medicine, especially paediatric psychosomatic medicine.

DW: That's very kind of you to say. And I suppose it is true. I tried to do so, anyway.

BK: And as part of your psychoanalytic training, you had clinical cases of your own – patients in ongoing psychoanalytic treatment?

DW: I did, but not at first. I think that the Training Committee had its reservations about me. I was an odd duck, no doubt. And let's not forget that I came from children's medicine, whereas virtually all the other medics had come from mental diseases – psychiatry – so although I was a doctor, I wasn't exactly *their* kind of doctor.

BK: Who influenced you most in your psychoanalytic training?

DW: I had good lectures from Jones and from Glover and from the others, people like Flügel who had trained as a psychologist – John Flügel – a very erudite man. And they all knew Freud personally. Jones, of course, knew Freud best of all. In fact, he would always pepper his talks with incessant personal references to "The Professor", or "Professor Freud". "As Professor Freud told me in Salzburg …", "When I heard Professor Freud introduce this idea in Vienna …", you know, that sort of comment. But it made it all very authentic. And we rather liked that.

BK: And you had supervisors with whom you discussed your training cases?

DW: Of course, but we didn't call them "supervisors". Not in those days. We called them "control analysts", don't you know! But yes, I did have supervisions, and they served a purpose.

BK: In what respect?

DW: I enjoyed my various control analysts … somewhat … but these people did not really inspire me or push my thinking forward, at least not greatly. They did, however, hold my hand through the experience. I had Miss Sharpe, Miss Searl, several others.

BK: Ella Sharpe and Nina Searl?

DW: Both spinsters, like many of the early women in the psychoanalytic movement. Not Sylvia Payne, of course. She had several sons, one of whom became a great athlete … rowed in the Olympics, I think. But many were spinsters, and a bit fanatical, a bit dotty. But good women, well-meaning women. Miss Sharpe had a more tidy mind, whereas Miss Searl had a rather more strange mind, and one day she disappeared. She simply left the British Psycho-Analytical Society. I think she became a psychic – you know, trapped in the spiritual voodoo world. There was quite a lot of gossip about her and quite a lot of concern … and, also, quite a lot of relief when she disappeared.

BK: And of course, you had a very profound experience with Melanie Klein.

DW: It would not be an overstatement to tell you that Mrs Klein transformed my world. Not only did she have a huge influence on my understanding of children and of the primitive and aggressive aspects of infancy, but also our lives became intertwined – Melanie's life and my life. She supervised me on my child work in the early days. And I helped her. I helped her a huge amount financially, you see, because I sent her patients – many, many patients – and that gave her quite a good income. I sent patients to many of the analysts, because I had access to an entire hospital – two entire hospitals, in fact – full of psychologically unwell children needing help. I filled a lot of practices, don't you know. But Melanie and I became entangled in other ways. I analysed her son.

BK: Erich Klein?

DW: Yes, but he changed his first name to "Eric", without an "h" at the end, and his second name to "Clyne", with a "C". I suppose he needed some distance from his mother.

BK: And you had other entanglements with Melanie Klein.

DW: Yes, it did not stop there with the analysis of Eric. Years later, my second wife, Clare – I suppose you know that I divorced Alice and remarried – well, Clare would come to have her training analysis with Mrs Klein. So we really did have quite a lot of involvement.

BK: Nowadays, a supervisee would never psychoanalyse the child – or indeed any relative – of his or her supervisor. We would endeavour to keep these roles more separate.

DW: Of course, that would be better. But in the 1930s we had so few analysts available, especially for child cases. We had no choice.

BK: I understand.

DW: So Melanie and I did become a bit embroiled in one another's lives.

BK: I believe that James Strachey had first recommended that you speak with Mrs Klein.

DW: That's right. Mr Strachey had an interest in my hospital work, but he wasn't a medico, and also, he didn't understand all the specifics of child work. He was bright and a fast learner, and he could grasp clinical, medical vocabulary quite quickly and had even been to medical school for a few weeks, I believe; but, still, he did not work with children. He didn't psychoanalyse children, and he didn't have any children of his own. So although he tried, he didn't know a lot about children, except what he had read in Freud's essays. And *that* he knew *extremely* well. But he had known Klein for many years – he helped to bring her to England, you see. And *Mrs* Strachey, too, had known Klein in Berlin. I think Mrs Strachey had analysis in Berlin after her analysis with Freud in Vienna.

BK: Yes, both Melanie Klein and Alix Strachey had psychoanalysis in Berlin with Karl Abraham, the founder of the German psychoanalytic movement.

DW: Yes, I suppose they did. Yes, I remember that, now you remind me. Would you like some more tea?

BK: Thank you, that would be lovely.

DW: Hopefully we can prevail upon Mrs Coles once again. But first, let us stretch our legs a bit, don't you think?

BK: What a good idea!

CUP 5

Mrs Klein and the "sub-Kleinians"

BK: We had begun to speak about Mrs Klein ...

DW: We'll just get through all of this about Melanie, shall we, and then I'll call for Mrs Coles again.

BK: That would be fine.

DW: Mr Strachey, you see, told me that Melanie Klein had come to England from Germany, and that she had begun to cause quite a stir in the British Psycho-Analytical Society, because not only had she made great strides in child work, but she had also dared to challenge the ideas of Miss Freud. And that was heresy, you see. Although Anna Freud had not yet come to England – that happened only in 1938, with the Nazis – we all regarded Anna Freud as the doyenne of child analysis. She really came to dominate the field in the minds of most people. And she was Professor Freud's daughter. So for Klein even to whisper a disagreement with Anna Freud ... well, you can imagine.

BK: But Jones supported Klein. And Strachey supported Klein. Given your important relationship with each of these men, you must have ...

DW: Indeed. I simply *had* to meet Mrs Klein. She came with all of these high recommendations.

BK: Of course.

DW: Do you know, I never quite figured out whether Jones's support of Klein represented his love of her work, and his recognition of her brilliance, or whether he simply needed someone to look after the ill people in his own family. On Jones's invitation, Melanie analysed Jones's wife – he called her Kitty, don't you know – *and* some of his children as well. And that seemed very important, because Jones could not have sent his family for analysis with one of his English disciples. He needed a senior person – an outsider – and so Melanie came over to London primarily for that purpose, *expressly* for that purpose.

BK: Ernest Jones took rather a risk, I suppose, in supporting Mrs Klein. After all, Klein had already become *persona non grata* among the Viennese Freudians, who regarded Anna Freud as the queen of child psychoanalysis.

DW: I have often wondered about that. I may be quite wrong – and I don't mind being wrong – but I have sometimes asked myself whether Jones's advancement of Klein – enemy to Anna Freud – may have represented the split-off hatred that Jones had towards Freud. Jones idealised Freud, but idealisation always has its shadow side. I have often thought about that. Because in bringing over Klein, Jones had thus offered huge patronage to a woman who rivalled the master's daughter!

BK: You could well be right.

DW: You see, even though Jones loved Freud, he might also have hated the dependence. We all have to become our own man, in our own right. And Jones may have resented his subservience to Freud.

BK: Very interesting.

DW: I think so.

BK: So you went to meet with Mrs Klein?

DW: She spoke very clumsy English. Even after all those years of living in England, she never learned to write well. Her writing heaves with a sense of burden, I think – a sense of weightiness. But, when one ploughs through it, one finds it absolutely brilliant. She really got to grips with the parts of children and of grown-ups, the unpleasant parts, perhaps better than anyone else had done. But she went wrong.

BK: Oh?

DW: Yes, where she went wrong is that she often thought that people had *only* unpleasant parts. She didn't know much about creativity, and although she pioneered play therapy with children, she didn't know much about play … though her people would disagree with me I suppose. She liked music, you know, but she couldn't play music. And she loved literature, but she couldn't write. And she loved to talk, but she couldn't give a speech … not a good speech at any rate. She had her limitations of character and ability. But she was brilliant, and I learned such a lot.

BK: You had supervision – or should I say "control analysis" – with her?

DW: Yes, control analysis. But I also discussed my hospital work with her, and she made very, very useful comments about the children's fears of their own aggression. I found that exceptionally useful, and I began to understand much better how such an idea might translate into psycho-medical terms. How children might attack their own bodies, in fact, with red-hot rage, for instance, becoming transformed into a high fever!

BK: Fascinating.

DW: And a bit mad, too, I suppose, or at the very least eccentric. The other doctors in the children's field thought so. But eventually, I started to win the children's doctors over to this way of thinking – some of the younger ones at any rate, men like Peter Tizard, John Davis, Ronnie MacKeith.

BK: And I believe that Klein spoke to you about her work with children in the context of your supervision sessions.

DW: Yes. I would often go to her for case discussions, and sometimes my mind would just go blank. I had hundreds and hundreds of cases on my mind because I would see hundreds of children a week … well, perhaps not hundreds, but certainly quite a lot. But Klein never worked in an institution. She saw two or three children a week, but she saw them every day, and she knew them intimately. And this gave her time and space to think about children and to remember children. And when I couldn't recall a single piece of my work – that is, my work with all these suffering child cases – Melanie would tell me about *her* cases, instead. And she did so in great, great detail.

BK: So you had a master class in child analysis.

DW: I did. I had a master class.

BK: And I believe you found her book on *The Psycho-Analysis of Children*, published in 1932, deeply moving.

DW: Once, I went back to see my family in Plymouth for a holiday, and I took Melanie's book with me. It must just have been published. And I went to Dartmoor, a favourite nature place of mine, not far from Plymouth. And I sat outside on the moor, and I read the book. Dartmoor is a wonderful place for reading. No one disturbs you on Dartmoor. And I found the book so remarkable – it quite blew me away – that I read the book again, right there on the moor! And then I read it yet again!

BK: Did Klein's book furnish you with a map?

DW: One could very well say that. A map, yes … a map. You see, I had all of this raw experience, and I had no one – apart from Mr Strachey, of course – with whom I could discuss it. And then Melanie wrote her book, and it said so much of what I had wanted to say, and it did so quite brilliantly, in spite of Melanie's somewhat weighty, Gothic style.

BK: And by Gothic style, you mean … ?

DW: Well, you know that Klein wrote very poorly, as I have said. She really sweated over her writing. It certainly did not come easily to her, in part because of being a native German speaker and then a Hungarian speaker. I never heard her speak Hungarian,

you understand, but I suppose she must've picked up something of the language, because of her time in Budapest with Sándor Ferenczi. But English did not sit well with her. With the benefit of hindsight, I think that the book suffers from Mrs Klein's somewhat obsessive quality – and this often gets missed, I think – the same obsessive quality which allowed her never to be wrong.

BK: Of course, Mrs Klein wrote her first book in German, and Mrs Strachey, your analyst's wife, had translated it into English.

DW: Yes, I had not remembered that. Precisely. At that point she did not have the confidence to write a whole book in English. She did later though, but with difficulty.

BK: You had a deeply intimate relationship with her, but this became increasingly fraught during the 1940s and 1950s.

DW: Yes, that is true. I think that we each felt a sense of betrayal by one another ... I betraying her because I would never allow myself to become one of her official cronies, and she betraying me because of a certain arrogance, a failure to really get to know about other people and their work, including my own. She had a dogmatic quality, and much of this got absorbed by her closest followers, especially people like Hanna Segal and Herbert Rosenfeld and, for a time, Donald Meltzer, all of whom, I thought, behaved in very uncollegial ways in our British Psycho-Analytical Society by always having to be right. Mrs Klein cultivated "Kleinites", as we used to call them, or "sub-Kleinians". And I hated this. Why could these people not be themselves?

BK: You experienced the Kleinians as being rather certain.

DW: More than that ... arrogant, I would say.

BK: And your papers often revel in doubt and uncertainty as well as independence of mind and spirit.

DW: Well, I hope that might be the case.

BK: I believe that people had often asked you to form a Winnicott society – an independent psychoanalytic association based around you – but that you had always refused to do so.

DW: Yes, I would blanch at the thought of anyone else being a Winnicottian. It can be very important not to have the answers. The analyst who has the answers, or who believes that somebody else already has all of the answers, will hardly need to talk to the patient to discover what the answers might be. Psychiatrists, you see, have all the answers. They meet a patient for five minutes ... three minutes, even ... and then they conclude the patient is schizophrenic. And they know that this means that the patient has a broken brain, and that the patient needs ECT, and so forth. There is no curiosity about the patient's history.

BK: And you experienced some of your Kleinian colleagues as having all of the answers already?

DW: Oh yes, indeed!

BK: But Hanna Segal and Herbert Rosenfeld pioneered work in the psychoanalytic treatment of schizophrenia. Wilfred Bion, too, also made contributions to this area of work. I suspect that they might well have shared your distaste for ECT.

DW: I certainly mustn't include them in my diatribe against the somatic psychiatric people, not at all. But even so, these Kleinians ... did you know that I was really the first person to call Melanie's followers "Kleinians"?

BK: I had read that in your correspondence.

DW: These Kleinians had, nevertheless, a psychiatric flavour to their way of working, in spite of being psychoanalysts. They would often make interpretations to the patient within minutes of meeting them ... sometimes within seconds. This became extremely clear to us all when they presented papers to the British Psycho-Analytical Society at our fortnightly Scientific Meetings. Instant interpretation, quick interpretation ... well, that is not a psychoanalytic strategy. That is a psychiatric strategy, I think.

BK: Throughout your published contributions, and in your unpublished correspondence, you have expressed various concerns about interpretation.

DW: Yes, man cannot live by interpretations alone. One should use them carefully, and sparingly; and they should generally be short … in length, I mean. I make long interpretations only when I am very, very tired. Unlike Melanie, whose interpretations could go on for ages …

BK: You have written about the importance of short interpretations, and I believe that you once committed yourself to the view that one interpretation per session will often suffice.

DW: Absolutely. And that one interpretation need not even be a "correct" interpretation. Even if we give the patient the *wrong* interpretation, the patient will often appreciate our efforts, our attempts at understanding.

BK: You certainly had reservations about the Kleinian approach to interpretation.

DW: Yes, Clare, my second wife, had an awful experience with Mrs Klein. Melanie interpreted one of Clare's dreams, and she went on and on, for an interminable period of time, and Clare felt as though Melanie had robbed her of her own dream. She really came home fuming! She then dropped out of her analysis for a while.

BK: I believe that you worked with patients who had had prior analyses from Kleinian colleagues.

DW: I had many such patients, and they came to me because they had had failed analyses with one Kleinian or another. Of course I had failures too. We all have failures. You know, I ought to mention that many psychoanalysts believe that they can make patients better solely with their interpretations. This is true to an extent, but only to an extent.

BK: You mentioned many years ago that the interpreting analyst might actually become a replacement for a depressed parent.

DW: Yes, yes. The interpreting analyst has the potential to help the patient keep alive, or to permit the patient to become alive, through being interested. It is the relatedness between analyst and patient, more than the interpretation itself, that strikes me as so fundamental.

BK: You might be interested to know that much of contemporary psychoanalytic and psychotherapeutic theorising concerns the absolutely pivotal role of the relationship between the clinician and the patient, about the attachment that develops between the two participants.

DW: I am glad to hear it. You must understand that I like the idea of making interpretations. They are fundamental. Of course they are. But they form only a portion of an analysis, and we mustn't forget that.

BK: I have a sense that one could almost teach a course on the modern history of psychoanalysis by teasing out the nature of your disagreement with Melanie Klein, because you had so much sympathy for her work and yet you became so estranged from it as well. Do your disagreements represent a so-called "narcissism of minor differences", as Freud might have argued, or do they stem from personal and interpersonal sources? Or can we think of them as truly substantial theoretical and technical differences?

DW: This is a vital set of questions, and the answer is "yes", perhaps, to all of your questions. Certainly Mrs Klein and I had a private falling out based on complicated personal feelings towards one another, especially as I had begun to find my own voice as I matured and grew. We were just fine when I was her junior, sending her lots of child patients. But when I became senior in my own right, when I became President, for example, and when I became more well-known and more in demand as a speaker and as a writer from a wider audience ... well ... I think some envy may have got evoked. She had a huge reputation within psychoanalysis, but I had a huge reputation, I suppose, both inside *and* outside psychoanalysis. She never went on the radio.

BK: Also, you knew quite a lot about her private family life from having analysed her son.

DW: And she knew quite a lot about mine from having analysed my wife.

BK: In retrospect, do you wish that you and she had not become so very entangled professionally and personally in this way?

DW: I do wish that we had had a broader base of membership within our psychoanalytic community, but at that time we had very few people to whom we could refer, so we all referred to each other and we all treated each other and so forth. Dr Jones had to bring Klein over from the Continent because he had no one in London to whom he could entrust the care of his wife and children, and they needed psychoanalysis very badly. But we've talked about that already, I believe.

BK: And Freud had analysed his own daughter. To whom else could he have dared to entrust her?

DW: We always suspected something of that kind, but no one dared to speak about that during my lifetime.

BK: Yes, shortly after your death the American historian of psychoanalysis, Dr Paul Roazen, who had interviewed you in 1965, published this important revelation.

DW: I remember Roazen. A clever young man. But I take your point. We had very incestuous relationships with one another back in the early days. Everyone knew everyone, both on the couch and off. And this did not help matters. Certainly, it compounded difficulties between Melanie and me. She wanted to supervise my analysis of her son Eric, but I refused!

BK: But surely, by the time your second wife, Clare Winnicott, had begun to train as a psychoanalyst in the 1950s, she could have gone to someone other than Melanie Klein? Given your deep relationship with Klein, I wonder whether Mrs Winnicott would have felt the analysis to be all her own, which strikes me as a vital part of a psychoanalysis. And even if Mrs Winnicott had a strong wish to have analysis from Mrs Klein, surely Mrs Klein could have advised her to seek analysis from someone else?

DW: I agree. But you must remember that I knew *all* the analysts at that time, and I knew them all quite well. And Clare knew them all through me, and through our dinners and parties and so forth. I mean, I had served on practically every single committee at the Institute of Psycho-Analysis and the British Psycho-Analytical Society, and I took up the presidency and all of that. And, of course, I had long been a Training Analyst as well, and I had treated so many of the analysts. But Clare did have a strong wish for Melanie. Clare knew that Klein would help her with her rage. And she did have some rage. And Klein was very good at analysing rage … and also in evoking it!

BK: I have often wondered about the ways in which you and Klein represent not so much different *theories* of psychoanalysis but rather different *styles*.

DW: Well, Melanie and I are both Freudians. We both sit at Freud's feet. She had once heard Freud speak in person, back on the Continent. She sat at his feet, quite literally. And I did too, in a more symbolic fashion. I got Oscar Nemon's statue of Freud bronzed and then erected outside the library at Swiss Cottage, on a high plinth, to boot. So one might say that she and I both sat at Freud's feet in our different ways. We are … were … both Freudians. But we disagreed, especially over envy, on the theory side, and interpretation – rapid-fire interpretation – on the technique side. But does that represent a fundamental theoretical difference? I don't know. But stylistically, yes, most certainly, we had our different textures and accents.

BK: Perhaps we can continue to explore these themes when we come to think about your adult psychoanalytic work in a more general way, later on.

DW: I see that you already have a lot more questions planned for me.

BK: Well, this does seem to be a unique opportunity to ask you all the questions that had remained unanswered at your death.

DW: In that case, we definitely need a top-up of tea. Good Lord, I realise that I had promised to ask for some more tea ages ago, hadn't I? But we did get rather caught up in Melanie. One can so easily get rather caught up in Melanie! I'll just pop out and …

[*At this point, Mrs Coles enters the room, once again, with a fresh pot of tea, and with yet more biscuits.*]

JC: I have your tea, Dr Winnicott.

DW: Mrs Coles, you have read my mind. You always read my mind, just as you have had to learn to read my handwriting.

JC: Yes, Dr Winnicott.

DW: My handwriting is very artistic, but very hard to read, especially when I write quite quickly. Lots of loops and squiggly lines. Mrs Coles knows that only too well.

JC: *Yes*, Dr Winnicott. Will there be anything else?

DW: Anything else? No, I don't think so, Mrs Coles, but we are rather ploughing through my entire life, and it is thirsty-making work, so I suspect more tea in half an hour or thereabouts?

JC: Very good, Dr Winnicott. I've finished typing your draft manuscript, Dr Winnicott. Would you like me to start typing up the tape from the first part of this interview?

DW: Oh would you, Mrs Coles? That would be most helpful.

JC: Yes, of course, Dr Winnicott.

BK: Are you really happy to do that, Mrs Coles?

JC: Oh, yes, you'll have the transcript and two carbons within the hour.

DW: This is really most good of you. I mean, I think that I have stopped paying your salary, haven't I? I mean, we don't really need money where we are, do we Mrs Coles?

JC: *No*, Dr Winnicott.

BK: Well, thank you so much.

JC: Do ring if you need anything further.

DW: Thank you. You know that we shall.

[*Mrs Coles exits the consulting room with the cassette tape of the portion of the interview undertaken thus far.*]

BK: My word, what efficiency! What loyalty!

DW: Joyce is an extraordinary woman. I spent years and years and years searching for the right secretary, and then, in the summer of 1948, I found Mrs Coles, and she found me, and it all went on from there. Did you know that she typed and retyped every paper, every book, every case note written by me. Well … everything. In fact, there would simply be no Winnicott without Coles.

BK: I had not intended that she should type up the tapes of this interview.

DW: Well, as I am no longer seeing patients – at least not formally – she hasn't had quite as much typing to do in these last forty-odd years. And she does like typing. She types and smokes at the same time. I don't know how she does it – typing while smoking – but she does it. Wonderful woman! You were hoping to publish the interview, weren't you?

BK: Well, I thought that we would have this discussion and then see what you think about it.

DW: I have had lectures published, and books published, but no one has ever published my tea! I rather like the thought of that.

BK: You know the long-standing literary tradition, popularised by the Germans, called *Tischgespräch*?

DW: My German is very poor. My French is much, much better.

BK: *Tischgespräch*, meaning "table talk" … publishing the private musings of great thinkers.

DW: Oh, I'm not a great thinker.

BK: I think that most contemporary colleagues would very much disagree.

DW: Oh, I can't believe that? Really?

BK: Oh, yes. For some, you have become a guru. And although you detest the idea of acolytes, there are, nevertheless, people who call themselves "Winnicottians".

DW: Good Lord. That's very surprising. Even though I resisted founding my own school. Well, recognition is important. But at the same time, I do think that each of us needs to be his own person, not someone else's person. Unless, of course, he or she has no other choice. Isn't that one of the centrepieces of my writing?

BK: I think that your work on the "true self" and the "false self" has become so fundamental in contemporary thinking, both inside psychoanalysis and outside.

DW: Yes, we can sit at someone else's feet, and internalise them – and we need to do that, for a time, as I did with Freud, and perhaps a bit with Klein – but then we have to become ourselves.

BK: Did Klein's followers not become themselves?

DW: Well, as to that, I really couldn't say. But I do wonder.

BK: And might it be possible that some of the self-styled Winnicottians have not become themselves? I suspect that some of them have adopted *your* self.

DW: Oh, I would hate for that to be the case. My most ill patients came to me because they had been living someone else's self, if you like.

BK: We have had a little digression from our chronological narrative, but I suppose we have also had a taste of how you underwent a very intensive psychoanalytic training, and then tried to become your own person. A "true-self" psychoanalyst, perhaps.

DW: I like that way of thinking about it. You know that John Rickman, my old friend – a lovely psychoanalyst, a truly fine man – he always used to tell prospective students that he would offer them a training. But he insisted that afterwards, they could do with that training what they liked. In other words, Rickman wanted young people to know that there isn't a blueprint for how one should be as a psychoanalyst.

BK: I believe that Rickman did not mind whether those who trained in psychoanalysis actually practised or not. I have talked to one of Rickman's students, and she told me that Rickman had allowed her to apply psychoanalytic ideas in creative arenas, such as organisational consultancy, for instance.

DW: Yes, he would have been very happy for a person with a training to develop the work in an original fashion. Not everyone needs to sit in a little room behind a couch all day long. There are no rules for how one develops a professional life. Certainly, my importation of psychoanalysis into paediatrics did not follow the rules.

BK: It always impressed me that in his technical papers Freud offered *recommendations* to his students rather than *rules*.

DW: Yes, of course he did.

BK: Your second analyst, Joan Riviere, translated Freud's paper on this very subject, which she entitled, "Recommendations to Physicians Practising Psycho-Analysis". And then your first analyst, James Strachey, revised the translation for inclusion in the twenty-four volumes of *The Standard Edition of the Complete Psychological Works of Sigmund Freud*.

DW: I know that paper, and I must have read it many times over the years, but I can't remember a jot of it. But it doesn't matter, because I have Freud inside me, in my bones, I've always thought.

BK: You never became a scholar of the psychoanalytic literature. But did that freedom from reading and reading and reading in an academic way help you to become a more original thinker?

DW: Oh I really don't know about that. I read, but not in the way that you read, because you have one of those minds that works historically. I can see that. Anna Freud had that way of thinking, so did Masud Khan, one of my pupils. They could find any quotation from Freud within minutes – seconds, even. I could never do that. They read line by line, in a Talmudic way, I suppose. But I never read that way. I suppose I absorb knowledge in a different way.

BK: How would you describe it?

DW: I don't know. I don't know how my mind works precisely. We can think about that. It works more laterally, I suppose … I can't quite be sure. Speaking of Freud's works, did you know that I presided over the banquet which we had arranged to celebrate the publication of Strachey's *Standard Edition* by the Hogarth Press? Clare helped a lot with the organisation of that, and Joyce, too, I suppose. I enjoyed that evening immensely.

BK: Mr Strachey and Miss Freud each received a complete set of the *Standard Edition* bound in red, while everyone else had blue bindings.

DW: You cannot know how happy they were to see this gargantuan project completed. It cost Strachey his eyesight, poor devil. He had spent nearly fifty years translating Freud from German into English. He went blind in one eye as a result, and he had very poor vision, I believe, in the other. He truly sacrificed himself for the psychoanalytic movement.

BK: Strachey certainly performed heroic work.

DW: A very substantial man, James Strachey. A real exemplar.

BK: Indeed.

CUP 6

Lurching towards war

BK: May we, perhaps, return to our chronology?

DW: Forgive me for meandering. But that is what I do.

BK: Oh, not at all. Would it be fair to say that as a result of your candidacy at the Institute of Psycho-Analysis, and your contact with Melanie Klein and others, you imbibed the Freudian ethos during your training years, but that afterwards you came to make it your own?

DW: That's right. I qualified round about 1933. I'm very bad at dates, but I think it was 1933, although I didn't read my full membership paper until '35. You can check all this, I suppose.

BK: Yes, you read your membership paper in 1935.

DW: How useful to be reminded of all this. I remember that evening very well – my first paper to my senior colleagues. I was so young then compared to my teachers! And I wanted them to like it, especially Mr Strachey, and Melanie, and Dr Jones.

BK: And you completed not only the training in psychoanalytic work with adults, but also the further training in child psychoanalysis.

DW: I was the first man to do so, at least in England.

BK: It might amuse you, or please you, to know that back in 1937, after you had qualified as a child psychoanalyst, Ernest Jones wrote a letter about this to Sigmund Freud. So Freud would certainly have seen your name in print.

DW: Oh my ... I find that very touching ... oh my!

BK: Yes, indeed. Jones told Freud that you had become the first male child analyst. Did people think it unusual for you, as a man, to be psychoanalysing children? I mean, when one thinks of Hermine von Hug-Hellmuth, Anna Freud, Melanie Klein, Marianne Kris, Berta Bornstein, Dora Hartmann ... all the great women pioneers of child analysis.

DW: Yes, here I am again surrounded by the "multiple mothers" of my past. Well, it helped me being a children's doctor and all that. Certainly, I had a kinship with babies and with children, which other men did not have. We can call this my feminine or maternal identification, I suppose. But thank god, I did have this aspect to me. It proved indispensable for my work, because I could relate to the infantile parts of my patients as a mother would. And also, I wanted to bring in fathers, you see. Child-care cannot be the exclusive preserve of only mothers. Babies need mothers, but mothers need fathers. I know that this is not always the case with modern family arrangements, but that is not the issue. The issue is that men are needed in the baby world, and I am rather proud to have helped get the men on board.

BK: So, you got through the training?

DW: Yes, I did, and I became a fully-fledged psychoanalyst. I read my membership paper on "The Manic Defence".

BK: In many ways, your membership paper reads as a fairly humble, fairly traditional piece of work. You pay homage to many of your teachers and mentors, Melanie Klein in particular, but also Ernest Jones, as well as Joan Riviere, Melitta Schmideberg, and Nina Searl. But some commentators have come to regard that paper as a real salvo of independence on your part.

DW: Well, I tried to suggest that mania might not always be manic, at least not in the more traditional psychiatric sense. I think that mania as a concept has had a very poor press in clinical circles. "The patient is manic", they say, as if to disqualify all aspects of the patient's energy and enthusiasm and creativity. "Winnicott is manic", they might say, but that isn't really the case. Not really.

BK: You certainly write in great detail about the dangers of manic defences, and about the way in which mania can be a defence mechanism which can be mobilised to deny reality, especially the reality of depressive feelings. But you also found a way to suggest that manic defences might be quite valuable.

DW: I think that you are right. I have not re-read that paper in half a century. What aspects did you have in mind?

BK: Well, I particularly like your reference to the music hall. If you recall, Dr Winnicott, you wrote about the flurry of manic excitement that can occur in a theatre when the dancers rush on stage, full of liveliness, full of exhibitionism of their bodies and their talents, and so forth ...

DW: Yes, that is manic. It is even manic defence. But it is also liveliness. It is life.

BK: Absolutely. In your paper, you even capitalised the letters of the word "LIFE", stressing your point all too clearly, I think. Yes, theatre can be manic, but it can be life.

DW: Oh, how wonderful to be reminded of this ... 1935 seems a very long time ago. And I did want to slip that remark into the paper, because Melanie and her cronies had, even at that early stage, already begun to talk about mania exclusively as a defence. And I found many of these colleagues very depressed – you know, these traumatised, displaced, homeless Jewish refugees who came to London ... many without spouses, and that would include Melanie. And many were quite depressed. In fact, whenever they saw signs of life in their patients, they interpreted it as mania. It *could* be mania, of course, or manic defence, but it could also be life. We must be careful not to knock the stuffing out of our patients in moments of joy!

BK: Do you think that certain psychoanalysts might envy the vitality of some of their patients?

DW: Oh, completely!

BK: What sort of reception did you have to your paper?

DW: Well, I can't quite remember. It was so long ago, and I gave so many papers since. But I think I had a good airing. Jones certainly liked it, and in many ways that was the most important thing.

BK: And your qualification as a psychoanalyst coincided with many other seminal life changes.

DW: Well, I stopped analysis with Mr Strachey about 1933, and also at this time Alice and I moved from Surbiton, which is in Surrey, to Hampstead. So we were finally in London, and that seemed very important for me. But that was not the only move that I had made. You see, I had also shifted my private office from Weymouth Street to Queen Anne Street, albeit still in the Harley Street area. And I also relocated from Mr Strachey's couch to Mrs Riviere's. And in terms of clinical appointments, I moved from the Queen's Hospital to … well, to nowhere. I just left The Queen's after more than ten years. I wanted to write and to develop my own clinical practice.

BK: A lot of change, clearly. But you also had a lot of continuity. You remained at Paddington Green Children's Hospital.

DW: Oh yes, that became my home away from home. My psychiatric snack-bar.

BK: We all love that description … "psychiatric snack-bar".

DW: I made that up myself. You see, I had a very good psychoanalytic practice on Queen Anne Street for private patients – mostly adults, but some children too. And I did see quite a lot of them five times a week. By the time I got my first couch, the tradition of seeing patients six days a week had become reduced to five. Analysts need their weekends, you know, because the work can make us hate our patients. So we need to be doing analysis, but we also need *not* to be doing analysis. Anyway, I had my private patients at Queen Anne Street, but I also had my other patients at The Green. And as I had said earlier, I had literally thousands of child psychiatric patients, and I couldn't give them all analysis. So I had to find a way to give them a snack instead.

DW: A snack instead of a five-course meal.

BK: Precisely. And that is why I came to think of The Green as my snack-bar.

BK: You developed play therapy and also your now legendary squiggle technique.

DW: Well, look, with some patients one must ask, "How much *can* I do for this chap?" But with other patients, especially young children, who are very pliant and often very resilient, I ask, "How little *need* I do?" So Queen Anne Street became the centre for doing as much as possible, and The Green became the centre for doing as little as might be necessary. And both proved to be very vital therapeutic endeavours, each effective in its own way.

BK: You received quite a lot of resistance from some quarters in response to your brief consultative work at Paddington Green.

DW: Although she never said it to my face directly, Miss Freud – who liked me, as I liked her – had, nevertheless, a special effrontery for this sort of work … these therapeutic consultations in child psychiatry. She kept the flag flying for intensive five-times-weekly child analysis, and I know from other sources that she worried that I might be diluting child analysis. But I did do proper child analysis … a lot of it … more than a dozen cases, perhaps. But it is deeply time-consuming, and not every child wants it, or needs it, or can afford it, or can get to it, or whatever. And parents won't always engage with child analysis. Not the parents of Paddington, at any rate. They would have run a mile if I had told them that they must bring little Johnny to the hospital every single day of the week. For starters, *I* wasn't there every day of the week, and even if I had been, even if I were, this could well have made little Johnny feel more ill than he really was. So I found a way of untying knots in children and in their families, and sometimes that could be done in only one or two consultations.

BK: I believe that because of your growing reputation in child psychiatry, parents from all over Great Britain would bring their children to see you, as many had no child psychiatrists in their region.

DW: Again, that's right. You must understand that when I began working, we had no formal profession of child psychiatry, just as we had no formal profession of paediatrics. In many ways, I had to invent them – or help to invent them, which would be more accurate – especially the whole area of child psychiatry. I was certainly one of the first. We didn't have child psychiatrists as such in the 1920s, except for odd-bods like Hector Cameron – a complicated man – another psychoanalysis-hater.

BK: So The Green really became your laboratory for experimentation and for developing child mental health techniques.

DW: Very much so. I had a large interviewing room at Paddington Green, and I would have several cases on the go at once. I had to. One child would be undressing behind a screen waiting to be examined physically. Another child would be drawing. A third child might be perched on mother's knee, while I took a family history. And we had visitors observing – social workers, health visitors, and so forth. It was quite a *mêlée*, but somehow it all cohered, and often it needed only one interpretation from me to take a child's symptom away. Child intervention is very powerful stuff. One doesn't need to treat a child for decades and decades. Often one meeting can resolve the presenting symptom.

BK: You worked with entire families at Paddington Green. Did people find that unusual?

DW: Melanie certainly found it unusual. But Melanie was not a medic. She never worked in a hospital in her life. She had a very antiseptic approach to the child. Anna Freud had worked in schools. She had her own school in Vienna and later her nursery in London, so she knew a little bit more about families than Melanie. But Anna Freud, also, had never, ever worked in a hospital. At least I don't think she did. And Melanie knew nothing about the real family. She refused to meet with the mothers and fathers. Anna Freud, it must be said, understood more about families than Melanie did, but she, too, did not know about them in the way that I did.

BK: Your colleague John Bowlby often recounted the story of his supervision with Melanie Klein. You may perhaps know this anecdote. Apparently, he had begun to work with a little child whose mother had recently become psychotic and had to be institutionalised. As a result, the child had no one to serve as escort to Bowlby's office, and so the analysis had to stop abruptly. Apparently, Mrs Klein became bewildered that the outside world should dare to interrupt a child analysis in this way. Bowlby told me that Klein insisted that the analysis should carry on, and Bowlby threw up his hands in exasperation when he explained to Klein that the child had no way of coming to see him. Bowlby claimed that Klein simply could not understand why the analysis should have to stop.

DW: I know that story ... yes, indeed. This is precisely my point. One must engage the families, otherwise they will attack the child's analysis and all of that. Yes, I tried to work with the families. The fathers came rarely. They had to work. In those days, if you were a working-class man in West London and you took time off from your post to bring your child to the doctor, you might well have got dismissed. The fathers of West London worked as barrel-makers, peanut-vendors, manual labourers, that sort of thing. They lived from hand to mouth. And taking a child to see the doctor, well, that was mother's job. So I met a lot of mothers and a lot of grandmothers, and even older siblings, but I did also meet some fathers – quite a few, in fact. More as the years went on. "The Piggle" ... you know "the Piggle", the little girl I worked with in the 1960s?

BK: Yes.

DW: Her father frequently came with her to sessions. What a lovely family they were! I saw them here at Chester Square though. But I digress again ... this is all by way of saying that I did use The Green as a space in which I helped to create a new psychoanalytically informed paediatrics-cum-child psychiatry, providing a total, overall coverage for the child. Bodily symptoms could be interpreted psychoanalytically and then cured. Psychical symptoms could also be cured in this way. And then, the balance of the family could be restored.

BK: Unlike a very great majority of your psychoanalytic colleagues who worked in private practice with perhaps four or five or even six intensive patients attending five times weekly, you worked with literally thousands of child patients. I think that no one has really come to appreciate the *magnitude* of experience that you had as a clinician, and the fact that you had a storehouse of clinical data shared by no one else. You had the intensive depth of experience of a Melanie Klein, but you also had a breadth that no one else had.

DW: Of course, one can denigrate a large body of experience. "Winnicott is manic", they might say. "He's with a child five minutes, and then he dashes off to another … and then another …" But that wouldn't be true. No, not at all. You are correct that I did have a large body of experience that no one else had had.

BK: I would imagine that with all of these clinical impressions swirling in your mind, and with all of these case files cluttering your office, and so forth, that you might have had a strong need to *write* about the work, to *teach* about the work, to process it, or even to get it out of your mind.

DW: Well, as my work at The Green developed, I returned for more analysis, and I went to work with Mrs Riviere. I needed a place to talk, I suppose, about all sorts of matters, including my clinical practice.

BK: You went back into analysis even though you had had a good ten years or so with James Strachey?

DW: I went back for at least three reasons. First of all, I needed to digest all of my professional work … most certainly. Second of all, I needed to find out whether I was going to be a sub-Kleinian or whether I was going to be myself. And so I went to Mrs Riviere, as she was Klein's closest disciple. And, perhaps of greatest importance, I went to Mrs Riviere because my marriage to Alice had really begun to disintegrate. Not from her point of view, I think, but from mine. So I had quite a lot to talk about.

BK: You stayed with Mrs Riviere in her consulting room in Bayswater for several more years. Did you find that a helpful experience?

DW: Of course I did, but partly because it taught me a lot about how to avoid becoming like Mrs Riviere.

BK: Marion Milner, your long-standing colleague and friend, used to describe Mrs Riviere as a bully. Even Hanna Segal, a fervent Kleinian, told me that she found Mrs Riviere quite a tough person.

DW: And Hanna Segal would know. She could be quite tough too. Did you know that I knew Hanna Segal before she became Hanna Segal? Yes, she was Dr Poznanska, or something like that ... a Polish name. She had been my house officer at The Green before she trained as a psychoanalyst. I do not know how much of an influence I had upon her, though, as she became an altogether different sort of practitioner. But that is very much another story.

BK: So you struggled with Mrs Riviere?

DW: I did. I struggled. Part of the struggle was mine, no doubt about it. Alice had begun to suffer from all sorts of anxieties. And I had to absorb all of that. But Mrs Riviere – herself a very fragile woman – a very masculine woman, with a highly developed false self – she would attack me with interpretations ... a lot of interpretations ... some of which were right, and some of which were wrong – in part because they were badly timed. But still, I found a way to learn a lot from the analysis. The war interrupted the analysis in any case, and I just continued to get on with it.

BK: Many questions come to mind about your analysis with Joan Riviere, and about your relationship to Melanie Klein, but I know these must be very personal matters, and you may be reluct...

DW: ... Oh, you can ask me anything. One of the advantages of a posthumous interview of this nature is that I can speak quite freely. You should feel free to do so too. What is it you want to know?

BK: Well, we could, I suppose, think about many aspects of your personal life, and about your marriage, and about your analysis, but I simply wanted to say that it must have become quite burdensome for you to have had so much on your plate.

DW: Hmmm ... yes, I did, didn't I?

BK: You had a very fragile wife at home. You had hundreds, if not thousands, of patients at work. You had a sometimes bullying analyst. And you lived in a country about to go to war. And you had already survived the Great War in which virtually all of your contemporaries from school and from university had died.

DW: Indeed, it was a very anxious-making time ... a very paranoid time for Great Britain, and we all got sucked into that, and into the anti-German frenzy, the anti-Jew frenzy ... and everything. It was horrible. And after the "Phoney War", we had the real war, the real Blitz. And civilians started dying. The whole of the national psyche became fragmented, a case of the true self suffocated beneath a national false self characterised by Churchill, and his smile, and his victory sign, puffing that cigar as though all were well. We created a great illusion of clubbing together, and of being strong by singing patriotically while fighting the Nazis. We did manage that. But we also fell to pieces. Everyone did.

BK: Perhaps we can speak about your own particular experiences during the Second World War, because I know that this proved to be a very important transitional period for you, both professionally and also personally.

DW: It was a crucial time in many ways. When war broke out, I became very worried. Of course I had the private worries, the private fears about my own safety and of Alice's safety. And she did almost get killed by a bomb. Terrifying. But I had more widespread concerns for the children. And then the government implemented this terrible idea of evacuating the children from London and the environs.

BK: In 1939, you co-authored a letter with John Bowlby and Emanuel Miller – fellow child psychiatrists – for publication in the *British Medical Journal*, warning other physicians about the potentially devastating psychological effects of evacuation.

DW: We have spoken about John Bowlby a bit already, haven't we? He and I had a great sympathy professionally, and also personally, although we never became intimate social friends as such.

BK: Bowlby told me that he regarded himself as "singing from the same hymn sheet" as you.

DW: A musical link … oh, I like that. Yes, he and I did see eye to eye about children and separation. We both knew that separation, though often unavoidable, could damage a child greatly. And then Emanuel Miller joined forces with us. People have come to forget Miller I think. I don't know why. He was a child psychiatrist long before me or Bowlby … well, a bit before us, anyway. He was a tad older than me. But he was a full-time child psychiatrist. He never became a psychoanalyst. And I think it is sad that psychoanalysts like to forget people who are not psychoanalysts. And Miller was one of these very good people. He made a huge contribution, wrote lots of books and papers. But he dropped off the radar somehow. In any case, the three of us did write this joint letter to the *BMJ*, as you mentioned. Because we knew what would happen.

BK: I suppose parents and government officials alike feared the terrible consequences of massive air strikes on London. But should a child's *physical* safety not come before a child's *mental* safety?

DW: No. I think not. Because without mental safety, a child has no physical safety. If a child has no mental safety, the child will become mad, or suicidal, or delinquent, and then the child's body will really be in jeopardy. No, just as one cannot separate mother and baby at the beginning, one cannot easily separate the physical from the mental here.

BK: And your concerns about the impact of evacuation on young children proved to be well-founded.

DW: When the war ended, I encountered so many cases of families that had previously been psychologically healthy, and that now had become ripped apart. Literally ripped apart. Do you know that some children who had been evacuated to Canada or to America did not see their parents at all for *six* years? Children evacuated that long often forgot their parents and could no longer draw upon them as good internal objects.

BK: I can tell you that in my own work with patients I have seen several elderly people (in the 1990s and the early 2000s) who had experienced evacuation as youngsters during the Second World War, and each came to me with a deeply profound depression.

DW: How horrible. The human cost of war – the psychological cost – is simply incalculable. So I tried to speak up about it, especially in relation to the children.

BK: Can we talk more directly about your war work?

DW: Yes of course.

BK: You remained in London, I believe. But most of your colleagues fled to the countryside, or joined the Royal Army Medical Corps.

DW: I stayed in London, you see. I wanted to. I had to. Again, my Wesleyan roots are showing. I simply could not abandon the ship. I stayed. And I had to work. But I couldn't work at The Green, as they had closed down the hospital for quite some time. And I had virtually no private patients, due to the evacuation of the children and the disappearance of most of the adults. You must know that many of the women took flight to Scotland and elsewhere. And all the men of a certain age went off to fight. I couldn't keep an analytic practice consisting solely of eighty-year-old men! So I got a job, really meant to be for one day a week, but in practice it turned out to be much more time-consuming. I took up a post as a psychiatric consultant for the Government Evacuation Scheme in Oxfordshire and the surrounding areas.

BK: This became the foundation, I believe, of your work on juvenile delinquency, among other topics.

DW: Well, as a general child psychiatrist, I had seen juvenile delinquency aplenty in London. Of course I did, particularly in my special geographical areas of East and West London. You know I came to call these children "antisocials", or "AST" children – in other words, those with an "antisocial tendency".

BK: Your work on the antisocial tendency has become widely respected.

DW: The war of 1939 created a whole host of psychological upheavals. Of course, we had the evacuations, and Oxfordshire became a key reception centre for evacuated youngsters. And those children went to lives in billets. Although I have no doubt that they suffered from the stress of separation and relocation, somehow or other most of them did manage. But I didn't look after those ordinary children. As a psychiatrist, I had a special role, working with children who had *already* demonstrated psychological difficulties in London, and *then* had to endure evacuation to the countryside *on top of that*. So in many ways, I got to meet a group of children – several hundred in all – whom one might describe as doubly cursed, doubly impinged upon.

BK: And these children lived in the hostels to which you consulted?

DW: Yes, these children lived in hostels dotted about the county of Oxfordshire, and some in Berkshire as well. I had to consult to five hostels in particular, but not just to those five, others also.

BK: What form of consultation did you provide in the early 1940s? Obviously, you did not have the resources to offer full child psychoanalysis to these children.

DW: Oh, no, I did virtually no formal psychotherapy of any kind. I would visit the hostels when I could, sometimes weekly, sometimes twice weekly, sometimes less frequently, doing the rounds, you know. And this was not an easy feat because of the petrol restrictions. But we found a way. As a doctor I had a special petrol allowance, and that helped greatly. Sometimes I took the train from Paddington Station. Anyway, I would visit these hostels, and I would spend time with the children, talk to them, draw with them, simply be with them. Sometimes I would even cook food with them. And that gave me first-hand knowledge. But mostly, I worked with the staff.

BK: You had some professional staff members under your supervision, but also some workers who had not had any psychological training at all.

DW: The majority of the staff in these children's hostels held no formal qualifications. Most had only a rudimentary level of literacy, with little basic education, and certainly virtually no higher education. These people did the bulk of the work, functioning effectively as the house parents. Sometimes we had two spinsters in charge, but I liked to have a heterosexual couple of mother and father, often with children of their own. So we had these house parents, you see, but also a few social workers. And from time to time, when I could arrange the budget with the authorities, I brought in some colleagues to do specialised psychoanalytic work with some particularly needy children. Miss Sheehan-Dare, have you heard of her?

BK: Yes, Helen Sheehan-Dare, an early child psychoanalyst. I believe she supervised you as a student.

DW: She did, Miss Sheehan-Dare. Yes she did, and I had found her solid. But at this point, during the war, she needed money, you see. Everyone did, so I had her come in to do a bit of psychotherapeutic work with the children.

BK: But you had one social worker in particular who became very important to you.

DW: Yes, Miss Britton. Well, that's what I called her for many years, "Miss Britton". And she called me "Dr Winnicott" … for many years, in fact. But we soon became close, and then, years later, after Alice and I became divorced, I married Miss Britton … Clare.

BK: We have mentioned Mrs Winnicott – the second Mrs Winnicott – several times so far, but not fully.

DW: Well, as you know, we met in Oxfordshire, when I consulted to these hostels for the evacuated children. And although we began as professional colleagues, we really did fall in love – a difficult thing to do, you see, because I still had Alice. In fact, Alice and I had just about got to the point of having our twentieth wedding anniversary. And at that time … well, one simply did not divorce … it would have been unthinkable … scandalous, in fact. But Clare had very special qualities. She came from a religious background, as did I. And she took a great interest in my work. And although timid in many ways at that time, she had sanity. She had a core, you see.

BK: I know that the decision to leave your first wife proved very painful.

DW: Yes. Yes, it did.

BK: But you divorced Alice Winnicott, and then you married for the second time. And Miss Britton became the new Mrs Winnicott and, I know, ultimately trained as a psychoanalyst. You must have had so many overlapping conversations about work.

DW: Yes, Clare could share my work. But she had her own work too. And I am proud to tell you – but perhaps you know already – that she became quite an important person in the Home Office, holding down a very big government post. She became the Director of Child Care Studies in the Children's Department at the Home Office.

BK: Did you know that after your death the Queen honoured your wife with a decoration? She became an OBE – Officer of the Most Excellent Order of the British Empire.

DW: That's wonderful. Wonderful news. She really dedicated herself to the Home Office, working in the special children's section, helping to promote social work training and standards and all of that. It nearly wore her out, but she did it. Oh, I am so proud and pleased to hear that Clare had received this recognition. What a shame I couldn't go to Buckingham Palace with her for the investiture ceremony. She had one, I presume?

BK: Very much so.

DW: Pity I couldn't go. Buckingham Palace is only just round the corner from this house in Chester Square, you know.

BK: You have the most incandescent smile on your face right now.

DW: Well, one's wife at Buckingham Palace ... How marvellous! You know, I had always hoped that somebody might have arranged a knighthood for me. Some people did try at one point, but this seemed not to happen.

BK: You certainly deserve a knighthood, Dr Winnicott.

DW: Well, perhaps someday they'll award the damn things posthumously.

BK: Although you did not receive an award from the monarch in your lifetime, I hope that it may be gratifying to know that that your articles always rank highest on the Psychoanalytic Electronic Publishing database.

DW: I have no idea what electronic publishing is, but I'm very glad to hear of this.

BK: Well, the Psychoanalytic Electronic Publishing service is an archive of essays – a veritable storehouse of journal articles – and your publications remain extremely popular, even more than forty years after your death.

DW: How happy-making!

BK: So, about these hostels in Oxfordshire, during the Second World War, and your work with the staff?

DW: Oh yes. I would basically run case discussion groups for the staff, and try to help them to understand the children. Many of the untrained workers thought these boys and girls naughty … simply naughty. But they were not *just* naughty, you see, and I tried to help the staff understand that the children's behaviour might also have a meaning. It might have a purpose. It might be conveying something.

BK: So you encouraged understanding, rather than discipline or punishment?

DW: We did indeed. We had to learn compassion, because these children were at risk, and they needed help, having been wrenched from their homes, their parents, their siblings, their surroundings … so disorientating. It was deeply devastating for them, all this loss. And of course they acted-out in ferocious ways. They would steal, they would hit, they would set fire to things. One of them set fire to a hayrick and caused a heck of a lot of damage and fear. They would truant, you know, run away, and the staff would have to scour the Oxfordshire countryside to find them. Real demons, some of these children.

BK: And did the staff consultation process help?

DW: Well, there you'd have to ask my wife and the others. But I think it helped a great deal. Certainly, we did a lot of good diagnostic work, and we saw which children improved from which sorts of interventions, and the like. I came to know a lot more about play. Miss Britton and I came to the conclusion that if children could play, well … that became a hopeful prognostic indicator of future health and possibility. We really worried about the ones with no obvious imagination or creativity. Children who couldn't play, you see. These were the very ill children.

BK: How did these children come to you during the war? How did the authorities know which children to send to your special hostels?

DW: Well, most of these tearaways began the war in ordinary billets, but they nearly drove their foster parents insane, and so they had to be billeted with us. But I'll let you in on a secret. I hand-picked quite a lot of them. I sent a number of my Paddington Green cases to these hostels, in part so that I could keep an eye on them. I think this helped greatly.

BK: And eventually you and Miss Britton – the future Mrs Winnicott – began to write papers about the experience.

DW: Poor Clare couldn't write for toffee in those days. It didn't come naturally to her, and she had very little confidence in her own professional abilities. But we worked, and we worked, and we shared drafts, mostly written by me, and she soon developed a fine mind and became, in the end, I think, a very good writer – certainly she became a very clear writer. She needed encouragement to find out that she had a remarkable brain. I knew it, but I don't think that she *knew* it, like quite a lot of ladies at that time. But she developed into a first-rate social worker and teacher. After the war, she had a very influential post, you see, teaching at the LSE.

BK: The London School of Economics and Political Science.

DW: Yes, and she taught the next generation of social workers. And I lectured for her there. Great fun.

BK: You became quite a team, both personally and professionally.

DW: We did. And, you know, she added ten years to my life. I always said that I would have died much earlier, had it not been for Clare. How old was I when I died? Let me think …

BK: Seventy-four years old – almost seventy-five.

DW: Well, without Clare, I know I would have died at sixty-five. No question in my mind about that.

BK: But how did you extricate yourself from the first Mrs Winnicott? From Alice?

DW: Oh, that didn't happen for quite some time.

BK: Of course.

DW: Now, I seem have got lost in my own story-telling. Where did we leave off? Oh, yes, we are still at war, aren't we?

BK: Yes, and I know that much else happened to you during the war years, apart from your regular visits to Oxfordshire.

DW: We had all those horribly strained conversations at the British Psycho-Analytical Society.

BK: They have come to be known as the "Controversial Discussions".

DW: I am not sure that I have the stamina to go into all that, but as the nation went to war, so, too, did we analysts. Meeting after meeting, Freudians pitted against Kleinians. Kleinians pitted against Freudians. Everyone hating Edward Glover. You know that Adrian Stephen – he was Virginia Woolf's baby brother – he organised a coup to get Glover out of office. Glover was too, too powerful, and everyone resented this. And Jones had been President forever, so these meetings had several functions. Get rid of the old guard, sort out the tensions between the developing factions, and, I suppose, try to relieve the morbid dread of being bombed every night by the Luftwaffe. An almost unspeakable time.

BK: I believe that you would sometimes hear air raid sirens blaring during your Scientific Meetings at the psychoanalytic society?

DW: Do you know, on one particular occasion, the sirens made a terrific noise. And I, being an air-raid warden in Hampstead at that time, knew the seriousness of this. I urged everyone to proceed to the basement for shelter. But the old dears kept arguing with one another about some arcane theoretical point, and no one took much notice. The analysts kept on fighting. If a bomb had been dropped on our building in Gloucester Place – that was before we moved to our bigger premises on New Cavendish Street – the whole of the psychoanalytic movement in Great Britain would have been extinguished in one go.

BK: How do you understand the theoretical disputes which erupted in these wartime psychoanalytic meetings?

DW: As Masud Khan would tell you, I really don't understand them. Masud was a great theoretician. He understood all the nuances of theories. He knew the difference between instincts and drives, between the superego and the ego-ideal, and all of that. I don't. Not in a detailed way. Only in a general way. So I may not be the best person to tell you what happened. But I do know that the Kleinians didn't like the way the Freudians practised, and vice versa. But as to our war-time discussions, quite a lot of them revolved around the nature of unconscious phantasy. How much does the infant know? How old is the infant when one first detects the presence of oedipal issues? And so forth. We argued and argued. But in the end, we didn't really resolve anything at all.

BK: The British Psycho-Analytical Society almost split into different professional organisations.

DW: We almost split ... we could easily have become two different organisations at that point. But we didn't. We managed not to split. But we splintered. We simply splintered. And we did so in a nasty way, and the Society became full of factions, with Klein's people forming their own cabal, and Miss Freud's forming theirs at the Hampstead Child-Therapy Clinic and often boycotting Society meetings, with only a few leftovers – me, Bowlby, Rickman, Adrian Stephen, Marjorie Brierley, and Sylvia ... Sylvia Payne, who became the new President – and we became known as the "Middle Group", or as "middle groupers". No one knew quite what to do with us. And Melanie never forgave me for not having declared myself to be a card-carrying Kleinite. Or perhaps I felt that by this point she didn't want me to be one of her people as I had too many non-Melanie ideas.

BK: One of your old supervisees, Miss Pearl King ...

DW: I really adored Pearl. You know she became my Deputy President during my second term of heading up the British Psycho-Analytical Society.

BK: Well, she had arranged to have all the minutes and notes of the Controversial Discussions typed up and published properly, and the full text runs to nearly one thousand pages. So even dogged historians of psychoanalysis find this a weighty tome to absorb.

DW: You know, when analysts spend so much time being silent with patients, they have a great need to talk ... and they talk a lot – outside the consulting room, that is.

BK: I do appreciate that.

DW: So I had war tensions in Oxfordshire, and war tensions in Gloucester Place with all these well-analysed psychoanalysts. Thank goodness the press never got wind of our many disputes. I suppose it wouldn't have interested them much, but if they had known how belligerent everyone became, it would have shamed the profession irreparably.

BK: Speaking of the press, we must mention that during the war years you developed another important aspect of your work – namely, radio broadcasting, and communicating to the general public.

DW: I did indeed.

BK: How did you come to be a seminal figure in mental health broadcasting?

DW: Is that what I am, a seminal figure? I like the phrase "mental health broadcasting". I suppose that is what I was doing, although I certainly didn't know it at the time.

BK: Well, you dared to speak out in public about mental health matters at a time when many of your psychoanalytic colleagues had neither the capacity to do so, nor the bravery to do so.

DW: I suppose you are hinting at the fact that we liked to keep ourselves to ourselves.

BK: In a way, this hardly surprises. You will remember only too clearly, I suspect, all the hatred that Freudians had to endure during the 1910s and the 1920s.

DW: Oh, yes, people thought us witch doctors, sexual charlatans, and goodness knows what else. People thought psychoanalysis very unsavoury. Perverts and all that, what with our putative interest in sex. In fact, we analysts really knew very little about sex. Much less than one would have thought. Like the general public, we also found it very difficult to talk to patients about their sexual lives, for instance.

BK: So for you, Dr Winnicott, to have allowed yourself to be put forward in a more public way, that took guts.

DW: I had really two principal reasons for speaking up. First, my concern about the mind of the baby, and about the mind of the mother and the father, you know, the topics that I addressed in my books on *The Child and the Family* and *The Child and the Outside World*. And all of that has to do with early life, and its challenges, and so on. I wanted people to know more about the psychology of the family. And then I had a second concern about ECT.

BK: Electroconvulsive therapy.

DW: Yes, and leucotomy, too ... you know, chopping out bits of the brain. And I wanted to speak out about these cruel treatments to a wider audience. I had very passionate views about these somatic therapies you see. I thought it a dreadful step for psychiatry to have taken – a deeply misguided step, in fact.

BK: I would be very grateful to know more about how you came to develop these interests.

DW: Certainly. Shall we deal with mothers and babies first?

BK: By all means.

DW: Back in those days – the 1930s, the 1940s – I had a real worry that no one knew how to talk to parents. Doctors would talk *at* parents, but they never talked *to* parents, or *with* parents about their fears and anxieties. Do you know that when I was a medical student, most of the staff at St Bartholomew's Hospital would not allow their patients to talk at all! It seems incredible, but it was true. The doctors would examine the patient, and then they would tell the patient what was wrong. They had little interest in learning *from* the patient. Except people like Tommy Horder – Lord Horder, as he later became ... Baron Horder, in fact – he was an exception. He liked to sit down by his patients' bedsides and listen to them, and those conversations would help to inform his diagnosis. So, you see, at the time when I first came into the medical profession, other doctors would simply talk *at* the parents and tell them what to do.

BK: What would the doctors recommend to parents?

DW: Oh, usually something silly. They might tell mothers to administer castor oil to their children, or they might advise sending the child to the country for some fresh air. Worse still, doctors often recommended that one should ignore the child or punish the child for bad behaviour.

BK: How the field has changed!

DW: Instinctively, I knew it to be wrong for doctors to talk *at* parents. I like to think that I tried to talk *with* parents about their children. Not to give advice, but to help them to see if the child's behaviour might have a meaning ... to see if the child made sense to anyone. That was much more important than prescribing a sedative at bedtime.

BK: Your philosophy of parent–child relationships and of doctor–patient relationships has a great correspondence, a great continuity. And this philosophy, it seems to me, also gave you something very original to say on the radio.

DW: You know, I can't quite remember how I first got to the BBC. Perhaps someone recommended me ... I don't know ... but certainly by 1939 I had begun to broadcast for the Corporation – you know, make addresses to the people from the studios at Broadcasting House on Portland Place. Great fun for me, really, quite an opportunity.

BK: And you developed a very special reputation as someone who never told parents what to do. You talked with them, and you respected their expertise.

DW: That is so. I suppose that having been a psychoanalyst, I already knew that one should never tell the patient what to do. Psychoanalysts can't advise patients whether they should leave their marriages or their professions. We can't tell them whether they should or they shouldn't commit suicide. We listen, and then, together, a solution may present itself. And this psychoanalytic way of being ... well ... I simply applied that to my work with children, and then it proved very easy for me to know that this is what I must broadcast. Everyone wanted me to give advice, like some mountebank columnist for a ladies' magazine. "Hit your child when he is naughty." "Hit him three times on the bottom." That sort of thing. But I don't believe in that, and so I didn't pander to those sorts of requests.

BK: You had your own very personal approach, steeped in a psycho-analytic accent.

DW: A psychoanalytic accent. That is quite a good way of expressing what I had tried to do. Yes, an accent. That is what I had.

BK: Did you enjoy the broadcasting work? You gave dozens of talks – scripted talks – on the radio, especially during the 1940s and 1950s.

DW: I did enjoy it immensely. I found it hard work, and I found the timetabling challenging, as I had all these patients, you see. And the BBC always needed me in the studio early in the morning. So I always had to do my broadcast, rush back to my office, see my patients, write the next script, and then attend to all the many other tasks that I had set for myself. Thankfully, I had much more stamina back then. That was before I died.

BK: You reached millions, I believe, with your radio broadcasts, and also with articles for popular magazines such as *The New Era in Home and School*.

DW: You know that Beatrice Ensor, a great educationalist, got me to write for her magazine. A lot of analysts wrote for *The New Era*, like Susan Isaacs, who trained alongside me as a child analyst. And when Beatrice Ensor stepped down, Peggy Volkov took over, and it was she who not only published many of my radio scripts in her magazine but also helped me to put them into pamphlet form. And those pamphlets sold many, many copies. They had a wide circulation. And the pamphlets became the basis of my two 1957 books, *The Child and the Family* and *The*

Child and the Outside World. And then we put those two volumes together into one book published by Penguin ... and that was quite a big deal, to be published by Penguin. That became *The Child, the Family, and the Outside World*, one great big amalgamation, and it sold tens and tens of thousands of copies, maybe more. It did have a great impact.

BK: That book really made you a household name.

DW: I suppose it did, at least a little bit. And I owe so much to Peggy ... to Mrs Volkov, you see. She had become my champion. I must say that I never really suspected how far and wide those little *New Era* articles might ultimately travel!

BK: So you devoted quite a lot of time and thought to your broadcasting work and to your popular writing work in the child and family field, but, as you have reminded me, you also campaigned quite vocally against somatic treatments – physical treatments – in psychiatry.

DW: When I worked at Barts, back in the late 1910s, mad people received really quite horrid care. We locked them up, we ignored them, we gave them purgatives. But we didn't cut up their brains as the treatment of choice. We didn't make their bodies convulse with electrical shocks. We treated them abysmally, but not as abysmally as the psychiatrists of the 1930s and 1940s! When the ECT and leucotomy craze began to grip the psychiatric profession, especially during the 1940s, I became increasingly outraged. How could physicians do this to people? Cut their brains up. Disgraceful. Of course, these psychiatrists – people like William Sargant, you know – they spoke with such conviction about how shocks and brain surgeries are really quite effective treatments, proven treatments. But I disagree. I saw patients at Queen Anne Street who had already had these treatments. They had submitted to these procedures, these tortures, and I can tell you that these were *not* effective treatments at all. The patients still suffered, and they suffered *more*, not less, by having been misunderstood by their doctors in the first place. They felt punished, not healed. And so, I thought, this must be spoken about, spoken *against*, and I did so, at virtually every opportunity.

BK: You wrote many letters to the editors of the leading medical journals of the period, and you helped to organise a symposium on electroconvulsive therapy at the British Psycho-Analytical Society?

DW: And I was really the first – perhaps the only one – to talk about the *sadism* of psychiatry. No one liked that. But the truth may not always be likeable.

BK: Did your outspokenness have an impact on psychiatric practice at the time?

DW: Not hugely, no. Maybe some people went to see psychoanalysts instead of psychiatrists. I had lots of letters from patients wanting analysis instead of brain surgery, but I couldn't see them all, and nor could my colleagues. We had so few analysts back then, and hence, so few vacancies, especially during the war period. Very sad indeed. *Very* sad.

BK: Some twenty years later, during the 1960s, Dr Ronald Laing – R. D. Laing – and others …

DW: Oh, I know what you're going to say. I knew this man Dr Laing. He was one of our candidates at the Institute of Psycho-Analysis, but then he disappeared, to become a guru. He mounted a much more visible anti-psychiatry campaign than I had ever done, with television, with big meetings, all of that. And he did it very well, I thought. You know that he wrote to me before he became famous. He asked me to read his first book prior to its publication.

BK: *The Divided Self: A Study of Sanity and Madness*?

DW: Yes, *The Divided Self*. And I did read Dr Laing's book. Took me a while to find the time to read it, but I did, and I thought it rather good. And I wrote to him, and I told him so. I rather like to think that I may have given him some useful encouragement. Essentially, I would agree with Laing – or should we say that he agrees with me – that madness stems from environmental failure, usually in the context of the family, you see. People are not born mad. They are driven mad. I think that is basically true.

BK: Having these bold positions, these vocal positions, on the radio, in magazines, in the letters pages of widely read, internationally renowned medical periodicals, you, too, became somewhat "famous".

DW: Yes, I suppose in a way I did have a certain fame. Not in the way that the Beatles had fame. Oh, are you a Beatles fan? I am. I mean I know they're not of my generation, but I find those boys very enjoyable. I think they know how to play. Yes, when they get onto the stage, the Beatles play. I don't just mean that they play instruments. No, they *play*. And that is why we like them. We want to be able to play like that. Their songs are good, but they are not musicians in the way that Beethoven is a musicians. But the Beatles could play, and that is what is important. They let their hair down. You know, I think that if the Beatles did not wear their hair long, they would not have become stars. They represented a lifting of repressions, literally letting down the hair.

BK: What a wonderful "take" on the Beatles. Thank you. I had not thought of them in that way before.

DW: Well, I like to think about popular culture. I think analysts are often too old, chronologically speaking, and we don't think about young people's culture enough. No, not nearly enough.

[*Mrs Coles re-enters the room with a stack of carbon copies.*]

DW: Mrs Coles, you've returned.

JC: I've finished typing up the interview, or at least the first part. Shall I start on the next section?

BK: That would be very kind, Mrs Coles, thank you.

JC: Shall I bring more tea, Dr Winnicott?

DW: We're all right, I think, just for the minute Mrs Coles. But thank you. We're deep into our work. We've started me off in 1896, and now, I think, we're up to the late 1940s. Although we've just been talking about the Beatles.

JC: Very good, Dr Winnicott.

[*Mrs Coles exits the room with another cassette tape, ready for more transcribing work.*]

DW: Look at these pages. She types so beautifully. Mrs Coles is quite remarkable. You'll have no trouble putting this interview together now, will you? I suppose it will be more a question of whether anyone will want to hear what I have to say. I'm not rambling, am I?

BK: Oh not at all. You speak so clearly, so engagingly.

DW: Do you think so?

BK: Yes, I do, Dr Winnicott.

DW: Well, in that case, let's press on, shall we. I mean, you can always share this interview – this *tea* – and *if* people find it of use, well then, that's marvellous. I like to be of use.

CUP 7

Surviving hatred

BK: So, the war ended in 1945, and during those years you had achieved a lot.

DW: Well, of greatest importance, I survived.

BK: Of course. Everyone must have worried hugely about a Nazi invasion and about survival.

DW: Oh yes, we all joked about what the Nazis would do to us if they took charge. I was definitely going to be shot and maybe tortured beforehand. Psychoanalysts are figures of great suspicion you know, and we would have been among the first to be rounded up. Of that I am quite certain.

BK: But you survived.

DW: I survived.

BK: And also, you had had established yourself as a key figure in broadcasting.

DW: Yes, and furthermore, I had come away from the war with a new theory of antisocial behaviour, linking it to deprivation, to abandonment, to separation, and all that.

BK: Bowlby also had undertaken similar work with juvenile delinquents.

DW: Yes. He looked at early loss. Criminal children who had lost their fathers in early life. That sort of thing. I looked at that too. We had similar preoccupations. But I think he did mostly research work. At some point, he virtually stopped seeing patients, stopped seeing people through the long process of psychotherapy.

BK: Did you and Dr Bowlby have a "sibling rivalry" of sorts?

DW: No, not at all. I always had a great affection for John. He was quite a few years younger, you know. And when he became a Fellow of the Royal College of Physicians of London, I took him for drinks … or perhaps for a meal, I can't quite recall … to celebrate becoming FRCP – quite a big deal for doctors. I was already an FRCP. I became one in 1944. No, I don't think John and I were rivals. I might use your phrase and say that Bowlby and I both spoke psychoanalytically, but with a somewhat different "psychoanalytic accent".

BK: I see. I believe I mentioned that when I interviewed Dr Bowlby in 1986, he told me that although you and he both sang from the same "hymn sheet", he regarded himself as a scientist and you as an artist.

DW: Did he indeed? Is that what John said? Well, is that rivalry, or accuracy? I *am* an artist, I suppose, a sort of an artist, but I would like to think that I am also a scientist. I mean, I had a scientific training. I collected data, and I collected a lot of data, and then I shared it. No, I am not so sure that I agree with John about that.

BK: Perhaps one can be both artist and scientist.

DW: Yes, both. Yes, I would like to think that in some small way, I am an artist and a scientist, working, you understand, for psychoanalysis, and for babies.

BK: I would agree.

DW: We have been speaking about the war, and about the upsurge in juvenile delinquency which I encountered in my work, and which Bowlby had detected as well, and all of that. And course, the war, though dreadful in every respect, gave me Clare, you see. Very important, that.

BK: But you did not marry Miss Britton straight off.

DW: Well, I had a predicament. I was still married to Alice, and I had been for over twenty years. I wanted to leave Alice, but I worried that if I did, she might break down. And so I didn't.

BK: You and the first Mrs Winnicott never became parents.

DW: No, Alice and I did not have any children.

BK: But you had children living in your house on Pilgrim's Lane, in Hampstead, I believe?

DW: We did. You may know that from time to time I had very disturbed children in my care, professionally, and sometimes they had no place to stay. Their parents had absconded, or had died, or had treated them savagely. And with very few good social services in place – this was before the creation of the National Health Service, you understand – Alice and I would sometimes take them in to live with us for a bit. And not just children, adult schizophrenics as well.

BK: May I speak frankly, Dr Winnicott?

DW: I would hope that after having shared so many cups of tea and so much conversation, you will be *completely* frank.

BK: Well, some of your critics, some of your *posthumous* critics, have looked upon your practice of taking in patients with great suspicion. With great concern …

DW: As though I'd lost the plot?

BK: Well, perhaps not quite so …

DW: But that I'd been acting-out in some way?

BK: Well, yes. I mean, after all, psychoanalysis prides itself on the exceptional clarity of the professional boundaries between patient and practitioner. Stopping the session at the fifty-minute mark, refraining from extra-analytic contact, and so forth. Our model of boundaries and structures provides both parties with a sense of safety.

DW: Oh, indeed. But one must remember that although the boundaries are extremely important, the patient is even more important than the boundaries. And these patients had nowhere to go. No one to care for them. Often no money. Often quite mad. And they needed saving from ECT and surgery. So when Alice and I took them in at Pilgrim's Lane, they really were pilgrims, you see, receiving charity – real old-fashioned Christian charity. I stand by my actions on that one.

BK: Do you think that practitioners of psychotherapy and psychoanalysis do not do enough for their patients? That we might lack a sufficient social conscience? I mean, we would never shop for them, or feed them in a concrete sense, or house them. And yet you *did*, at least with some of your more vulnerable patients.

DW: Psychoanalysis is a wonderful gift for neurotics. Simply wonderful. I know of nothing better. But then a neurotic can *use* psychoanalysis. Ill people can also use psychoanalysis, but they need something *other* than psychoanalysis – or, I should say, they need something *in addition to* psychoanalysis. They need management. They need housing. They need soup … literally soup. I have fed soup to my ill, psychotic patients. Not all the time, but from time to time.

BK: These "experiments" with psychotic patients, with deprived patients, with traumatised patients, have evoked a great deal of controversy. The Kleinian psychoanalysts, for example, who also worked with schizophrenic individuals, have lambasted you for being uncontained. They have argued that one can, and should, work with a schizophrenic person within the formal structure of psychoanalysis, five times weekly.

DW: Well that is true, perhaps. But I know from direct experience that some of those patients also committed suicide. All of the major Kleinian analysts of my time – and I am thinking of two very well-known Melanie-followers in particular – had suicides on their books. One can fail in any treatment arrangement, or succeed in any treatment arrangement. And I, too … I also had suicides. And I have written about this. I never tried to cover it up, you see. A suicide is part of the price of working with those *already* suicidal.

BK: But do you think that having such patients living at Pilgrim's Lane helped them or hindered them? I mean, you did not spend much time in your house, owing to your heavy workload at Queen Anne Street and at The Green, and so Mrs Winnicott, whom you had described as a fragile woman, and who suffered, I believe, from narcolepsy … well, she might have resented nursing these "in-patients".

DW: Certainly, that may be so. It was an experiment. But I do think my intentions were good. And the experiment did save many lives. These people would most certainly have died on the streets otherwise, and some would have killed themselves in hospital rather than submit to ECT. I am pleased that you have raised this delicate question. And I am pleased to say that I stand by my actions. But we must keep researching. That is certainly so.

BK: You know, psychoanalytic work has become so codified and so routinised nowadays, that we all work quite naturally, quite automatically, within the fifty-minute boundary. If a patient needs more than fifty-minute sessions five times weekly, we encourage the patient to access social services, hospital services, general medical practitioner services, and so forth. And often, this works quite well.

DW: Yes, the profession has become more formal. This is good. A science needs its formality. But it also means that experimentation becomes harder to do, and true creativity in clinical work becomes harder to deploy.

BK: You may recall, Dr Winnicott, that for many centuries the Belgian village of Gheel devoted itself almost entirely to the care of the mentally ill. Rather than institutionalise patients in primitive lunatic asylums, the whole village would take "mad" people into their private homes and care for them there, just as you and the first Mrs Winnicott had done.

DW: That I did not know. How fascinating!

BK: And you may or may not know that throughout much of the nineteenth century, and into the early twentieth century, Continental psychiatrists and asylum doctors would regularly live with their patients and take their meals together, side-by-side, in the hospital. So your "experiments" at Pilgrim's Lane have a long historical context.

DW: That is really most interesting. I did not know that.

BK: Well, no doubt we could speak much more about this topic, but I have brought only four cassette tapes with me, and I really would like you to have the opportunity to tell the whole of your story. So shall we continue with our historical arc?

DW: By all means. I think we are now at 1946 or 1947, thereabouts.

BK: Can we resume with 1947, particularly February of 1947?

DW: So specific?

BK: Well, on the 5th of February 1947, you first presented your landmark paper on "Some Observations on Hate", which you published two years later as "Hate in the Counter-Transference". Most contemporary practitioners regard this as one of your very best papers. Indeed, some workers have come to view this as your *most* important essay.

DW: It is a short paper. But I sweated a great deal to write it, and I had a certain amount of trepidation about having written it. I think it is quite provocative. I think it is hard to digest, even though it is so short and, I hope, reasonably clearly written.

BK: Well, you put forth a rather profound thesis – namely, that most analysts hate their patients, especially their very ill patients, and that caring for the severely ill can be burdensome.

DW: That is a fair summation, to be sure. But I want to be very clear about what, precisely, I mean when I say that analysts hate their patients. We don't hate our patients. We love our patients. They come to us suffering, they come in pain, and we are trained to help them to feel better. We love them, we are concerned for them, and we want them to be healthier, more integrated, you see. But we can also come to hate the ill part, the burdensome part, the needy part, the part that treats us like a toilet, and so on. We have the potential to be hateful about the ways in which our patients can abuse us. And they *can* abuse us, make no mistake about that.

BK: You based your remarks about the potential for analysts to hate their patients on the interactions that you had observed between mothers and babies. You argued that analysts hate their patients, just as mothers hate their babies, or *can* hate their babies.

DW: Well, mothers love their babies. But they hate them too. They hate them for many reasons.

BK: In the published version of your paper, you listed no fewer than eighteen separate reasons why mothers hate their babies.

DW: You counted them?

BK: Well, I have taught your paper to students for many, many years.

DW: It is odd to think that a paper that I started to write in 1946, and finished in 1947, and published, with revisions, in 1949, has now become something that one teaches.

BK: It has become a classic, known the world over.

DW: How very odd. How very gratifying.

BK: Coming back to the eighteen reasons …

DW: Yes, well, you see, it is only too easy to adopt the sentimentalised view of mothers and babies: "Mothers love their babies. Mothers would give their lives for their babies." And so on, and so on. Of course this is true. Mothers do love their babies, as we know, but let us also remember that the baby has also caused the mother a lot of grief along the way. The baby may have created much physical discomfort for mother during pregnancy. The baby may have made the mother feel that her body was being ripped open during delivery. The baby may even have endangered the mother's life during the perinatal period. And then, afterwards, the baby wakes mother up all throughout the night. The baby expects and deserves absolute care, and this is taxing. This is exhausting. And this can be hate-inducing.

BK: In your paper you used the extraordinary word "scum". Although "scum" has now become a common term of derision, I know of no other professional writer in the 1940s who had used that word hitherto.

DW: I think colleagues did wince when I suggested the baby treats the mother like "scum". But it is true. The baby often does not take the mother into consideration. Mother is treated like an object to satisfy baby's needs. There is a certain ruthless quality about this, don't you think?

BK: Some women would claim that you have painted a rather biased and unflattering picture of the mother–baby relationship, and that they did not mind at all being awakened at 3:00 a.m. for a feed. These mothers would insist that they felt loved and needed by their babies, and useful to their babies. Such parents would insist that they felt not at all resentful towards their infants.

DW: Well, those would be the more healthy mothers. Not all mothers are as psychologically healthy as others. And even with those mothers, I would wonder about an unconscious hatred, a split-off hatred which would manifest itself somewhere, somehow, in spite of the mother's denials of her hatred. You know, it cannot be accidental that every mother and father loves to sing that lullaby, "Rockabye Baby on the Tree Top". You know the lullaby, of course. It ends with the cradle tumbling down, crashing to the ground, and, presumably, killing the baby. In this way, quite unconsciously, we all express our hatred of the needy, demanding, burdensome baby, while still being able to love the beautiful baby in an untainted way.

BK: In many respects, you have urged us to be more honest, more frank, more complete in our understanding of ourselves and of our feelings towards babies.

DW: More honest, yes, absolutely. It is much better to acknowledge the hatred consciously than to act it out unconsciously. And this applies not only to mothers and babies, and to fathers and babies, but also to analysts and patients. Analysts hate their ill patients just as mothers and fathers can hate their babies.

BK: And you had some very ill patients at the time, I believe.

DW: When I wrote this paper, "Hate in the Counter-Transference", I really found myself in deep, deep struggles with a very psychotic person whom I had treated since 1930 or thereabouts. In the end she stayed in analysis with me for twenty years or so – a very long time. A very long time indeed. And she tried to drive me mad … drive me mad so that she would not have to feel mad herself.

BK: What did she do?

DW: She would threaten suicide all the time. One can dismiss that as hysterical, of course, but she wasn't hysterical. She really meant it. And it is therefore a huge burden for a doctor to have a patient always in a suicidal state.

BK: You managed her for a long time in analysis. In view of the intensity of the suicidality, did you consider hospitalisation?

DW: Oh, of course. She had many periods in a psychiatric hospital. But this did not diminish her wish to die. She made horribly abusive comments to me. And, of course, she struggled with her erotic wishes towards me as well. Everything burdensome that could occur in a psychoanalytic treatment had, in fact, occurred with this patient. And, in the end, she did commit suicide. A horrible blow for her, and for me. And I loved her deeply, in many ways, like a daughter … the closest that I ever had to having a daughter, really. But I hated her for having this illness. I hated the illness. I hated her parents for not having given her a better start in life.

BK: What a tragic experience for your patient, and what a huge loss for you.

DW: Well, it was a huge loss. But I also had to find a way to learn something from it. And this patient taught me a great deal about how people become schizophrenic. And I tried to pass on that knowledge to the profession. She taught me that schizophrenia results from environmental failure. Not from genes, not from biochemistry, not from physiology. Of course, there is all of that. But in her case, and in the case of so many like her, there had been a failure of environmental care, of environmental provision. And her mother had not prevented her baby – my patient – from feeling dropped again and again and again.

BK: Do you support, then, the much-reviled notion of what the American psychoanalysts came to call the "schizophrenogenic mother"? You may know that this theory about parents contributing directly to their children's madness had deeply angered a very great number of people at that time and had brought psychoanalysis into disrepute in many circles, irrespective of whether this might be a valid concept or not.

DW: Yes, that would make sense. From my own point of view, I wouldn't blame the mother in that sort of way. No, it is not a term that I had rushed to use, but I know what is meant by it. I agree with the idea, but I wouldn't put it in quite that way. And yet, the early parenting has a huge responsibility for what comes later.

BK: I see.

DW: Never blame mothers. They do that quite enough themselves. In a way, that philosophy is what lies at the heart of my wartime radio broadcasts. Instead of blame, one must offer empathy for the mother, and a recognition of her struggles, her difficulties, and her fears that she has already done a bad job. At the same time, one must allow for the reality that some mothers do actually do a bad job – often a very bad job.

BK: So what should we do with all this unconscious hatred? How do we make it conscious? What should the mental health worker do when he or she feels hatred towards the patient for being difficult, for being a burden, for projecting the hatred onto the analyst or into the analyst?

DW: One must talk about it, but probably not to the patient. The analyst must put the hatred into words. Maybe the analyst must talk to his or her own analyst, to a colleague, to a supervisor. Just as the mother must talk about the hatred of the baby to the father, or to whomever. One mustn't burden the baby with the hatred. But one must unburden oneself of the hatred. But not to the patient, and not to the baby.

BK: How did colleagues react to the paper back in 1947?

DW: Well, I think most of them did not quite know what to make of it. Miss Freud never engaged with this paper, although she did absorb other aspects of my work and cited other contributions that I had published.

BK: I remember having lunch years ago at the old Hampstead Child-Therapy Clinic – since renamed the Anna Freud Centre – and one of Miss Freud's elderly colleagues told me that Miss Freud insisted that countertransference should never enter the treatment situation. It should be analysed away in the clinician's own training analysis.

DW: Precisely my point. We all have this countertransference hatred, however much analysis we have had. And we should be honest about it. And use it. Melanie had a similar avoidance reaction. She, too, did not really engage with my paper. I think she had already managed a different way of dealing with hatred in the consulting room.

BK: A different way?

DW: Well, I say this with some trepidation … some analysts attack the patient with their interpretations. They bombard them with long interpretations – often very long and very frequent interpretations. And they may be correct interpretations, spot-on interpretations, but they castrate the patient's mind nevertheless. They flood the patient, and they corrode the patient's capacity to think or even to develop thought. And although Melanie was brilliant, she was also a very angry woman, and she took out some of this anger on her patients, many of whom became quite angry people themselves. Of course, no one else will tell you that, but it is true.

BK: A powerful observation.

DW: Melanie could never have grappled with my "Hate" paper, you see, because it touched too close a nerve for her. You know that so much hatred had developed between Melanie and her own children – all three of her children – well, I had best be careful what I say, because I analysed one of them. But one of her sons died in a mountaineering accident, which may not have been an accident at all. And then Melitta …

BK: Melitta Schmideberg, her daughter.

DW: Yes, Melitta. She was an analyst too. But she came to hate her mother. She called her mother "Mrs Klein" in public meetings. She argued against her mother at every available opportunity in Scientific Meetings and so forth. I could say more, but I won't.

BK: Anyone who has read Professor Phyllis Grosskurth's biography of Melanie Klein – published some fifteen years after your death – knows that Dr Schmideberg wore red boots in defiant celebration when she learned of her mother's death.

DW: That I did not know. But I am not surprised. Red boots ... it says it all.

BK: But you must have had your own reasons for being so aware of hatred at this time.

DW: Oh I think so. I think so very much.

BK: Can you help us to understand what had sensitised you to this topic, in addition to your very painful and long-standing struggle with your suicidal patient?

DW: Well, we had just come out of the war. And everyone was full of hate. We liked to think that we weren't hateful. We didn't want to think that we enjoyed killing the Germans and the Japanese. We became like schoolchildren, you know: "They attacked us. They wanted us dead. So we had to kill them." But did we have to drop two atomic bombs on the Japanese? And when I say "we", I mean, of course, the Americans, who are our allies. And we Britons ... well, we helped to make those American bombs, and then, afterwards, we made some of our own.

BK: So the Second World War served as quite an important, albeit unspoken, backdrop to "Hate in the Counter-Transference".

DW: I think it did. And I had private struggles too, but I kept those to myself.

BK: Your marriage to the first Mrs Winnicott? To Alice?

DW: Yes, Alice had become a burden, in spite of my love for her. She became a burden, and ... you see ... although I did not plan it this way, I fell in love with Clare. But I couldn't leave Alice. I didn't think that she would be strong enough for me to leave her. And that became a burden.

BK: And then you had a heart attack in January of 1949?

DW: I did. I almost died. Perhaps I should have died, given the strains on my heart. But I survived.

BK: Did the frightening proximity to death allow you to reappraise your future?

DW: Inevitably one does in such circumstances. And then, when I recovered enough to return to work, and so forth – not straight-away, but some time after – I told Alice that I had found some-one else. And then we divorced. And after a suitable interval, I married Clare. It was a painful, painful period, but one with a good ending for me. Not, I fear, for Alice, and that has troubled me greatly. Because she was a good woman, you see. A woman one could love. But a burden nonetheless.

BK: Although heart attacks result from many causes, not least from compulsive smoking, I believe that you regarded your own coro-nary thrombosis as having psychogenic roots.

DW: I smoked incessantly. We all did in those days. So that may have had something to do with it ... may have had quite a lot to do with it, actually. But I had a broken heart as well, or, I should say, a heart on the verge of breaking, and my thrombosis became the expression – the symptomatic expression, I suspect – of that conflict.

BK: But you recovered.

DW: I could not tell you that I recovered, because I kept having more coronaries over the next eighteen and a half years, but let us say that I improved. Although not without challenges. Alice was, regrettably ... how can I say this ... not the best of nurses. Mrs Coles, who had only just begun working for me a few months previously, did quite a lot for me. I might have died, but for Mrs Coles. But I recovered sufficiently, and then I decided that I should have to leave Alice, and so I did. I left her slowly, in stages, throughout 1950, spending more and more time away from Pilgrim's Lane. But, eventually, I did – I left her completely – and ultimately, we sold the house and moved on. Alice went off to live by herself in Berkshire.

BK: And you married Miss Britton?

DW: I married Clare, in December, 1951, after my divorce became finalised. We had a lovely wedding, and I never once regretted my decision. You never met Clare?

BK: Sadly, no. I had tried to make contact with her back in 1984. I even rang her house to speak to her, in the hope of inviting her to speak at a conference, but unfortunately, she had died only just a few days previously.

DW: So she lived until 1984? She had thirteen years more after my death. It saddens me to think of Clare dying.

BK: You finally had a wife with whom you could share your domestic life as well as the minutiae of your psychoanalytic work.

DW: Yes, Clare read quite a lot of my papers. And my books. She came to my talks. And we did work together, though we didn't really write a great deal together. I rather like the fact that she had her own work. She did more than anyone else to put the social work profession on a proper footing in Great Britain. A really proper footing. And she earned my deepest esteem for that. And she trained as an analyst too. And she saw patients. And she took on the Home Office job, working to raise standards of training for child-care workers ... I could go on. Yes, we had a real partnership.

BK: But you had no children.

DW: Clare and I very much wanted to have children. But it did not happen. I was already nearly sixty years old, and she was well over forty, so ... you understand.

BK: Of course.

DW: But I had many students. Many students. And I held seminars – seminars for child psychiatrists, for paediatricians, for psychoanalysts, for child therapists. Sometimes I put them all together at our new home in Chester Square – in this very house. It still feels most odd to be back here again.

BK: I can well imagine.

DW: But I had lots of very good seminars with my students, with these bright, younger people. I think that all of the teaching that I undertook really helped to clarify my thoughts, you see.

BK: The 1950s proved to be a very creative decade for you. Apart from your textbook on children's medicine, which appeared in 1931, and your two pamphlets of broadcast talks, which appeared in the 1940s, you had not quite managed to produce a full-length psychoanalytic book until shortly after your sixtieth birthday.

DW: That remains a huge regret. I should have written many more books – many, many more, in fact. I had always wanted to. But one can't punish oneself. The guilt is bad enough. I went to my death with many unwritten books in my mind, but what with married life, committee work for the Institute of Psycho-Analysis, patients, hospital work, correspondence, etc. ... Anyway, thank God for Peggy Volkov. As I said, she pushed me into doing those two books in 1957. And that set the ball rolling for those books which I did manage to complete before I died.

BK: *The Child and the Family: First Relationships*, and *The Child and the Outside World: Studies in Developing Relationships*. I believe that Dr Janet Hardenberg helped you with editing those.

DW: Yes. She was a fine person. The wife of my junior at The Green, Herman Hardenberg, a very solid child psychiatrist and analyst. You see, once those books had come out, and once we sold them to the Americans, and to other countries, too, I got quite excited about proper publishing. And this, combined with gentle prodding from Mrs Coles, and from Masud, well ... I finally managed to get more and more out there.

BK: Masud Khan, of course.

DW: Yes, Masud Khan. He played a hugely facilitating role in helping me to put many of my books together.

BK: Masud Khan had a considerable involvement in your life in later years, or should I say that you had a huge involvement in his life.

DW: I came to know him shortly after his arrival in this country. He had come from India – well, Pakistan, really. But it was all India in those days, before the partition. He was one of the Muslim Indians. And he came here to train. Started with Miss Sharpe as his training analyst; then, when she died, he got passed along to Rickman – John Rickman, my friend – and then, poor Masud, he had another trauma. Rickman dropped dead on him too. So he'd had all these terrible losses. And he needed more analysis, so he came to me.

BK: Did you have reservations about taking him on as a patient, as you had already had quite a bit of contact with him in one form or another? After all, he had, I believe, come to observe your child psychiatric work at the Paddington Green Children's Hospital, and he probably attended your lectures and so forth.

DW: Indeed. But we were such a small community of analysts in those days, everyone knew everyone, and we simply had to manage these multiple relationships. And Masud and I did have these multiple relationships. Yes, he came for analysis.

BK: But I believe that his first wife had some consultations with you as well.

DW: I had best not say too much about that. It got a little confusing at times, but we managed.

BK: And you allowed Mr Khan to help you with your manuscripts.

DW: He offered, and I really couldn't say no. He was such a brilliant scholar. He knew his Freud, and everything else. One of those people who could read psychoanalytic journals cover to cover and remember exactly who said what, and when, and where they had published it. Quite a skill. Quite a gift. I can't do that. I have no head for academic references. So Masud often stuck the references into my papers. He insisted. I would have been very happy to have published my papers without those references. I think for myself.

BK: Well, perhaps we shall return to Masud Khan later, as he has had a big influence on your posthumous reputation.

DW: Oh, dear, that sounds ominous. Did he come a cropper? I always worried what might happen to Masud after my death.

BK: Well, he did have a very great struggle and, I believe, caused a lot of harm.

DW: It saddens me to hear this, but it does not surprise me entirely. No doubt we'll come to that.

BK: In the meanwhile, can we return to the question of your books? Your books have become the primary vehicle through which subsequent generations of mental health professionals have come to know you.

DW: After those two books for Tavistock Publications, you know, *The Child and the Family*, and *The Child and the Outside World*, I had thus established a proper relationship with a publisher, and this allowed me to get my collected papers – my professional psychoanalytic papers – out into the world. Well, I had lots of papers, but Masud helped me, and Joyce – Mrs Coles – also helped me to assemble the best of the best. And that became *Collected Papers: Through Paediatrics to Psycho-Analysis*. Masud's brother, Tahir, did the photo for the inside back flap of the book jacket. A photo of me.

BK: Since your death, that book has come to enjoy several reprintings, but the publishers had ultimately shortened the title, removing the words *Collected Papers*, because, I suppose, you had subsequently produced further volumes of collected papers. So most people know your 1958 book quite simply as *Through Paediatrics to Psycho-Analysis*, or *TPAP*.

DW: I like *TPAP*.

BK: And that book of papers has become legendary, a real masterpiece, containing some of your most extraordinary contributions, including your seminal essay on countertransference hatred, about which we have already spoken.

DW: Oh, but don't forget my transitional objects paper. That's quite an important one, I think, and "Primitive Emotional Development", and the others.

BK: I agree. All of those papers form the spine of many a psychoanalytic education.

DW: How gratifying. You know, one writes and one writes, but one never quite knows what others will do with one's writings. So it is good to know that people have read those papers and have come to remember them.

BK: Very much so.

DW: Do you have a favourite chapter from *TPAP*?

BK: I would be very hard-pressed to choose a favourite, as I have drawn upon all of those wonderful essays.

DW: Oh, but do tell me. The other papers in the book will be able to manage their jealousy!

BK: Well, having begun my clinical career working with people diagnosed as "schizophrenic", I turned to your paper "Psychoses and Child Care" quite early on. That had an immense impact on me and on my work.

DW: I remember that one very well. I first delivered that at the Royal Society of Medicine.

BK: The RSM.

DW: Yes, indeed. You know I had a long relationship with the RSM. That is where I cut my teeth as a young children's doctor, going to their meetings, long before I knew much about psychiatry at all. I did a lot of work for the RSM back in the 1920s. And then, shortly after marrying Clare, I became President of the RSM's Paediatrics Section. Most enjoyable, but far too many boring committees, listening to radiologists chattering away. In the end, I just did my own thing, and I bunked off the committees. But tell me about "Psychoses and Child Care".

BK: Well, I thought you demonstrated a great deal of bravery in writing that paper.

DW: Bravery?

BK: Yes. Because in that paper, you really state quite boldly that psychosis stems from failure of environmental care. In the early 1950s, that must have irritated the geneticists and the biochemists, the ECT people and the psychosurgeons.

DW: Sargant and the others never read my papers.

BK: You have already mentioned William Sargant briefly.

DW: He was an Old Leysian like me.

BK: Old Leysian?

DW: Yes, he went to the Leys School, as I did. But we each took psychiatry in totally different directions. I would like to think that I tried to steer psychiatry down the right path, and he down the wrong one. No, he would not have read my paper.

BK: This may be quite gratuitous gossip, but I can tell you that one of my teachers had shared an office with Sargant on Harley Street, back in the 1960s. And he told me that Sargant used to scream at his secretary constantly, really bullying her.

DW: Well, Mrs Coles might have some thoughts about that. I know that I do. You see, I think that the way in which a doctor treats his secretary very much reflects how he might treat his patients. And I do think that Sargant and his crowd – though proud, educated professional men – certainly bullied their patients into having these operations on their brains.

BK: I wonder how much choice patients would have had in the 1940s and 1950s.

DW: Virtually none, I expect. No, William Sargant would never have read "Psychoses and Child Care". But I am glad that you liked it. I did try to say that psychosis has something to do with the way the mother treats the baby. Not a popular theory. But a necessary theory.

BK: I really regard that paper as a crucial contribution to our understanding of madness.

DW: Has it stood the test of time?

BK: Well, psychiatry has become very anti-psychoanalytic in recent decades, and many psychiatric workers have little patience for psychoanalytic theorising about the aetiology of schizophrenia. They would argue that case material as such does not constitute proof of anything. So, to be fully truthful, your paper has not made an impact on psychiatry. But on psychotherapy it has, most definitely!

DW: That saddens me.

BK: But we may have reason to be a bit more hopeful, because after decades of proto-somatic theorising, psychiatry has, finally, begun to recognise the importance of early intrafamilial experiences. Certainly, we now have a great deal of data about the large number of psychotic patients who had experienced physical abuse and sexual abuse during early childhood.

DW: How sad. That, too, does not surprise me. That would constitute a massive impingement ... a really ghastly failure of the environment to facilitate growth.

BK: Yes, I agree.

DW: And the other papers in *TPAP* that please you? I really do love that acronym. *TPAP* – how marvellous!

BK: Really, it would be too hard for me to ...

DW: Oh, I'm just having fun. It's so nice to meet someone who likes my work.

BK: I wish that we had time to consider all of your papers and all of your books in turn, but I fear that in doing so, we would be taxing Mrs Coles with far too much typing.

DW: Don't let that stop you. She's very fast, and very accurate. Queen of the carbon paper, don't you know.

BK: By the 1950s, I think we can begin to see some repetition in your writings – discussing the same phenomena from different angles – but also, one can begin to recognise the emergence of a fully-formed theory of human development, and of a clinical technique which devolves from it. Do you think I might prevail upon you ... I know this may be quite a chore ... but do you think I could ask you to give us all a potted summary of your theory of human development, in sequence?

DW: In sequence? I know what you are trying to say. I never wrote it out in a tidy, orderly way, did I?

BK: Well not exactly ...

DW: Shall I have a go, then?

BK: I think it would be extremely helpful to young students who wish to embrace your work. After all, your collected books and papers and correspondence – the published ones, that is – fill nearly twenty volumes … and as we speak, various scholars are busy preparing further volumes of your writings. So it can be quite a daunting task to study your multitudinous contributions.

DW: So a bit of order would be helpful.

BK: Very much so. Though one would be loath to lose all the nuances and subtleties of your work as well.

DW: But I see your point. I did write up some of the lectures that I delivered to my students in book form, but I believe I died before I finished it.

BK: Well, you may be pleased to know that in 1988 those lectures did appear in print under the title *Human Nature*, edited by members of the Winnicott Publications Committee.

DW: There is a Winnicott Publications Committee?

BK: Well, that group has recently completed its work, so it no longer exists, although it had functioned very successfully for many years, during which time its members prepared many of your unpublished papers for publication. But there is still a Winnicott Trust charged with the administration of your literary estate. And a Squiggle Foundation, too, which provides public lectures on Winnicottian themes.

DW: How marvellous. A Squiggle Foundation!

BK: Yes.

DW: Well, at least my thoughts won't be lost. How gratifying that these people are looking after my ideas in this way.

BK: *Human Nature* is, I believe, a good starting-point for trainees, but you introduced so many new concepts, so many neologisms, into the psychoanalytic lexicon – words and phrases like "transitional object", "squiggle", "true self", "false self", "good-enough mother", and so on – I think a crash course in Winnicottiana might be of great value.

DW: Very well. Let's have a whirl.

CUP 8

A crash course in Winnicottiana

BK: If you could begin, perhaps, by explaining your views about how a neonate becomes a grown-up – how a baby matures – that would be indispensable to students and, I think, to seasoned practitioners as well.

DW: I can try. But I warn you, I am not an orderly thinker.

BK: How does a baby come into the world? What might be the baby's psychological state at the time?

DW: Well, perhaps we need to begin by asking the question as to *why* a baby comes into the world.

BK: Yes, of course.

DW: Years ago, I made a passing reference to the stage which I called being "conceived of". In other words, we all begin not only as a twinkle in our parents' eyes. We begin as a phantasy in our parents' minds. They have already given birth to a baby in their heads long before sexual intercourse occurs. So, I suppose what

I am trying to say is that development and character-formation start long before the baby comes into the world.

BK: I think you are trying to formulate an idea about the unconscious wishes in the mind of the mother and father which precede a baby's birth.

DW: Some parents bring a child into the world in order to love the baby. Others do so because they want someone to hate. And the foetus becomes the fulfilment of those conscious or unconscious wishes. So, in many respects, our personalities become formed, at least in part, long before the fertilisation of the ovum.

BK: In other words, primitive, unconscious parental phantasies can exert a determinative power on the child's eventual state of mind?

DW: Very much so. A child will know intuitively whether his parents really wanted to have a baby or not. But early parental phantasies will not be the only determining factor.

BK: Oh, yes?

DW: Round about the time of the birth, the mother's experiences – her perinatal experiences – will have a further impact upon the child. You know that many mothers have truly suffered at the hands of very envious midwives. And many midwives – at least in my day – would infantilise mothers and humiliate them, keeping them passive and helpless in a hospital bed, criticising them for not breast-feeding properly. These sorts of unfortunate interactions can make the mother feel sad and persecuted; and that will impinge upon the baby.

BK: I believe that modern midwives have a much greater understanding of psychology than those who practised in the 1930s and 1940s.

DW: Oh what joy to know!

BK: So, following on ... the baby's state of mind will depend very much upon the mother's state of mind, right from the start.

DW: This may seem quite simple, quite obvious. But I can tell you that in my day, few people, if any, recognised this very simple fact.

BK: You had to fight for the obvious.

DW: I had to fight for the obvious. You see, the mother will have a state of mind in which she can either function well as a primary caretaker or function less well. And if she is well, then the baby has a better possibility of being well. And if the mother is ill …

BK: This preconceptual, pre-infantile period – shaped by parents' unconscious phantasies, and then by perinatal experiences – all of this has a very large role to play in the baby's ultimate character development.

DW: Yes. The baby will be very much beholden to the early atmosphere created by the grown-ups, long before the baby arrives!

BK: And what about the actual birth itself? Would you agree with early psychoanalytic writers such as Dr Otto Rank that the very physicality of birth itself could be traumatic?

DW: I had a copy of Rank's book in my library, you know. Once, I even loaned it out to a patient. I think his work is very interesting, and we don't talk enough about it in psychoanalytic circles. Birth, you see, can be exceedingly traumatic for both mother and baby. Birth can occur so very quickly.

BK: But the mother has some time for preparation … psychological preparation.

DW: Thank God biology has given the mother nine months to ready herself for the arrival of the baby. That allows her time to greet the baby in her mind. But the baby does not have the same privilege. You see, when the labour process begins, the mother may often experience pain, but she knows that in six hours, in ten hours, in fifteen hours, there will be an end to these pains, and that she will have a beautiful baby as a reward.

BK: But the foetus?

DW: The foetus has no such guarantee that labour will end. I have often thought that the foetus, suddenly propelled from the relative calm and consistency of intrauterine life, will experience unbearable anxiety as birthing begins – propelled down a long, dark tunnel, if you will, with no reassurance that this process will ever cease. I think that birth might well be very frightening for the baby.

BK: That makes a great deal of sense. Nowadays, we have much more knowledge about intrauterine life – knowledge that you would not have had access to in your lifetime.

DW: How fascinating. Do tell me.

BK: Well, in recent years, safer and more sophisticated methods of ultrasound scanning have allowed obstetricians to see right inside the womb, and to observe exactly how the foetus responds to light, to sound, to music, to movement, and so forth. And we know that the foetus does not simply lie suspended in amniotic fluid – rather, he or she will react strongly to external stimuli, especially during the second and third trimesters. So if the mother feels anxious, she will transmit this in a variety of ways to the foetus, who will often become distressed in consequence.

DW: This confirms what I had always suspected. In fact, I knew this already from my own work, although I did not have the scientific data to provide confirmation. But I knew this intuitively from my intensive psychoanalytic work with regressed patients, because, you see, when one has a regressed patient on the couch, this resembles an intrauterine environment. And when the analyst crosses or uncrosses his legs unexpectedly, or coughs, this impinges upon the patient, rather in the way that a sudden jolt might impinge upon a foetus *in utero*.

BK: That makes a great deal of sense, Dr Winnicott.

DW: So, you see, we have this incredibly sensitive neonate, and this incredibly sensitised mother, and they begin to have a relationship where everything that happens has an impact, especially for the newborn baby. And the baby will be alert. Make no mistake about that.

BK: Of course.

DW: The baby knows precisely what should be happening, and will experience pleasure if that happening actually happens. But the baby will also experience pain if something fails to occur. In other words, if a feed takes place, the baby knows it. And if a feed does not take place, the baby certainly knows that too!

BK: Tell us, please, more about what happens postpartum between the mother and this very sensitive, very alert baby.

DW: I notice that you have asked me about the mother and baby, rather than about the father. And that is probably correct. Of course, we have some fathers who act like mothers.

BK: Nowadays we would call them "primary caretaker fathers".

DW: That is a good term, I think. But in most instances, we are talking about a mother. At least, in my day that was the case. So we have this mother, and she has a series of tasks to perform in order to provide her baby not only with the physical nutrients needed to stay alive and to thrive but also with the psychological ingredients required to develop a mind ... to become mentally healthy.

BK: When you speak of tasks ...

DW: When I speak of tasks, I do not mean mechanical, timetabled tasks in a Truby King sort of way. We spoke about Truby King a while back, and you know my views about his rigidity. Perhaps "tasks" is not quite the right word. I mean, rather, a series of undertakings – psychological undertakings – which have no starting time and no stopping time. They become the bread-and-butter tasks of mothering, and they go on all the time.

BK: I believe you identified three functions, or tasks, or undertakings, in particular.

DW: We could certainly speak of three tasks of motherhood.

BK: And how would you define these primary tasks of the mother?

DW: First and foremost, the mother must "hold" the baby. Of course, this is so obvious that it almost does not need stating, and yet it also needs stating very emphatically. And here, I think I would use the word "hold" in two different senses – both physical and psychological. Most crucially, the mother must hold the baby in her arms.

BK: Physically?

DW: Yes, physically. In other words, she must provide the infant with a cradling environment in which the infant will feel enveloped, enfolded, and protected from the outside world. The infant must be held onto, but not in a constricting way, and not in a smothering way, but, rather, in an ordinary way that makes the baby safe and happy. And the mother must not drop the baby on the ground in a "Rockabye Baby" sort of way. She must hold onto her newborn son or daughter, and keep the baby aloft. All of this represents a part of good holding.

BK: But you also mentioned psychological holding as opposed to physical holding.

DW: Yes, holding happens at two levels – first, the physical holding, as I have stated, and, second, the psychological holding, which one might describe as a kind of "holding in mind". One holds a little person psychologically by thinking about him, or her – and really holding ...

BK: In mind.

DW: Yes, that's right. It might be as simple as remembering that one has actually *had* a child in the first place, and that this child might need a drink, or a blanket, or a cot, or a breast, or what have you. Forgetting about the baby means that one has not held the baby in mind, and that way lies madness!

BK: So the mother must become an adept at holding, with both her left arm and her right arm – the physical holding – and also with her thoughts and memories and attentivity – the psychological holding.

DW: Exactly. And if the mother can do this satisfactorily – and it is a great blessing for us to know that most healthy mothers *can* do this quite naturally, quite automatically – then the baby has a very good chance, indeed, of becoming sane. Of being mentally healthy. But if the mother cannot do this, either because she has never been held in this way, or because she hates her baby for some reason ... or even, whether, due to her own traumatic state she has no space for the baby in her mind ... well, then the baby will begin to suffer primitive psychological agonies.

BK: But how marvellous to know that in your experience, most mothers do have the capacity to lay the foundations of infant mental health and child mental health as a matter of course.

DW: Yes, that is where I am a Darwin man through and through. By reading Darwin at school, I suppose I learned that one does not need to *work* at human evolution. It simply unfolds as a matter of course. Similarly, one does not need to study holding or practise holding. A healthy mother will do it because she knows about her baby's needs in a deeply-felt way, and she can make it happen, almost automatically.

BK: You mentioned that the mother has two other tasks, apart from this combination of physical and psychological "holding".

DW: Indeed, she must also be able to demonstrate "handling" of the baby, which is not quite the same as "holding". I suppose we might say that in holding the baby, the mother keeps the infant safe and prevents her baby from falling, both out of her arms and, also, out of her mind. We could think of holding as a physical and mental cradling of the child.

BK: And handling?

DW: With handling, we have to look in a more detailed way at how the mother actually touches her child. Does she handle the infant in a rough way? In a smooth way? In a seductive way? Does she stroke the skin so that the baby feels comforted, or maybe irritated? All of this, you see, constitutes handling. It is the nitty-gritty, moment-by-moment interaction that takes place between a mother and her baby.

BK: Does the quality of handling set the tone of the relationship?

DW: Very much so. And no two mothers will handle their babies in the same way. But healthy mothers will do handling quite well.

BK: And the third task?

DW: We call that "object-presenting". Essentially, this might be defined as the mother's attempt to introduce the outside world to the infant. You cannot have a mother who keeps the baby stuck on her breast all day long, wrapped up in a symbiotic psychosis or a *folie à deux*. The mother must eventually begin to share the baby with the outside world and guide the baby through the outside world. She must point out objects and accustom the baby to objects other than herself.

BK: Would father be included among those objects?

DW: Perhaps. We could indeed think of it in that way. But we must also include the grass in the park, the blue sky outside, the kitten on the window ledge. The attentive mother will guide her baby through each of these objects in turn: "Look, that's Rover ... he's our little puppy dog." And so on. You see, the infant has the important job of making contact with reality. And the mother helps the baby to accomplish this. And when she does, then the baby can become mentally healthy.

BK: Presumably, the mother who can hold, handle, and object-present creates a very safe, very comfortable and, at the same time, a very stimulating world for her baby.

DW: Absolutely! And when all of those components work harmoniously, in tandem, we find ourselves in the presence of a sturdy mother–infant situation, and we find ourselves in the presence of health – real mental health.

BK: And I know that you came to think of this sort of healthy mother as an "ordinary devoted mother". Your radio producer Isa Benzie, back in the 1940s, rather liked that term, I believe.

DW: Miss Benzie – yes, she was a highly skilled radio producer for the BBC, and she really understood my work. She really got it. And when I happened to mention the phrase "ordinary devoted mother" during one of our meetings – very much *en passant*, you understand – she seized on it, and she exclaimed that we must do an entire radio series all about the "ordinary devoted mother". And so we did. And that turned into a very popular pamphlet, and that really got me known in a very particular way.

BK: You became somewhat famous.

DW: Yes, I suppose I must have done ... a bit.

BK: You found a language that mothers could understand.

DW: Oh, yes. I wanted mothers to feel that they knew as much about how to look after a baby as the so-called experts. In fact, I really wanted to acknowledge that the healthy mother knows *more* about her baby than the experts do. And Miss Benzie allowed me to talk to mothers in this way, on the radio.

BK: And you received fan mail, I believe.

DW: Heaps and heaps of letters from mothers telling me that they had really wanted to hold their babies and comfort them during crying spells, but that their doctors had told them not to. They thought that by comforting a crying baby they might be indulging or spoiling the child.

BK: Your advocacy of the nursing mother must have proved to be a real godsend to many young parents.

DW: Well, they wanted to trust their own instincts, but the experts often discouraged them from doing so. And we had a lot of very unhappy parents and babies as a result.

BK: So the ordinary devoted mother provides both safety and stimulation.

DW: Yes, that's right.

BK: But you also wrote an entire paper about the phenomenon of "Primary Maternal Preoccupation", back in 1956. How does the "ordinary devoted mother" differ from the mother who manifests "primary maternal preoccupation"?

DW: Here we have Winnicott the neologist! Do forgive me. Essentially, the ODM and the PMP – I would sometimes use these initials, you see – essentially, they are the same thing. The ordinary devoted mother is one who, in the first weeks and months of the baby's life, devotes herself with such intensity of preoccupation to the baby, that the baby becomes her sole purpose. She becomes empathic, if you like, and tries to put herself into the infant's place. She throws herself into the identity of being a mother with such fullness, and the baby feels this, and feels protected and loved and all the rest. So to be a devoted mother, one must be a primarily preoccupied mother.

BK: Some of your latter-day critics have accused you of idealising the mother, or of emphasising only the warm, gooey, loving aspects of parenthood. What about the mentally ill parent, the persecuted parent, the hateful parent?

DW: We've already talked about my essay on "Hate in the Counter-Transference", so you will hardly be surprised when I tell you that the ordinary devoted mother also includes hate in her repertoire. The ordinary devoted mother must allow herself to hate her baby, because the baby can be such a nuisance. But the healthy mother who is ordinarily devoted and primarily preoccupied can deal with her hatred by handing the baby over to father or to a nanny or to granny. Or she can put the baby in the cot for a nap, so that she can have a nap herself. But she deals with the resentment and the intrusion, and she continues to be preoccupied. The unhealthy mother, by contrast – and I saw many in my time – well, she may harm the child, often because she has no one to hold her up.

BK: In your writings, you often used the term "impingement". I find this a very resonant description of the way in which some-one – or something – in the environment impinges upon the potential peace and joy of the baby's world.

DW: The unhealthy mother tries to be ordinarily devoted. She tries to be preoccupied. But she just cannot quite manage it. She screams, she shouts, she neglects. And all of these moments of distress constitute impingements. I have also described these moments as environmental failures, and when these occur in profusion, then the baby becomes pregnable to a psychosis. The baby's original potential for madness becomes exacerbated.

BK: We have not yet talked about the "primitive agonies".

DW: It sounds like a play from antiquity, doesn't it? Dame Sybil Thorndike starring in *The Primitive Agonies*! Oh, I rather like that.

BK: Well, there is something Greek tragedy-ish about the depth of the fears that you have described in the infant's mind.

DW: Indeed. But let me answer your question more directly. The reason that the ordinary devoted mother must give herself over to devotion and preoccupation, and must hold and handle her child, is because the child comes into the world with the poten-tial for experiencing a deep, primitive, archaic terror. The child asks: "What am I doing here? Who will keep me aloft? Will I stay in one piece? Will I stay afloat, or will I keep falling forever?" ... Oh dear, I've put it rather badly, haven't I – because, you see, the child doesn't even have a concept of "I". The baby feels simply terrified of disintegrating. And the mother helps to pull the baby together. That is a better way of phrasing it.

BK: So you would concur with Mrs Klein about the role of psychotic anxiety in early infancy?

DW: Well, it is not so much that I concur with Melanie, but rather that I saw these primitive agonies in my clinic at Paddington Green, and in my work with schizophrenic people in states of regression. Their dreams provided me with all the evidence I needed that these patients felt themselves to be falling into pieces – quite literally falling into pieces. That was the fear. But Melanie knew this. And I did too. So in that sense, we had an agreement.

BK: In your publications, you spoke not only about the baby's fear of going to pieces, and of the fear of falling forever, but also of losing hope and then dying.

DW: Yes, those are the primitive agonies, make no mistake.

BK: So, in Winnicottian developmental psychology, babyhood represents a potentially frightening experience, but one that can be remedied by the healthy ministrations of the healthy parent.

DW: That's absolutely correct. That's right. The healthy parent – and let us not leave fathers out of the equation – the healthy parent can mop up a lot of the madness.

BK: You will remember Harry Karnac, I think, the founder of Karnac Books.

DW: Oh, dear Harry Karnac. Is he still alive?

BK: He died in April 2014, well into his nineties.

DW: How splendid to have lived so long. Do you know that I am actually the person responsible for Karnac Books? I used to go into Harry's shop on the Gloucester Road, and I think I asked him outright to start stocking my writings. And then I seem to remember telling him that psychology – a new discipline back then – will really have a future, and that he would be doing something rather unique by specialising in psychology books. And so he did. He started to sell psychology books and nothing but psychology books – the first person in the world to do that!

BK: Well Harry's old shop on Gloucester Road has since closed down, but Karnac Books still flourishes with a newer shop in North London, on the Finchley Road. And Karnac Books not only *sells* books, it also *publishes* books. In fact, Karnac Books will be publishing the text of this interview, if you are happy with the transcript which Mrs Coles has already started typing for us!

DW: Oh, that is very interesting. Yes, I would be very happy for you to publish this conversation, if you think it would be of interest to people.

BK: Harry Karnac came to mind just a few moments ago when you mentioned that the healthy parent will "mop up" the infant's madness.

DW: Yes.

BK: Well, literally twenty years ago, I interviewed Harry for the biography that I wrote about you.

DW: I should certainly love to read your book.

BK: I can give you a copy. But I suspect that you know most of its contents already!

DW: Even so.

BK: Well, Harry told me that you had once described the infant's psyche to him as a piece of "blotting-paper". If we understood you correctly, the infant's psyche absorbs everything.

DW: How nice to be reminded of that little phrase. I don't think I used that in my writings.

BK: I think not.

DW: But I would agree with myself. The infant has a porous psyche – aware of everything. It picks up everything. And, yes, it needs the parent to blot up the mess. That's right. We might describe the mother as a blotting-paper for the infant's mind. I support that idea. Yes, I do.

BK: I realise that we have begun to reduce the complexity and the richness of your many books on developmental psychology to a few pithy phrases. I hope that you will not object.

DW: No, we must be simple. We must be concise. As you say, we cannot expect psychology students to read all of my books – not all at once. They must come to each one at their own pace. And that will take time. I mean, after all, it took me decades to write all my books, so it should take students at least a little while to read them. No, I think you are helping me to systematise my developmental psychology in a more linear way. And as I am not a linear man, this is quite good for me.

BK: So in the world of Winnicott, the earliest weeks and months of life might be characterised by the quality of the interaction between a baby and a caretaker. The baby enters the world in a state of potential terror, fearing annihilation, fearing falling forever, full of unthinkable anxiety. And the parent – either mother or father – then becomes the blotting paper that makes the baby feel safer, through devotion, through primary preoccupation, and so forth. And then we have health.

DW: You see, the baby needs the mother for health. And the mother needs the baby. And the mother who loves and needs her baby then satisfies her baby. The two cannot be separated at this point. And for this reason, I believe, I once got up at a meeting and announced that there really is no such thing as a baby.

BK: Yes, that has become an oft-quoted Winnicottian catchphrase: *"There is no such thing as a baby."*

DW: It's quite simple, really. If you take a baby away from a mother at this point – at this early point – you have a dead baby. Because the baby cannot survive without the mother. The baby cannot really be thought about without a mother. Together, they become an essential unity.

BK: Thus far, we have not yet spoken about your important emphasis upon "dependence" – upon "absolute dependence" – in infancy.

DW: Perhaps we should have begun this little lesson in developmental psychology by mentioning those ideas. In a way, one could define my whole approach to human growth and development as an exercise in the management of dependence.

BK: Please explain.

DW: When baby first appears, he or she cannot do anything without assistance. The baby cannot prepare its own supper. It cannot change its own nappies. The baby is really wholly, completely dependent upon the caretaking of a grown-up, usually a mother. In this sense, the baby lives in a state of "absolute dependence".

BK: In your writing, you also described this as "double dependence", and, I believe, on another occasion as "extreme dependence".

DW: Absolute dependence, double dependence, extreme dependence – it's really the same. The baby cannot master the dependence, because the baby doesn't have the motor capacities to move, or the cognitive capacities to think like a grown-up. The baby has a great deal of helplessness. So the ODM – the ordinary devoted mother – must respect the infant's absolute, double dependency, and must help out, by bringing food, by bringing a blanket, or a smile, or what have you.

BK: And when the mother meets the baby's needs, then the absolute dependence becomes less terrifying.

DW: Correct. The absolute dependence gradually becomes transformed into a state of what I had come to think of as "relative dependence". The baby is still dependent, but only relatively so. And then, as each of us progresses through the life cycle, we spend quite a long time in the stage of "relative dependence", because we become better able to look after ourselves. When we learn to hold a fork, when we learn to tie our shoelaces, when we learn to dress ourselves, we become increasingly less absolutely dependent, and more and more relatively dependent. Do you see?

BK: Yes.

DW: And the relative dependency becomes increasingly sophisticated. So at five years old, we need to depend upon Mummy or Father to put food on the table. But at twenty-five years old, we become less dependent, and we can earn money and buy our own food. All of development can be framed as a relationship to the phenomenon of dependency. And if the absolute dependency of earliest infancy is met, then the baby can grow and become less dependent.

BK: But do any of us ever reach *independence*?

DW: No. And nor should we. No one should be completely independent. We all need people, and we need them for the whole of our lives. But certainly, we can move "towards independence". And so, I always insisted on describing this last stage of development not as "independence" but, rather, as the stage of "*towards* independence". That is, I think, a more honest way of describing what we are looking at.

BK: Would it be correct to say that in many ways dependence might be considered to be the most important quality in the Winnicott scheme of development?

DW: Yes, it is a marker of achievement. It is a diagnostic marker. We need to know whether the infant has progressed from absolute dependence to relative dependence. And likewise, whether the grown-up has progressed from relative dependence to *towards* independence.

BK: I find this very helpful. Freud, as you know, had a clearly articulated notion of psychosexual developmental stages in which the newborn progresses from an oral stage to an anal stage to a phallic stage, and so on. And Klein, of course, had outlined a progression from paranoid-schizoid modes of relating to more depressive modes of relating.

DW: And don't forget Erikson and Mahler.

BK: Yes. Erik Erikson and Margaret Mahler each have clear linear models of progress.

DW: I had a great deal of time for Erikson's work – or, I should say, I *have* a great deal of time for Erikson's work, because I still rate it highly. It is such a shame that my British colleagues never really embraced his writings.

BK: Would it be too tidy to think of the Winnicottian stages as, first, absolute dependence, followed thereafter by relative dependence, and followed, finally, by what you call "*towards* independence"?

DW: Not at all. That is exactly what I am trying to say to you.

BK: And what about your extremely famous concept of the transitional object, as well as the related concept of transitional phenomena? How does all of that fit into the theory?

DW: Do you know, I once stumbled upon a book written by that American dramatist, Arthur Miller. And this particular book – a children's book, mind you – is called *Jane's Blanket*. And Miller wrote the book, I believe, for his daughter, all about a blanket. Quite literally.

BK: A transitional object?

DW: A transitional object, indeed. Now, Arthur Miller is a great playwright, a great author. And I think he must have known a lot about psychoanalysis. After all, he was married to Marilyn Monroe, and she had been a psychoanalytic patient, first with Marianne Kris and then with Ralph Greenson – both colleagues of mine. I knew Marianne Kris, who was herself very close to Freud. Of course, she and her husband Ernst came to London round about 1938, as refugees from the Nazis. And then she and he went to America. And I knew Ralph Greenson from international psychoanalytic congresses – a very creative man, very likeable. Anyway, Miller had exposure to these two people through Marilyn. But I also wonder whether Miller had ever read my papers directly.

BK: Because he wrote a book called *Jane's Blanket*?

DW: That's right. You see, early on, through my work with infants at Paddington Green, I came to know that in the early, early stage of life – those first days and weeks – the baby needs to cling to the mother for physical survival, and for psychological survival, too. But then there comes a time when the infant also begins to notice the rest of the world and begins to have a need for a bit of separate space. Sometimes the mother will introduce the infant to the world. But sometimes the infant will discover the rest of the world by himself or herself. And at first, the baby might start to suck on a bit of blanket, a corner of a sheet in the cot, perhaps. The baby might even start to make gurgling noises or even little musical noises. All of these bits and bobs represent something which I think of as "not-me". These are, in fact, what I have come to call *transitional phenomena* – quite literally, different types of phenomena which help the little baby to make the *transition* from mother's breast towards an independence of his or her own.

BK: This makes a great deal of sense, of course. But I am so struck that no psychoanalyst or developmental psychologist had studied this previously. This transition from mother's breast to the outside ... well, it's so foundational.

DW: I agree. It is the very bedrock of relatedness.

BK: So transitional phenomena assist the infant in relating to something other than mother or father.

DW: Yes, these phenomena provide a potential space in which something can happen.

BK: And the transitional object, as distinct from transitional phenomena?

DW: Well, the transitional object is a very special kind of transitional experience. It is an object, you know, an actual object, which the infant finds for himself or herself. It might be the child's blanket, but equally, it might be a teddy bear or another soft toy. Generally, these objects help the child to become calmer. They serve an anti-anxiety function, perhaps at bedtime. And the mother knows that this particular object is special. This is *Jane's Blanket*.

BK: I see.

DW: And the blanket, the doll, the teddy, whatever – all these objects help the infant to make the *transition* from mother's breast to whatever is not-mother's breast ... to the outside world. And so I came to think of the blanket as a prototype of the transitional object. It is often something soft and cuddly, like a breast, but it belongs to the infant, not to the mother. Although it may have elements of the mother and her breast. Indeed, the transitional object is based on the mother's breast.

BK: Yes, please continue.

DW: You know that some infants enjoy having a bit of mother's milk on their teddy bears? In that way, they can have a transitional object that is part-mother, part-not-mother, and so on. You see?

And the object must be a reliable transitional object. It must not change. If the child chooses a teddy bear, then he or she must be able to keep the same teddy bear constantly. Mother must not give it a bath and spoil its fur or change its smell. Only the child has permission to use this object ... and, also, permission to mutilate it as necessary.

BK: So the transitional object helps the infant to make the transition from absolute dependence to relative dependence?

DW: Indeed.

BK: And, as you indicated in the title of your book, *The Child, the Family, and the Outside World*, the child must find a way to join the family but, also, to engage with the world outside of the family as well.

DW: Yes, that's it. And the transitional object assists us in this process. It also gives the infant warmth. It serves a multitude of functions, but above all, I think, it eases the transition towards the next *tranche* of development. And all of this takes place somewhere between round about four months of age and twelve months of age. But we mustn't be prescriptive about it.

BK: And the transitional object will be used by the young child – used in a creative way – to facilitate growth and development. In fact, if I understand your writing adequately, the infant's engagement with the transitional object becomes the very basis of play.

DW: Play is crucial, and it develops from this experience of playing with the corner of a sheet, or with a sound emanating from the baby's mouth, and so forth. These play experiences become more and more sophisticated as the baby grows, becoming shared play with other children, and then shared play with other adults. Putting on a play in a theatre, for instance, is an expression of *play*, because, here one *plays* with other grown-ups to make a play, quite literally.

BK: So, cultural experience – shared cultural experience – derives from infantile experience.

DW: Yes, I think it all stems from the infant's use of an object. It doesn't really matter which object the baby uses. It is more important that the baby *uses* an *object*.

BK: I find that very helpful. And this use of what you call "potential space" …

DW: Potential space, well, that's the space that becomes created when the infant learns to trust in the environment. When he or she can trust the environment not to become annihilating, then the infant can start to learn to play. And play takes place in potential space.

BK: Thank you. That really makes a great deal of sense.

DW: You know, it really does all fit together, all this jumble of theory that I have created. Talking about it in this way does make me realise that it coheres. It is actually a whole. That is a great relief. You know it has been quite some years since I've talked about it. But it still makes sense. I'm so relieved that I still remember something of what I wrote!

BK: I find your explanation very clear and very profound.

DW: And my writing?

BK: People often find your writing remarkably lucid, but also, at times, remarkably enigmatic, cryptic, oblique.

DW: How interesting.

BK: I think that your book *Playing and Reality* …

DW: Written just before I died … or, I should say, completed just before I died, because I had, in fact, written sections of that in the 1950s!

BK: Yes, *Playing and Reality*, in particular – the book in which you elucidate the concept of transitionality and the concept of play most fully – well, many students and many sophisticated practitioners, too, find this text rather challenging.

DW: Oh good. I am glad that it is challenging. It certainly challenged me. Some more tea for you?

BK: No, no, thank you.

DW: When we grow up protected by a good-enough mother, it becomes hard to separate. I mean, if mother is good, or good-enough, why should we ever leave? But we must leave, we must separate. Eventually, we become too big for mother, and so a little girl or boy needs to find a way towards independence. Therefore, clinging to an actual, concrete physical object – this transitional object – helps the differentiation process along. And it can be a two-way process.

BK: The mother can help.

DW: The mother can indeed offer help. For instance, if one thinks of the mother's voice, for instance, one can see how the child can hang onto the sound of the mother's voice, even if she is calling out from the next room. The child can derive comfort from knowing mother is there, and yet not there at the same time. But the voice helps the transition from the breast to separateness. Do you see?

BK: Yes, I do see. You have really thought carefully, and observed carefully, how, precisely, the young child becomes a more individuated person.

DW: Individuated is a very good term here. I think that the Jungians use individuation and I am not entirely certain if I am using individuation in exactly the same way. I have never been very good at precise definitions of concepts. But I think that this is what they mean. Did you know that I was the first person to invite a Jungian analyst to speak at the British Psycho-Analytical Society?

BK: Dr Fordham, I presume?

DW: Yes, Michael Fordham. A very solid man, truly a fine man. He shared my background in child psychiatry, and we became close colleagues during the war – the Second World War. I brought him along to lecture, but I don't think my colleagues thought much of Jungianism, more's the pity. People can be so frightened of new ideas or new accents. But yes, I brought Fordham along.

BK: Why do so many psychoanalysts struggle to entertain new ideas from colleagues?

DW: Oh, that's very simple. Spending all day in session, as we do, in what I think of as the "white heat" of the consulting room, we have to deal with so much chaos. So, when we congregate at night for meetings, we like to have our preconceptions and our prejudices reinforced. We really do not have much time or space for novelty. It suspect it is too threatening.

BK: That makes great sense, though it saddens me that those with the training to be so open-minded can also be so closed-off.

DW: Yes, it saddens me too.

BK: So, if we may return to the developmental trajectory of the infant …

DW: But of course …

BK: I think you have now given us a very clear, very concise distillation of your ideas about how the mother holds the baby, in a state of devotion and preoccupation, and how this holding then allows the baby to grow from absolute dependence towards independence.

DW: Yes, we got there in the end.

BK: And if the mother provides such an environment, we think of her as being a "good-enough mother" who has given her child a "holding environment" and a "facilitating environment".

DW: That's right. My, my, I have invented a lot of terms. And one more term, if I may …

BK: Of course.

DW: "Going-on-being". This is a very important idea.

BK: Yes.

DW: If the mother is good enough, and if the environment is good enough, then all of this will contribute to ongoing growth and development, and to the fact that first the infant, and then, the child, and then, the adolescent, will all manage to reach adulthood. I think of this as "going-on-being". And mother's ministrations make the child believe that being can go on.

BK: Offering a sense of survival …

DW: A sense of survival. Yes. The object must survive.

BK: Before we conclude this portion of our talk …

DW: And then, we must have another drink, or a snack of some kind, don't you think?

BK: Oh, yes. I just wanted to ask about how health manifests itself in the child who has had the fortunate experience of growing up with a good-enough mother in a facilitating environment.

DW: Well, I have always thought that such a person will be mentally healthy. And by mentally health I don't mean "sane". Sanity is all right, but at the same time, it is a pretty limiting concept. Some of the most boring and restricted people I know are sane. We are poor indeed if we are only sane.

BK: You have mentioned this very notion in your writing.

DW: I believe I have.

BK: And that idea – that sanity might not always be the ultimate benchmark of health – has gripped quite a lot of people.

DW: Yes, sanity is important, but it's not the whole story. The healthy person shows himself or herself to be healthy by having the capacity to be alone, by having the capacity to be concerned about others, and by having the capacity to play.

BK: Each of these concepts deserves its own paper, or book, and thankfully, you have written those for us already. But briefly ...

DW: Briefly, we often think of aloneness as a terrible psychiatric state, usually linked to isolation and depression. But when the child has internalised a good and nourishing mother, then the child can play alone and yet still be in the presence of the mother. And we take that kind of experience with us into adulthood ... of being alone in the presence of the mother.

BK: How beautifully phrased ... being alone in the presence of someone else.

DW: Well, in that sort of situation, aloneness need not be loneliness; rather, it might be a great opportunity for private creativity. Like what I do when I stay up into the small hours painting – I am alone, but very much with my good internal resources, you see.

BK: Many authors have quoted your deeply moving observations about being alone, and of being alone in the presence of the mother. But you have also extended this notion, I believe, in your observations about the importance of being able to hide – not simply being alone, but actually hiding.

DW: Oh, yes, that is very important, both developmentally and clinically, in an analysis. I think you must be referring to my notion that *"it is joy to be hidden but disaster not to be found"*.

BK: Precisely.

DW: That is a very key notion for me. You see, the child must feel that he or she has the right to hide from mother. The mother who never permits separation, who never permits potential space for the child to play, well … that is an intrusive mother. But by the same token, the mother who abandons the child has lost the child. One must let the child hide, but one must also know where to find the child as well. But one can only find the child after one has allowed the child to make himself or herself disappear if the child needs to do that for a time.

BK: Your comments very much call to mind your extremely important idea of the "incommunicado", that part of the mind which must, for sanity's sake, remain inviolate and protected from the intrusions of the other.

DW: Oh, I remember writing about the "incommunicado". I rather like the idea that we might all need to feel that we can keep something of our mind to ourselves. In fact, I feel it essential that each of us must have the right to keep our minds to ourselves. The mother who impinges and needs to know everything in the child's mind is cruel.

BK: And analysts can impinge as well.

DW: Yes. In fact, the analyst who insists on knowing every single thought and fantasy, before the patient is ready, is also cruel. If one insists on barging into the patient's mind, well … that is the hallmark of an invasive, impinging analyst.

BK: Years ago, as a student, I participated in a training seminar with a very elderly psychoanalyst who reviled your notion of the "incommunicado". This man thought you rather stupid, I hate to say, as though you never knew anything about psychoanalysis. He used to say that any analyst who allows his patient to keep secrets, or to have an "incommunicado" part of the mind, has not done a very good job.

DW: Thank you for telling me about this. I feel very sorry for this man, and even more so, I feel very sorry for his patients. Of course secrets can be dangerous in psychoanalysis; but, invading secrets in an unbidden way can cause the analysis to disintegrate.

BK: So the capacity for healthy aloneness seems to be quite vital for you.

DW: Absolutely, quite vital, indeed.

BK: And you regard the capacity to be alone as one of the great achievements of the healthy personality. And now tell us, please, if you would, about the capacity for concern.

DW: Well, that, too, stems from good-enough mothering, you see. To have acquired a capacity for concern means that one has triumphed over narcissism, the pathological sort of narcissism, and that one can be empathic towards others, concerned about others. In many ways, we cannot have civilisation without being concerned for others, and knowing that others will be concerned for us. The criminal, you understand, cannot have concern. The criminal does not have the capacity to be concerned, not in the way that you or I can be, because of an impairment or an impoverishment of the superego. And that brings us speedily onto the capacity for play.

BK: Since your death, entire books have appeared about Winnicott and play.

DW: It is a very important concept, too important to summarise. It is so essential to mental health. And by play, I don't just mean playing a game of cards or a game of football. Play can come in many forms. It can be the play of conversation, the play of ideas … the play of anything, really. It must reactivate some of our early childhood pleasures, and it must not be work. It must be a very separate area which lies between love and work, I think. It's very hard to define, and it cannot be accidental that on my deathbed I had only just received the page proofs for the last book that I wrote, *Playing and Reality*. It took me that long to get the darn thing finished, even though it is one of my very shortest books. But I am glad that I ended with play … so crucial to human beings.

BK: *Playing and Reality* has become an international psychoanalytic classic.

DW: It is not, I think, an easy book, as we have already stated, but nor was it meant to be. It is very nuanced, I suspect.

BK: No, I would agree. It contains many subtleties and many profundities. But it really highlights the concept of play in a very careful way, in a very bold way … in a way that no one had accomplished previously. Dr Juliet Hopkins, the niece of Dr John Bowlby, once said to me that she thought that Freud would be remembered for emphasising love and work as the key ingredients of mental health, and that Winnicott would be remembered for emphasising the role of play.

DW: I remember her with great fondness. She came to me for case discussion about one of her child patients. She was a bright young student at the Tavistock Clinic, training to be a child psychotherapist.

BK: Yes, she has written a chapter about that experience for a book on Winnicottian approaches to infant and child mental health, which I edited in your honour.

DW: If I had known that people would be writing up their supervisions with me for publication, I would have endeavoured to be much more alert!

BK: I wonder whether you need a little break, Dr Winnicott? I fear that I have taxed you with all of these questions about complicated theoretical matters.

DW: Let's ring for Mrs Coles, shall we?

[*Mrs Coles re-enters the room with more typed pages of the interview.*]

JC: Some more tea, Dr Winnicott?

DW: No more tea just now, Mrs Coles, but I think this gentleman and I might like a sandwich. Does that appeal to you?

BK: Oh, thank you.

JC: I can do smoked salmon for you, Dr Winnicott. You always loved smoked salmon.

DW: Yes, fine. We still have more work to do here, and it is thirsty-making work and hungry-making work, Mrs Coles. Might we have a sherry, instead of tea, perhaps?

BK: Well, if you insist ...

JC: Very good, smoked salmon sandwiches and some sherry.

DW: Is that an odd combination? I think it is, but I like it. You know, when I used to have meetings with my old publisher, he would serve me smoked salmon. And, well ... I think it helped us to work better.

JC: And here are some more pages of your interview, typed with two carbon copies.

DW: Lovely. We will look at these later.

JC: Yes, Dr Winnicott.

[*Mrs Coles exits the room.*]

BK: On this whole subject of play, I have always thought that you have been such a great source of inspiration on how to play.

DW: We can't imitate someone else's play. That's not playing. We must find it for ourselves.

BK: Oh, that much I have certainly gleaned from your writings. I suppose what I want to convey ...

DW: Is that I know how to play?

BK: Yes.

DW: I do, you know. I can be silly. I can be a child. But I also know how to work. But I play, too.

BK: So many of the people whom I interviewed while researching your biography told me lovely stories of you as an archetypal expert in play.

DW: What did you hear?

BK: Well, I shall never forget your goddaughter, Dr Elisabeth Swan, the former Elisabeth Ede, telling me that you would often come back home at night to Pilgrim's Lane, after a day at the hospital, and that you would pretend to be the Walt Disney character

"Donald Duck", and that you would quack like a duck! I suppose you share the same name "Donald".

DW: Yes, she and her sister Mary spent a lot of time at my house. They used to call me Uncle Donald Duck, or something similar, if I remember. That was such a long time ago. But yes, that is playful. We could play together, those girls and I. They were healthy girls, and so, they played. I always thought that if a child can play, then we can think of that child as an essentially healthy person. The children who cannot play are the ill ones.

BK: Some of your detractors might dismiss you as silly … a grown man quacking like a duck. How would you differentiate between play and silliness?

DW: I like that question. We don't think enough about silliness, do we? Silliness is all right. But play isn't silly. It is very serious. And when I pretend to be Uncle Donald Duck, I am being very serious. I shall have to think about this some more. It is a very interesting area.

[Mrs Coles comes into the interview room with food and drink.]

DW: Mrs Coles, we are trying to think about being playful. Can you remember when I have been playful?

JC: You have *often* been playful, Dr Winnicott.

DW: Oh, thank you for these smoked salmon sandwiches – they look simply lovely – but tell me, Mrs Coles, you must have some associations, some particular memories of me playing.

JC: Dr Winnicott, do you remember the time you wrote a song about my car? To the tune of one of the songs from *My Fair Lady*?

DW: Good Lord, I do, Mrs Coles. I used to make up words and tunes, and all sorts of little poems, and quips, and even pictures. Yes, these are not great works of art, but they are playful. They are moments when one can allow the unconscious to pop out, with no fear of censure, and with no need to edit. I suppose that is an important part of play.

BK: I understand.

JC: Dr Winnicott, will there be anything else?

DW: No, Mrs Coles, but do take a sandwich for yourself.

JC: I will eat later, thank you, Dr Winnicott.

[*Mrs Coles departs once again.*]

DW: This smoked salmon is yummy. Even the dead have appetites.

BK: How comforting to know!

CUP 9

The white heat of the consulting room

DW: But look, I have been rambling. Even so, I feel we have covered a great deal. Is this the sort of stuff that you wanted from me? Because I do like to be of use, I really do.

BK: It has all been hugely helpful. Thank you. I hope that students might be able to use the text of this conversation as a map to guide them through the ever-expanding thicket of Winnicottiana.

DW: Oh, good. But look, we still have a bit of tape left, I can see. Let's use it properly. What else do you think people will want to know?

BK: Well, I would hardly have the temerity at this point to ask you about your theories of technique, of psychotherapeutic and psychoanalytic practice. That would take us into very deep territory which, I think, cannot be encapsulated in a brief chat. But perhaps …

DW: Some general thoughts about it all?

BK: Yes, some general thoughts would be deeply appreciated.

DW: With pleasure.

BK: You have already described the clinical encounter as having the capacity to generate "white heat". Presumably, both the psychotherapist and the patient have the potential to become very anxious, very engaged, very intimate, very bewildered …

DW: Yes, yes, indeed. That is what we do. We create a space in which a multitude of powerful affects can be unleashed. And for this reason, we need a technique. Freud knew this. We need a technique that can provide us with a holding environment, a structure, a roadmap.

BK: Yes, we would all benefit greatly from learning more about your map.

DW: Now, let us think about technique. The first thing to say, especially now that I am deceased, is that the analyst or therapist must not die. I'm really not being funny, you understand. I'm not playing. I really do mean that. If we can keep alert, awake, alive – not be dead – then we have already done something very important for the patient, you see. It didn't help that I died on some of my patients, and that pains me greatly.

BK: So many of our patients will have had broken attachments, painful abandonments, bereavements, misattunements …

DW: Yes, so many of our patients have had a little death every day, or even a big death. And we have to promise ourselves that we will not die. And by not dying … well … the very act of the analyst's survival becomes curative in its own right. So, first off, we should not die.

BK: When should a psychotherapist stop working so that he or she could thereby reduce the likelihood of dying on a patient?

DW: Do you know, when I was about seventy-two – yes, it must have been about seventy-two – a nice young analyst from the Institute of Psycho-Analysis came to see me. I think that she might have been a member of the Training Committee which vets candidates, and she had heard – quite correctly, you understand – that I had offered an analytic vacancy to a potential trainee. Well, she and the other committee members thought that I was too old to start a new, potentially very long-term analysis of a candidate at this point, especially as I had had a massive heart attack in New York City only a short time before. And of course, she was right. The committee members were right. It was omnipotent of me to think I could start what might turn into a ten-year analysis. And so we made other arrangements for the trainee.

BK: I had heard that story from the woman who came to see you. Isabel Menzies Lyth. After your death, she became quite a prominent psychoanalyst and writer in Oxford.

DW: Isabel Menzies. I remember. Though I don't think she was married yet when I knew her. But the point is … we have to hold our own death in mind. So, in answer to your question about when analysts should stop working, I confess that I don't know the answer. Certainly many clinicians work into their seventies and eighties, but perhaps they should not begin any new analyses at that age.

BK: I know some elderly colleagues who use their seventies and eighties for offering supervision and consultation, for offering time-limited therapies, and for completing long-term work begun years previously. Does that sound a reasonable approach?

DW: Oh, very reasonable. We must try to retire before we die. And that, alas, I did not manage to do. I still had several people in therapy – not many – and I think I had only one patient of really long standing, but, I think, someone who could manage my death.

BK: So what else must the clinician do, or how should the clinician be in the consulting room?

DW: Well, I think I wrote somewhere about the importance of not dying, not falling asleep, and all of that. This links in to my point, and that is about the crucial role of reliability. Above all else, one must be reliable. You see, reliability reduces the impact of what I have called "impingement".

BK: If I remember correctly, you once defined the very essence of psychotherapy as reliability meeting dependence.

DW: That is absolutely the heart of it, reliability meeting dependence.

BK: And I think in this way you have really underscored an important similarity between the newborn baby undergoing infancy and the client or patient undergoing psychotherapy.

DW: Oh that is very much deliberate. You see, the baby, at the beginning, is doubly dependent. But so, too, is the patient, the analysand. "Client" is not really a word that we used in my day, but I know what you mean. Anyway, these people – these patients of ours – they are very dependent. They feel that they cannot function without us. They feel tormented by dreams and fantasies and anxieties. And though they are definitely not babies – at least not in the concrete chronological sense – they do have very baby-like anxieties which make them depend on us. So that is a good reason why we must meet the need through the reliable provision of care.

BK: What you say might be rather obvious at one level, but it is also truly foundational nonetheless.

DW: It would be silly for a doctor to say that a patient needs oxygen to survive. Everyone knows that. But yet, it is completely true. So we need to start with the basics: not dying, and being reliable. Those are the cornerstones, not only of good clinical work but also of good mothering or fathering, call it what you will.

BK: So, extrapolating from your developmental concept of "primary maternal preoccupation", would you agree that the psycho-therapist or psychoanalyst needs to offer the patient a "primary analytical preoccupation"?

DW: I agree with you entirely. With a new patient, we really throw ourselves into the process wholeheartedly. We spend a lot of time thinking about this person, reviewing our notes, memoris-ing the family history, and all of that. We attend to the patient in the way that a mother attends to the newborn. After a long time of working, we don't need to think about the patient in that same way. The patient is more independent of us, less doubly dependent. Perhaps the patient can analyse his or her own dreams without our help. But new patients cannot usually do that, and so they need our constant preoccupation. Primary Analytical Preoccupation … I rather like that turn of phrase.

BK: Well, it is essentially your phrase, Dr Winnicott.

DW: Yes, yes. Do have another smoked salmon sandwich. I know that I am going to have another.

BK: So, when one has provided the patient with a clinician who will not in all likelihood die or fall asleep or be unreliable, what then?

DW: Well, then one needs a setting – a very reliable, dependable setting. Psychoanalysis cannot be done in St James's Park, though we have all been tempted to work outside on a hot summer's day! It must happen in a quiet private office, and it must happen in a professional way. You know that I always wore a suit to work, no matter what the weather. I never saw a patient in my shirtsleeves, or without a tie.

BK: I dress in exactly the same way.

DW: Well, in my day it would have been unthinkable for any professional to have dressed casually, whether a mental health professional or someone running a shop. But since the Beatles, well … everything changed, and the world became a much more informal place. But *we* as clinical practitioners simply cannot be informal. That does not mean that we have to be stuffy. We are interlocutors of the intimate, so we can't be stuffy. But we can still be professional. We have to be formal and intimate at the same time – a very special art form, I think.

BK: And what are the other features of the professional setting, apart from the suit and tie?

DW: Well, I like to use the couch. Not always, you understand … but often. And I think that the couch gives us something very spectacular, something that even Freud did not realise. It allows the patient to lie down, to rest, to talk without being looked at. Of course it gives us all of that. We know that. But the couch is also the mother's body. And the pillow at the head of the couch, well, that is the nipple. With the couch, we offer a very primitive gratification of a symbolic breastfeeding experience. That is what I have learned from some of my most regressed patients.

BK: And with this setting in place, one can then offer traditional psychotherapy or psychoanalysis.

DW: For the most part, that is true. I am classically trained, you know. Both of my analysts, Mr Strachey and Mrs Riviere, had been Freud's patients. So my technique is really very classically Freudian – my soul is really very classically Freudian – although some of my colleagues might not believe that. But it is true.

BK: Oh, I do believe you. I have talked to many of your former patients, and quite a few of them have assured me that you practised classical psychoanalysis. One lady told me that you always opened the door on time, allowed her to free-associate on the couch, and that you would make interpretations about her material from time to time. She painted a picture of you as a very, very classical psychoanalyst.

DW: And I am – or, rather, I was. But that is what one does for one's healthier, more neurotic patients. They can tolerate the classical provision of a fifty-minute session once a week or even five times a week. But the more ill patients cannot manage that. They go mad with the completely classical framework, or they can do.

BK: I suppose that we have come to the very topic that your most fervid critics have found most contentious about your technique – namely, your treatment of the more regressed patients. Can you tell us what modifications you made in your work with the more psychologically vulnerable?

DW: It really grew out of what the patients required. What they wanted, and what they needed. Over a very long time. And here, you see, we must remember that I am a hospital physician, and that I have worked with thousands of cases. It is all well and good for my colleagues in psychoanalysis to tell me that all one needs is a couch and a transference interpretation and so on. I had patients who refused to eat food for weeks at a time and who came perilously close to death. I had patients who went cottaging, looking for sex with little children, patients who became schizophrenic and who threatened to kill themselves every day. And so on. You understand what I am saying? And some of them could manage the Freudian structure, but many of them could not. Sometimes the rage would be so intense and could not be kept tidy in a fifty-minute hour.

BK: So you developed other ways of relating to patients. Can you tell us what you did?

DW: Well, I worked with these people psychoanalytically, but not antiseptically. Let me tell you a story. I had a patient – a woman – who had a very athletic body. In fact, I had better not say too much, but let us simply say that she worked in a profession that allowed her to have complete control of her body, in a very athletic way. She could do things with her body that the rest of us can't. Anyway, one day, while lying on the couch mid-session, this lady did a somersault. She actually did a backwards somersault from the couch, believe it or not, and she landed up in my lap, as I was seated in the chair behind her.

BK: Quite incredible. I cannot imagine anyone being agile enough, or desirous enough, to do something like that.

DW: Nor could I, but that is my point. When one sees a wide range of patients, one meets people who do not fit into a mould.

BK: But what did you do?

DW: Well, I functioned like a psychoanalyst. I knew that if she remained on my lap, she might worry that I might have an erection, even though it was not a very erotic situation. And so I explained that I was going to stand up. And then I did stand up, quite slowly, and consequently this person very gently slipped down my legs onto the floor.

BK: Gosh.

DW: I then asked her to get up, as it seemed clear that she would not get back onto the couch. And then she started pacing up and down the room, and I paced too. And I put my hand on her shoulder, because I sensed that she wanted some contact, and I had already got her off my lap. So, by having my hand on her shoulder – well, I felt that was a good way of maintaining the physical link without making it into a sexualised link, and without subjecting her to the shame of recoiling from her wish for symbolic physical contact. And so we paced up and down the consulting room, and I asked her to free-associate, and to tell me what had been going on in her mind just before the somersault.

169

BK: Fascinating.

DW: So in this way we could try to understand the meaning of the symptom and try to understand the behaviour.

BK: That is the sort of situation that does not happen very often.

DW: Well, Michael Balint ... you know Balint, don't you?

BK: I never met him personally ... but yes, I know his work, of course. But I did have the pleasure of interviewing his third wife, Enid Balint.

DW: One of my dear colleagues ... also a patient of mine.

BK: Yes, that has become quite well known.

DW: Anyway, Michael Balint had a patient who did a cartwheel in the room.

BK: I remember that story. But I have heard critics say that more independent-minded analysts – people like you and Dr Balint – must, somehow, have done something unconsciously provocative – that you had been "uncontained" – and that you had elicited such seemingly unusual behaviour in the first place.

DW: That is a possibility. An analyst who is a bit mad can certainly make the patient a bit mad. But it is even more frightening to think that this could happen to an analyst who is a bit sane. You must understand that what we might well have here is the patient's regression, the patient's feeling of safety, which allows her to show us her madness. A very rigid, very sane analyst actually frightens the patient, and as a result the patient cannot be a "true self" patient.

BK: I know that you treated many, many analysands who had already had previous analyses.

DW: I was always the analyst of last resort, especially during the 1950s and 1960s. People came to me after they had already undergone two or three or even four previous analyses. Failed analyses, often. With colleagues of mine from the British Psycho-Analytical Society. But these patients had not felt seen, or understood, or anything like that. They had to pretend to be sane. And they did not have a satisfactory experience, even though their analyst had thought that they *had* had a satisfactory experience. Only in work with me did these patients feel that they could really expose their true selves.

BK: I understand that with one patient, you sat on the rug of your consulting room, and then listened to the radio together. Is that really the case? And that you also fed your patients soup? Most analysts and therapists would cringe at the idea of something like that.

DW: But why? Why should they cringe? Of course our boundaries are important, and of course we must stick to our professional task, our typical way of working. But the analysts who would cringe at the thought of listening to the radio with a patient are probably the analysts who have not worked in a hospital for very long. Melanie Klein never, ever worked in a hospital, and we must remember that. Never. Most patients do just fine with a prescription from their general medical practitioner, and that is a very tidy, very professional transaction. But if a patient has a bullet wound, with blood and guts spilling out, then a simple prescription absolutely will not suffice. The doctor must use other methods. The doctor might have to get his or her hands covered in blood. Do you see what I am saying?

BK: Yes, Dr Winnicott. You present a very compelling argument that different patients have different levels of need, whether physical or psychological.

DW: Or both.

BK: Some psychotherapists and psychoanalysts would argue that a patient can listen to the radio anywhere, anytime, but that the fifty-minute hour needs to be used for the very special purpose of listening, talking, understanding.

DW: Well, quite, but then those analysts had not met my particular patient. This person – the one with whom I listened to the radio – needed me to sit down and to be quiet, and to provide an ordinary experience of listening to the radio together – something that this person had never had growing up.

BK: So, is psychoanalysis therefore a "corrective emotional experience", to use the phrase coined by Freud's disciple, Dr Franz Alexander?

DW: Of course it is. But psychoanalysis is not the same as mothering. But it is *like* mothering in many ways.

BK: I know that, on various occasions, you have described yourself as a "research" analyst, with reference to cases of schizophrenia and other severe manifestations of psychological vulnerability. Would you be good enough …

DW: To explain? Yes, of course. You see, we know quite a lot about the neurotic, but we know much less about the psychotic. And therefore, we must do research. We must do primary research in our clinical practices in order to find out how one can treat these patients, how we can structure the setting, and all of that. Because, in truth, we simply do not know. Not with the same degree of certainty as we have with the neurotic. If we cannot do research, then we will never know.

BK: So would you regard your technical experiments – long sessions, feeding soup, listening to the radio, and all of that – as part of clinical research?

DW: Some of my colleagues believe that psychoanalysis began in 1895 and ended with Freud's death in 1939. And that with a couch, with free association, and with interpretation, we have all that we need to know. But would medicine have stopped at Hippocrates? Would science have stopped with Sir Isaac Newton? I don't think so. We must keep investigating, keep researching. Sometimes, with the more ordinary neurotic patient, we can practice a standard analysis, but with the more troubled person we must become research analysts and figure out what works and what does not.

BK: Yes. I suppose that your reputation as an analyst – as a research analyst – has suffered greatly since your death in 1971, especially because of what happened to your one-time patient Masud Khan, with whom you had a somewhat non-traditional relationship. Do you think we might be able to discuss that?

DW: What happened to Masud?

BK: Well, after your death, Mr Khan deteriorated greatly – quite a bit in the 1970s, and even more so in the 1980s. He became deeply depressed, he suffered from pronounced alcoholism, and he got into physical fights with girlfriends, in public, and with his colleagues too. He is rumoured to have had an affair with a patient – the spouse of a trainee at the Institute of Psycho-Analysis, in fact – and much, much more. His patients discovered him in all sorts of states of decompensation, and one analysand even arrived for a session and found Mr Khan prostrate on the floor, writhing in agony, because his wife, the ballerina Svetlana Beriosova, had just assaulted him.

DW: This breaks my heart ... it really does.

BK: Perhaps most worryingly of all, just before his death he published a book which became instantly notorious, in which he spewed forth a whole litany of deeply shocking anti-Semitic remarks.

DW: Did he get any treatment? Any assistance?

BK: I know that Anna Freud tried to help him, and his personal physician also tried to help, as did some friends. But nobody seemed quite able to stop the deterioration – a deterioration which became compounded by a deadly carcinoma, which finally killed him in 1989. And, of course, because Masud Khan had often talked about you as his analyst and had often written about you and had edited many of your books, and so on, everyone still associates Khan with you. And everyone knows that you supervised him and that you then analysed him. And also, everyone knows that during the analysis – and certainly after the analysis – you and he collaborated on various publication projects. In other words, you had an extra-analytic relationship with him and, thus, a lack of clarity, some might argue, about the purpose of your relationship. And all of that has given rise to private rumours and public assertions that you failed him.

DW: I see. I cannot say too much, because Masud Khan was my patient. But, as I believe I have already mentioned, he came to me after his first analyst, Miss Sharpe, had died mid-treatment, and then, a few years later, after his second analyst, Dr Rickman, had died, also mid-treatment. Both of these training analysts had died on Masud within a few years of one another, and this proved to be devastating for him. And so, I told him that it would be very important for me not to die on him. And I didn't. We finished our work, and I had not yet died. And he became much, much better and, also, quite highly creative.

BK: I have had the privilege of reading Khan's unpublished work books – his diaries – and in one the entries he wrote that the work that you and he undertook had helped him to conquer his catastrophic sense of object-loss.

DW: I think so.

BK: But after your death, he gradually became worse and worse. And it remains a matter of both historico-biographical conjecture and clinical conjecture as to how much of this deterioration can be attributed to your death, even though you had long since ended the analysis by this point. People worry that he had become unhealthily dependent on you, and that any positive changes did not become internalised.

DW: I admit that this is a tragedy. And if I had lived, I would have done something to try to stop this, and Masud would, I know, have come to me to try to stop this. But I am deeply, deeply sorry to hear about his final years. What a waste of a great mind. And he had a truly great mind. He knew Freud better than anyone, perhaps apart from Miss Freud, and he applied Freud in such creative ways, in his papers. He wrote some deeply, deeply sensitive papers.

BK: That is the awful paradox. He had such brilliance … and such destructiveness … and a great deal of anguish, no doubt.

DW: Indeed.

BK: And of course Mr Khan's behaviour put his lifelong psycho-analytic colleagues in such a quandary for the longest time. They kept hearing stories about his unprofessional behaviour, and yet they also knew him to be a tireless worker on behalf of the British Psycho-Analytical Society. Pearl King once told me that but for Masud Khan's insomnia, the administrative infrastructure of the British Psycho-Analytical Society would have collapsed, because Mr Khan stayed up so late on so many nights doing so much paperwork, library work, committee work, etc. But eventually – especially with the publication of his anti-

Semitic book, in which he attacked patients in a shockingly cruel manner – the Ethics Committee finally removed him from the membership roster. And, although it pains me to say it, quite a few senior psychoanalysts have held *you* responsible and have used the Masud Khan scandal as a means of tarnishing your entire corpus of writings.

DW: Oh dear. Well, it is better to talk about these matters rather than keep them secret. I liked Masud greatly. We were colleagues, we were friends, we worked closely together. And yes, he was my patient. He came to me as an already qualified psychoanalyst, wanting, if you like, a postgraduate analysis – a top-up – after he had already had two previous analyses. And we did good work together. I suppose we are omnipotent if we presume that psychoanalysis will automatically inoculate a person against breakdown later in life. It can't, and it won't. It can help reduce the likelihood of breakdown – greatly so – but it cannot control every feature of a person's life, no matter how good the analyst.

BK: And of course, even if one has had a brilliant experience of psychoanalysis, one can still experience traumata in later life, which, if sufficiently severe, can overwhelm an ego structure.

DW: I think that is absolutely right. But fortunately, most people do improve in a deeply internalised way, at least in my experience.

BK: Of course, I am remembering that you worked with some twenty thousand patients, as well as tens of thousands of parents of child patients, during your fifty-year career as a physician …

DW: Just over fifty years, actually.

BK: Of course. And most of the patients with whom you worked got better, often very much better … and stayed better! I know this, because I have met approximately one hundred of your former patients, and virtually all of them have talked about your clinical abilities in the most glowing terms.

DW: That is good to know.

BK: And after your death, your wife, Mrs Winnicott, received letter upon letter from grateful patients, singing your praises in remarkable ways, telling her that no one had ever understood them or helped them in the way that you had.

DW: Also very gratifying to know.

BK: So the Masud Khan scandal has made some people very wary. Perhaps it might be important for you to know that since your death quite a few people in the psychoanalytic field have written papers excoriating you for your involvement in Khan's breakdowns, and for your involvement in the cover-up – or, at least, in turning a blind eye. Ethical standards have become much, much more stringent in the mental health professions during the last several decades, and nowadays people treat these matters very, very seriously indeed. And patients have a very clear means of complaining about a practitioner if they have suffered mistreatment in any way.

DW: I understand. But I cannot offer a complete explanation of what really happened to Masud. Partly because I do not know. If a patient develops cancer ten years after a successful chemotherapy, can we hold the former oncologist accountable? This is a medico-ethical question. But let me say this: I never turned a blind eye. I knew about Masud's difficulties – at least those that had occurred during my lifetime! And I kept meeting with him to try to work it through. He might have been much, much worse off if he had not had the analysis, don't you know.

BK: Well, when certain psychoanalysts have since come to hear about what happened to Mr Khan, they have subsequently begun to review your other departures from – or developments of – classical psychoanalytic technique, and this has made many people nervous … very nervous, in fact.

DW: I never pretended that departures, or developments, from psychoanalytic technique should become the gold standard.

BK: I understand. But many have seized upon the fact that with some extremely fragile people, you would often see them for two-hour sessions, instead of for fifty-minute sessions. And this knowledge has made certain colleagues anxious, because the fifty-minute hour has become sanctified.

DW: But if a surgeon started to undertake heart surgery, he or she wouldn't stop after fifty minutes. "Oh, I'm sorry, Mr Smith, but our time is up, and we'll have to do the suturing tomorrow, in our next session." The surgeon would stop only when the work was done. I found that my patients became unbearably mad when I ended the session too quickly. But I offered extended sessions only with the very mad. And sometimes I would do so with sane colleagues who had come from a long distance.

BK: Well, having studied your appointment diaries from 1949 until 1971, I can confirm that you had, indeed, offered most of your patients a traditional psychoanalytic hour, and that you started your sessions, in most instances, on the hour. But I did see a number of diary entries where either you, or Mrs Coles, had blocked out two-hour chunks, often at weekends, in order to see the more fragile ones.

DW: That is right. That is precisely right. But I can see how this can get very complicated and also very misunderstood.

BK: I hope that someday someone will write a very carefully researched book about your actual clinical practice, because I think that a scrutiny of what you really did and what you have been rumoured to have done, and so on, would be very instructive, and we could all learn a lot from it.

DW: What a good idea. Will you do that?

BK: Well, I am still hard at work on a fuller biography of you. I wrote a short-ish biography of you which appeared as part of the celebrations for your centenary in 1996, as you know, but there is still a much longer one in the pipeline. I shall try to deal with some of these issues in the forthcoming book.

DW: Oh good. I think we need a more thorough contextualisation of the Masud situation. But I do wish I could see him, and that we could talk to him. Because I suspect that much had happened to him that we do not know about and which might shed light on his final chapter.

BK: Shortly after you died, a very intelligent, very thoughtful man called Dr Christopher Bollas came to London to train as a psychoanalyst, and over a long time he has been a passionate student and scholar of your writings. He even helped Mrs Winnicott to prepare some of your writings for posthumous publication. Anyway, Dr Bollas has recently co-authored a book entitled *Catch Them Before They Fall: The Psychoanalysis of Breakdown*, in which he described the way in which he would – very, very occasionally – provide intensive, multi-hour treatments for fragile patients in deep distress. He waited until he had reached a point of great seniority and respect in his long career before writing about this, because of the anxiety of deviating from – or should I say *expanding upon* – classical technique.

DW: I would like to read that book.

BK: And I think that many people still have a fear or an anxiety of going outside the typical Freudian parameters, whatever the reason. I know that I do. I work only in fifty-minute sessions, and this offers a great comfort for both parties – for both client and clinician.

DW: Yes, Freud gives us comfort when we enter the murky waters of the unconscious mind. He gives us landmarks, otherwise we can get lost at sea. And the genius of the fifty-minute hour is that it can serve as a buoy in choppy waters. I speak as a former Royal Navy man, you understand!

BK: And your technical developments, Dr Winnicott ... your expansions of classical technique – whether "on demand" treatment, whether long sessions, or what have you – all of these innovations inspire both admiration as well as fear among practitioners. And also genuine research curiosity.

DW: I can understand that very much. More tea?

BK: Thank you, but no.

DW: Well, we certainly needed the smoked salmon sandwiches to fortify us during this last bit of the discussion. Our gentlemanly tea became a very blunt conversation.

BK: I hope that you do not ...

DW: Mind?

BK: Yes.

DW: No, you had to raise these questions. Clearly, a lot has happened since 1971, and I need to know about it all. And modern readers need to know as well, so that they can decide whether to bother with me or not. People might think that there is a Freudian Valhalla, and that we are all sitting up there watching the proceedings down below, but I can tell you, it's not true! This all comes as a great surprise to me.

BK: I understand. Suffice it to say, Dr Winnicott, that in spite of the Masud Khan "scandal", if I can use that word, your papers still receive the highest citation ratings of any psychoanalyst on the Psychoanalytic Electronic Publishing database – even more than those by Freud. Your article on the transitional object has scored more "hits" than any other psychoanalytic publication, and has done so for the past several years.

DW: What are "hits"?

BK: Well, since your death, most people write with a computer – which is a very fancy form of typewriter ...

DW: Perhaps Mrs Coles would like to have a computer.

BK: I think she seems happier with her typewriter, judging from these interview transcripts and the carbon copies.

DW: Maybe so. But look, I don't want to outstay my welcome. Is there anything else we need to talk about, or shall we stop?

BK: Well, we began the interview in a strictly chronological fashion, trying to paint a picture of your life history. But then we became rather immersed in examining *some* of your theories.

DW: Where did we stray from the path?

BK: I had noted that during the 1950s, you had produced so many books and papers, and that you had begun to lay the foundations of a very substantial theory of developmental psychology ...

DW: And then we got sidetracked. Well, perhaps not sidetracked. Perhaps we went in deeper.

BK: Well, shall we resume with the formal biography round about that period of time? The 1950s.

DW: Oh, yes, let's do that. Anything else to drink? Oh, no, that's right, you've already said no. My memory can sometimes get a bit hazy. I suppose we've both had quite enough tea. But there is more if we need it.

CUP 10

A psychoanalytic maestro

BK: So, perhaps you would be kind enough to continue with your personal story, round about 1950.

DW: Of course. In 1950, I had made the painful decision to leave my first wife and to marry Clare. You see, in January 1949 I had the first of what would be several heart attacks, and Alice and I became increasingly estranged during this time. She found looking after me quite difficult. I had always been the doctor, and now, you see, I had become the patient. And to complicate matters, Clare loved me, and I loved her. We had got to know one another increasingly well during the war years when I had worked in Oxford and she, also, had worked in Oxford. So I told Alice that our marriage must end. I just told her straight out.

BK: How painful.

DW: It was very painful, because I still loved Alice. But I loved Clare in a different way. And so I divorced Alice – or, technically, I think she divorced me. But we ended, that is the main thing, although I stayed in touch with her right until the end. We wrote to one another, you understand. I think she had a very sad life after our marriage, a very lonely life. But if I had stayed, I think I would have died.

BK: And you married Clare Britton and moved into a new home.

DW: It was rather a financially rash decision, but I think it paid good dividends in terms of joy. I took a lease on a huge house in Belgravia ... in fact, the very house in which we now find ourselves! You realise that it is really not the sort of place where psychoanalysts live. I was the only one in this part of London back in my day. But I wanted a fresh start with Clare, and so we settled into this grand house in a grand square, not far from the Queen and Buckingham Palace. We had a very happy life together in that house. And I suppose I got tired of living in one place and working in another, of the daily commuting from Hampstead to the West End. And so – not at first, but eventually – I moved my consulting room into this house in Chester Square, and there I remained. Clare and I had a lovely marriage. We played. We danced. It really was a great experience.

BK: I am so pleased for you both. And did the happiness of your new marriage influence your work in any way?

DW: Oh, in every way. It allowed me to become the theoretician of play and creativity and health, rather than just a theoretician of madness and breakdown and misery.

BK: What a profound comment.

DW: Yes, Clare did all of that for me ... and more.

BK: And you became increasingly active in professional circles, not only enjoying the rigours of a full clinical practice ...

DW: Yes, I had my private practice here – in this very room, in fact.

BK: And you continued to work at the Paddington Green Children's Hospital.

DW: Indeed.

BK: But you also took up important leadership roles.

DW: Very much so. I had already served as the chair of the Medical Section of the British Psychological Society where we had these Wednesday night meetings, you see, and where we could have doctors and psychologists, Freudians and Jungians, everyone really, all together in one room. The Medical Section eventually folded – I don't know why – but it really turned out to be the one place in the British mental health community where everyone had a voice. It did not pretend to be an exclusive club. I have often thought that our Institute of Psycho-Analysis – though I love it – is an exclusive club, and that we were not very good at speaking to the outside world. The Medical Section of the British Psychological Society, by contrast, allowed everyone to come on board, and that was very special.

BK: And you also became deeply involved at the Royal Society of Medicine.

DW: Yes, that one rather took me by surprise. Not long after my marriage to Clare and the move to Belgravia, I became the President of the Section of Paediatrics at the RSM. That was an odd thing to do because really, in truth, I had let my physical paediatrics go to pot by this point. I was a paediatrician, but not a *physical* paediatrician. I didn't prescribe drugs for children with infections or perform tonsillectomies. No, I was a paediatrician who was really a psychologist, and I dealt with all the psychosomatics, all the nervous breakdowns, all of that. But I was, at heart, and by background, a paediatrician, and some people thought it would be a good idea to have me as President.

BK: You chaired meetings about very high-technology paediatric matters.

DW: Yes, and though I admired and respected it, I didn't always understand it. But I think it turned out to be very important for British paediatrics to have had a psychoanalyst in such a visible position. It allowed paediatricians to take psychology more seriously, even if I didn't really have the most up-to-date knowledge about the medical side of paediatrics at my fingertips.

BK: And you did introduce some important psychological topics into the paediatric discussions at the Royal Society of Medicine.

DW: I am very pleased that I had arranged for John Bowlby and Jimmy Robertson, and his wife Joyce, to show their film about children in hospital ... I did that, you know.

BK: What a landmark film!

DW: You've seen it.

BK: Yes, we still use that film in teaching more than half a century later!

DW: I am glad to hear of it. You know, in my day, most hospitals forbade parents to visit. Not The Green, of course, we were too psychological there, and we did allow parental visits. But in the 1920s, the 1930s, in most places ... well, it was pretty grim, and the children suffered. Parents would be turned away and not permitted to see their children. And Bowlby's colleagues, the Robertsons – I think Jimmy Robertson trained in social work or some field like that, I'm not sure – well, they took a camera, and they filmed the very moment when parents said goodbye to their hospitalised children ... and ... you know what happened. The children went to pieces. They suffered deeply from the loss of parental contact. Deep, deep melancholias. A child can have a very deep melancholia you know. And the Robertsons captured this on film. And by showing the film at the Royal Society of Medicine, well ... the evidence was incontrovertible, and from that very moment, paediatric practice in Britain started to change, and doctors let the parents have more visiting time and even came to encourage visits!

BK: You must be very proud to have had a hand in that.

DW: Hugely proud. Don't forget, Bowlby and I jointly co-signed that letter in 1939, with Emanuel Miller, warning people about the psychological dangers of evacuating children. We knew that separation could destroy the soul, but no one else really understood that. So Bowlby and I had already come to appreciate this long before the Robertsons had made that film. But the film made it all much more visible, much more easy to see, although many people found it painful viewing.

BK: So, you held these key posts in the British Psychological Society and in the Royal Society of Medicine. And you also had two terms as President of the British Psycho-Analytical Society?

DW: Yes, from 1956 to 1959, with John – John Bowlby – as my Deputy President for some of that time. And then again from 1965 to 1968. Very happy times. I couldn't have done it, however, without Joyce. Not without Mrs Coles, especially as most of the job involved writing letters! And she did all my letters for me, beautifully typed, and thus I could keep in touch with a whole range of people. You know, when analysts died, the President would have to write a letter to the family members, write the obituary, all that, and more. It did involve a lot of paperwork, and a lot of chairing of meetings, and I wasn't very good at the administration. But somehow it worked out all right.

BK: What did you accomplish during your two terms as president?

DW: Oh, it's hard to say, but something that has made me incredibly proud is that I got the Freud statue bronzed. You know, Oscar Nemon's statue of Freud. It had just been sitting in his studio, but I got all the analysts to give us money, so that we could get it bronzed – a very expensive process, as it transpired – and then we managed to have it put on a plinth. And we had a big unveiling ceremony of the statue by the library in Swiss Cottage, in North London. I feel very proud of that, so that we could really, at last, sit at Freud's feet. I hope this alone proves my devotion to pure Freud.

BK: The statue still stands proudly in North London, although in recent years it has found a new home outside the Tavistock Centre in Belsize Park.

DW: Well, as long as it can still be used, and still be enjoyed.

BK: Very much so.

DW: Yes, the 1950s and 1960s. So much happened that I cannot really summarise my life. Lots of patients, lots of books, lots of papers, lots of meetings, lots of evenings with colleagues, lots of evenings with Clare.

BK: You became a truly prolific author during the 1950s and 1960s.

DW: Yes. You know, I had always wanted to write umpteen books and papers, but I never managed to write quite as much as I had wanted. At some point, I made a New Year's resolution, and I promised that I would have to devote myself more fully to writing. And I *did* write, but not as much as I would have wished.

BK: But you published one paediatric textbook, two pamphlets, three volumes of radio broadcasts and other pieces for members of the public, two volumes of high-level professional psycho-analytic papers, one volume of essays for general mental health professionals, and countless chapters, essays, articles, reviews, and so forth, all during your lifetime, with two more books appearing in the immediate aftermath of your death in 1971.

DW: Gosh, how extraordinary!

BK: And then many, many more books appeared posthumously throughout the 1970s, 1980s, and into the 1990s.

DW: Mrs Coles did a great deal of typing, didn't she?

BK: But you still had more to say.

DW: I had much more to say, and I still do now. So it is very pleasing to have this opportunity to talk with you. Just because one has died doesn't mean that one has finished speaking!

BK: Contemporary sixteenth-century accounts of the execution of Mary, Queen of Scots, had claimed that after her beheading, her lips continued to quiver for a full quarter-of-an-hour.

DW: Yes, how fascinating! I'm afraid I can't explain the anatomy and physiology of all of that, but I do know that the dead still need to speak.

BK: And you spoke very loudly, albeit in your soft voice, by broad-casting on the radio. You managed to transmit your work and your ideas not only through the printed word, but you remained, also, a broadcaster across most of your professional life.

DW: We have, I know, already talked a bit about my radio work. But did you know that I was one of the first psychologists to appear on television? Possibly *the* first British psychoanalyst to have done so! I don't know about that, but I think I may well have been!

BK: Did you find that frightening?

DW: Quite frightening in many ways, but rather natural in others. It had almost never been done before.

BK: So in that respect, too, you are quite a pioneer.

DW: I did have funny looks from some of my colleagues, but by that time I had become such a senior figure, they would have forgiven me much. And I was old. People don't envy the elderly, you know, because they know that we are about to die!

BK: But one wonders what anxieties you triggered among your colleagues by appearing on television. Psychoanalysis had been such a denigrated field for so many years, practised by only a tiny handful. One would have thought that colleagues would have appreciated your efforts to be an impressive spokesperson for psychological matters.

DW: Yes, I really did more than most, perhaps more than any of my colleagues, in bringing psychoanalysis out of Gloucester Place and later out of New Cavendish Street, and into people's homes and minds. Of that, I am proud. As for my colleagues, I don't really know the source of their anxiety about public relations. Unless it is do with primitive envy, or the wish to be greedy … you know, a need for psychoanalysts to keep psychoanalysis to themselves, like those chubby little children who hoard all the sweets!

BK: You were the first proper media psychologist in Great Britain, and thus a great ambassador for psychological ideas.

DW: It is now too late in our conversation to be falsely modest. But you are right. I did become a pioneer. And I am glad of it. As we speak about it more, I do think the others were envious, and they cloaked their envy in an accusation that I had watered down psychoanalysis.

BK: Well, I think we know that not to be true. After all, whose work has survived the test of time?

DW: Am I the first psychoanalyst to have agreed to this posthumous interview?

BK: Yes, you are, Dr Winnicott.

DW: So you haven't managed to resurrect some of the more conservative, inward people, have you? You have asked to interview *me*, and I am rather glad of it.

BK: So, here you are, working with patients, heading up major national organisations, broadcasting ...

DW: And teaching. We mustn't forget my teaching. I had been the most passionate of teachers you know. I loved working with my students.

BK: And you taught in so many places.

DW: Yes, throughout the '50s and '60s I had two regular commitments, teaching the child development students at the Institute of Education, which is part of the University of London. I had been doing that since Susan Isaacs had asked me on board in the 1930s. And also, at the LSE, which was, and I suppose still is, also part of the University of London. Clare taught there too. She headed up the social work training for a long time. Both the Institute of Education and the LSE gave me regular, weekly opportunities to hone my theories of development and technique.

BK: You did more teaching for students of child development and social work than for students of psychoanalysis.

DW: Yes, that is most certainly the case. I taught at the Institute of Education and at the LSE infinitely more often than I did at the Institute of Psycho-Analysis. You know, in spite of being President of the British Psycho-Analytical Society, they used me very sparingly as a teacher – very badly, in fact. They spread the teaching around too much, and not always among the best people. For years, I gave maybe one or two lectures and often no more ...

BK: That might come as a surprise, especially as you are so well known as a psychoanalyst. One would have thought that you would have done a lot of teaching for prospective psychoanalysts.

DW: Very little, really. And never in a sustained way. But I had a lot of supervisees, and I thereby had quite a bit of influence. And all the analysts listened to my broadcasts and read my papers. Or so I would like to think. But at any rate, my words certainly got about.

BK: Do you suppose that if you had devoted yourself exclusively to classical five-times-a-week psychoanalysis, your colleagues in the British Psycho-Analytical Society might have "used" you more fully, more enthusiastically, in the teaching curriculum?

DW: Oh there can be no question that many would have wished me to be just like them – you know, treating a training patient, followed by another training patient, followed by yet another training patient; maybe a talk or two to the Scientific Meetings every other year. Certainly, they resented the fact that I got about, spoke on the radio, lectured to midwives, undertook brief consultations. My "on demand" work certainly evoked some suspicions among Anna Freud and her group of child analysts.

BK: Because you sometimes consulted to children, such as "The Piggle", who lived outside London, and who could not readily attend for five-times-a-week psychoanalysis.

DW: Could not attend, and did not *need* to attend, five times weekly. Some found this notion shocking, you see, and they claimed that my work could not really qualify as true analysis.

BK: It seems striking how "po-faced", how stern, some of your colleagues had become during the 1940s and 1950s, even into the 1960s – as if living in an orthodox ghetto.

DW: That is a reasonable way to describe it.

BK: The idea of "on demand" treatment, offering a piece of psychological work to a child as might be needed, seems hardly shocking in an historical perspective. Freud, after all, spoke about "fractional analysis" (sometimes translated as "fractured analysis") which he certainly practised.

DW: I remember that phrase, "fractional analysis".

BK: Referring, of course, to a fraction of an analysis, as opposed to the standard whole.

DW: Yes, Ernest Jones and I sometimes talked about "fractional analysis". If Freud could offer fewer than six sessions per week, perhaps I could do so too. Sometimes a part is greater than the sum of the whole, don't you think?

BK: You had, of course, great support from Mrs Winnicott and from Mrs Coles while developing and practising your work.

DW: Yes – my two wives, if you like. Clare looked after my body and soul, and Joyce looked after my work. I think Joyce would say that she looked after my body too. Certainly she cooked for me when I was ill and Clare had to be out working at the Home Office. So I am fortunate to have had the care of these two very loyal, very remarkable women. Very fortunate indeed.

BK: But your health suffered greatly in 1968.

DW: I nearly died. In fact, I think I *did* die, or I thought that I had died. Yes, I was very ill.

BK: You had gone to New York City.

DW: That's right. I had an invitation from the New York Psycho-analytic Society, which is the oldest psychoanalytic group in America. And I had offers from other places, too, like the William Alanson White group in New York. They are also analysts, but much more modern. Anyway, Clare and I flew to New York in early November of '68, and we both became very, very ill with this Asian influenza. It was quite a virulent flu, not dissimilar to the one that we had back in 1918, when I was a medical student. I knew that we could both die.

BK: But you soldiered on, and you gave your paper to the New York Psychoanalytic Society, didn't you?

DW: Oh, yes, it was a grand affair, and all the men had to wear dinner jackets, which I thought a bit incongruous, what with all the American boys fighting and dying in Vietnam at that time. It seemed very out of touch. And they were out of touch – out of touch with their own warrior-like parts. And they gave me a very cold reception. Although they comported themselves as if in a gentleman's club, they gave me a very un-gentlemanly reception.

BK: But they had invited you, as a two-time President of the British

Psycho-Analytical Society. They wanted to hear you speak. And you knew many of them from international congresses and liked them. And they liked you.

DW: Well, three things happened on that night ... 12th November, '68. I remember the date, you see. First of all, I spoke very badly – a bit vague and dithery, I think – because I wasn't well. I really wasn't well at all. Also, I think that although many of them knew me and liked me, quite a lot thought I sounded like a British Kleinian – and they had been taught to hate Kleinians because of the rivalry with the Anna Freudians. And Anna Freud, of course, had a great foothold in the New York group.

BK: And the third factor?

DW: Well, I gave a very new paper on what I called "the use of an object" – another of my controversial papers, I suppose, although not controversial to me.

BK: You suggested that the patient needs to be allowed to *use* the analyst as an object to gratify needs and so forth, and to survive psychically.

DW: That's the gist of it. The patient uses the analyst. The patient discharges affect and also communicates something very profound about his or her internal world, and all that. But I think I made it sound too complicated and too mysterious. And they just didn't get it. Or maybe they *did* get it and didn't like it. After all, if you are an analyst, wearing a dinner jacket (or "tuxedo" as they all said in America), then you wouldn't be able to hold a regressed patient's hand or sit on the floor with a regressed patient who wants to use you, or even rip you to pieces with rage ... throwing things at you ... and all of that.

BK: I can sense the potential for confusion.

DW: You must remember that American psychoanalysis at that time had a huge allegiance to traditional psychiatry, to traditional medicine. Most analysts had to have the MD degree, whereas in Great Britain this had never been the case. In my experience, the Americans took huge pride in their status as physician–analysts, and, consequently, I don't think they would have enjoyed being described by me as people who get "used".

BK: So they attacked you?

DW: They applauded, but only a bit. And yes, they made some theoretical comments, which were essentially critiques. Afterwards, I turned to one of the young psychologists in the audience, and I whispered that I now understood why the Americans had gone into Vietnam.

BK: You felt bombed.

DW: I did. And I went back to my hotel room, and not long thereafter, I had a massive heart attack, and nearly died.

BK: What a horrible, frightening experience. And to be so far away from Chester Square.

DW: Clare and I had to stay in New York for six weeks or so. It nearly bankrupted us, because of the American medical fees. They had no National Health Service, you understand. Seriously, I almost lost everything. It cost so much money.

BK: You must have wanted to send the bill to the New York Psychoanalytic Society.

DW: The thought had occurred to me. Some of its members came to visit – some of the old guard, who had known me for years. Very kind people. Very dear people. Others wrote. One of them brought me a book to read in my hospital bed. But on the whole, it was pretty ghastly.

BK: So you returned to London in a very debilitated state.

DW: Yes, and I could not resume work for quite some time. I started off bit by bit, but I did not return to full steam for several months. And then I had to be quite careful, for obvious reasons. But gradually I resumed with patients, with writings, with teaching. I worked at a slower pace, undertaking a bit less work, but only a bit. 1969 and 1970 turned out to be very busy years, when all was said and done, crowned by the unveiling of the Freud statue in October of 1970. I knew that I had to stay alive for that. But I was very ill at the ceremony – an outdoor ceremony in Swiss Cottage, held on a very, very cold day – and I thought that I might die.

BK: But you lived for another three-and-a-half months.

DW: Yes, I died in January 1971 – on the 25th of January, I think. I'm not good at dates at the best of times, but on that occasion I really wasn't thinking of the calendar.

BK: Mrs Winnicott told her intimates, people like Mrs Coles, that you died at about 4:00 a.m. on the morning of Monday, 25th January.

DW: Clare would know. Did she find the body?

BK: Yes, she had fallen asleep, and apparently when she awoke in the middle of the night, she found you.

DW: I am sorry that she had to find me. But she is a strong woman, and she knew that it must happen. She was no one's fool, and my death would not have come as a surprise. We talked about my impending death … a lot. But I am sorry for her, because we had such a great love, you see. Such a great love.

BK: You had a spectacular funeral at the crematorium at Golders Green, in North London, packed to the rafters with family, with friends and colleagues, with patients. People spoke about your remarkable contributions to the world. I think you would have enjoyed it.

DW: Did you go?

BK: No, I was only a child at the time.

DW: Yes, of course.

BK: But I spoke to many, many people who did participate, and they all described it as a truly great tribute to a truly remarkable man.

DW: How pleasing to hear. And how wonderful to have this opportunity to come back to life for a few hours. Tell me, did I have good music at the funeral?

BK: Yes, a concert pianist played the piano – a special grand piano imported into the crematorium for the occasion.

DW: We've not talked much about my musical side.

BK: In some ways, I have always thought of music as one of the most important aspects of your life – and, indeed, of your work.

DW: It is, but that might be something to talk about at another time. Perhaps you could invite me back?

BK: Well, that would be a great treat.

DW: What do you know about my music?

BK: I know that you played the piano with great facility and that you enjoyed sharing your pianistic accomplishments with others, often performing at seminars and so forth.

DW: All true.

BK: And I also know that you speak like a musician. You have musical cadences. You speak with pauses, with rests, with rhythms, and with textures. You modulate your dynamics.

DW: I have always thought that the musicality in my voice had a healing property for patients – just as the mother's voice becomes a healing object, potentially, for the baby. The voice allows the baby to know that mother is there, that she is alive and alert. I used my voice in that way with patients.

BK: But also for private play, for private joy.

DW: Above all else, yes, I suppose.

BK: Tell me about Gilbert and Sullivan.

DW: You know of my love of Gilbert and Sullivan?

BK: Marion Milner first alerted me to your interests in that direction.

DW: Of course, people don't realise it, but Gilbert and Sullivan were the Beatles of their day. They were very popular. Well, that is underplaying it. They were the epitome of chic, of culture, or wickedness, of cleverness – of everything, really.

BK: Today Gilbert and Sullivan evoke a great deal of suspicion in people. Many find them "twee", or "arch", or even silly. Certainly many regard them as dated.

DW: How ridiculous. They are pungent social critics. They have a wonderful clinical eye. I suspect they might have made very good analysts. They were supremely intelligent.

BK: Perhaps in our next conversation we can think more about G. and S.

DW: Oh, good, I look forward to that, because I think you cannot really understand Winnicott without understanding Gilbert and Sullivan.

BK: Do you have any final thoughts, Dr Winnicott?

DW: Well, I began my life in a tradition of Wesleyan Methodism, devoted to service. That philosophy allowed me to become a full member of the Winnicott family. We all became objects to be used. That is what we did in my family, and in the Christian family at large. Needless to say, we did not think of it in quite that way. But we were, truly, objects to be used.

BK: And this allowed you to become a physician and a psychoanalyst?

DW: It didn't allow me to become one. It *insisted* that I become one. And so I did.

BK: And you devoted half a century – actually, more than half a century – to the care of patients.

DW: You know, I remember once saying to a patient – this was a patient who had had many tragedies in her life – and I said, "I'm sorry that your life has had to be so difficult", or words to that effect. I couldn't take away all the pain, but I could acknowledge it to be real. She did not expect me to take away all the pain. It was there, and she knew it. But she cried, I think, and she felt deeply, profoundly moved that I had confirmed that the pain really did exist.

BK: I think that nowadays we would speak about the psychotherapist offering validation or witnessing of the client's experience.

DW: That fits. I validated this woman. And I felt touched, too. For me, the art of therapeutic work is for two people to meet, in a room, in private, and to be touched. Not touched in the same way. The analyst will have a different experience from that of the patient. But something touching must occur. And I tried to research the best way for that to happen. Yes, I am sorry that some people have had to have such painful lives.

BK: And you did so much to help people and to accompany them on their pain-filled journeys.

DW: I think we are not trying to be sentimental here. I think we are being honest. We serve and we strive to reduce pain, or at least to keep people from being lonely with that pain. That is the essence of the work with patients. And if we succeed – if the pain goes away – then we have the opportunity to have play and pleasure.

BK: To the outsider, our work looks so simple. Two people sitting in a little room, talking, chatting, listening, nodding their heads. But it is essentially an encounter based on the search for meaning, for understanding, for pleasure, for relief from pain.

DW: It is. Very much so.

BK: During my training, I had the great privilege of having had supervision with a lovely man – a very special man, called Dr Bernard Barnett.

DW: Oh, yes, of course.

BK: He was a very young psychologist at the time of your death, and afterwards he trained as a psychoanalyst. He had heard you speak at a conference back in the early 1960s. And he spoke very warmly of you.

DW: I am sorry that I did not live long enough to know him better.

BK: He has a lovely turn of phrase. He describes psychological treatment as a very special form of "intensive care".

DW: Oh, I really like that. That fits with my way of thinking precisely. Though he has put it rather better. "Intensive care". Yes, that is primary maternal preoccupation ... that is primary analytical preoccupation, to use your phrase. It is the analyst or therapist devoting himself or herself to the patient. It is care of an intensive kind. And when we sit with the patient day after day, year after year, we give intensive care. Whether we cure them or not, we care intensively. Lovely.

BK: We've not seen Mrs Coles for a little bit.

DW: She must still be busy typing. She works so hard for me.

BK: Please thank her for her extraordinary work today. And for her many years of typing and editing and caretaking of you.

DW: Without Joyce Coles, there would be no Donald Winnicott.

BK: And how can I express my thanks to you?

DW: No, it is I who must thank you. Perhaps we shall meet again.

BK: I do hope so. Thank you again, Dr Winnicott.

DW: These tapes will be turned into a book, I believe?

BK: Would you be agreeable to that?

DW: I would enjoy the experience of publishing another book, in spite of being dead. What shall we call it?

BK: I had been thinking *Tea with Winnicott.*

DW: I rather like that. But now, I must return, as I have a patient to see.

BK: A patient?

DW: Oh, yes, there is still quite a lot of work for psychoanalysts and psychotherapists in the after-life.

BK: So full retirement is not really an option.

DW: Absolutely not. Well, I must now leave you and dear old Chester Square, with a shake of the hand, and with a smile. How gratifying still to be alive after one has died!

EPILOGUE

How I came to meet Winnicott

Regrettably, I never had the opportunity to meet Dr Donald Winnicott in the flesh. I have, however, had the great privilege of studying his life and work in great detail over more than thirty years; and consequently, I have learned deeply from his writings and from his teachings.

In 1996, I published the very first biography of Winnicott, based on a study of his collected works and his private correspondence, as well as interviews with family, friends, colleagues, and former patients. Since completing that book – rather a short volume, less than two hundred pages in length – I have developed my research work more extensively, having read not only all of his published contributions many times, but also the numerous surviving drafts of his manuscripts and typescripts which contain his original, hand-written annotations. Furthermore, with the kind permission of the Winnicott Trust, I have had the great privilege of studying his deeply extensive correspondence, consisting of literally tens of thousands of pages of print. In fact, I may be the only person obsessional enough to have read through the entire collection of Winnicott's unpublished letters – housed in archival repositories on both sides of the Atlantic Ocean – not once, but twice, and sometimes even thrice. In preparation for my 1996 biography, I had interviewed approximately two hundred people who knew Winnicott personally; subsequently, since publication, I have interviewed a further seven hundred or more.

Although none of this painstaking scholarship can replace the experience of having known Winnicott directly, I have, I trust, acquired a sufficiently rich and, hopefully, accurate grasp of both his life and his work. Certainly, having studied his complete unpublished correspondence – housed partly in London, partly in New York City, and partly in other archives and private collections scattered throughout the world – I would like to think that I have absorbed something of Winnicott's musicality, by which I mean the rhythm, the tempo, and the phrasing of his private speech. I have drawn upon this multi-decade immersion in the world of Winnicott in order to bring him to life in this interview.

Much of the dialogue contained in this reconstruction comes from actual passages or turns of phrase that I found again and again in Winnicott's private, unpublished letters. Other passages derive from my interview material. It struck me as quite extraordinary just how many of my interviewees could quote precise conversations that they had had with Winnicott years earlier. Of course, when considering such oral history data, one must allow for the possibility of some elaboration over time. But even so, Winnicott obviously exerted such a great impact on his colleagues and on his patients that large numbers of these people had ready access to many especially memorable conversations with Winnicott, which had remained in their minds for decades. It would not be at all uncommon for an interviewee to exclaim, "I shall never forget Donald's precise words to me on that occasion. He said ..."

Additionally, I had the real-life pleasure of knowing Mrs Joyce Coles. During the early 1990s, I tried valiantly to locate Mrs Coles, of whom many of informants had spoken, knowing that she would be an indispensable source of information about her long-standing employer. But quite a number of Winnicott's close associates believed her dead, not having had contact with her in over a quarter of a century. And yet, in spite of the rumours of her death, I could find no obituary of Mrs Coles; and therefore I harboured the hope that she *might* still be alive.

As it happened, Miss Irmi Elkan, a very elderly psychoanalyst who had once worked closely with both Donald Winnicott and Anna Freud, told me that years previously, she and Mrs Coles had found themselves, quite by happenstance, on the same walking holiday. Miss Elkan thought that she might have an ancient address for Mrs Coles, and with great generosity she then ferreted out a tattered, handwritten address book, and she did indeed locate a telephone number for Mrs Coles. Miss Elkan explained that she had not rung that number in some twenty years and cautioned me that it might no longer be in service. Undeterred, I rang, and a feeble voice answered the telephone. When I asked whether this might be the home of Mrs Joyce Coles, the elderly lady on the other end of the line introduced herself as the very woman I sought. Apparently, she had recently had a horrific car crash, from which she nearly died; and she had only just returned to her flat in West London that very day! Had I rung a week before, or a month before, I would have had no answer, as Mrs Coles lived alone and had no answering machine. And had I not had an answer, I might well have assumed her dead, as many had led me to believe.

Yet in spite of her fragility, Mrs Coles invited me for a visit. Of course, I offered to postpone any such meeting, as I did not want to intrude upon her convalescence. But she insisted that I come at my earliest possible convenience. That very weekend, on the Sunday morning, I went to see her, intending to stay only for a short conversation. In fact, Mrs Coles spoke so fully and so engagingly about her time with Winnicott that I ended up spending the entire day. I then returned for a great many lengthy visits thereafter, during which time Joyce regaled me with a cornucopia of unpublished stories and anecdotes of her association with Winnicott, which had lasted from September 1948 until January 1971, as well as her relationship with Clare Winnicott, which had endured until the latter's death in 1984.

As my friendship with Mrs Coles developed, she gradually entrusted to me the safekeeping of a rich and rare archive of Winnicott letters, papers, postcards, clinical notes, index cards with case reports, memorabilia, and other materials, not to mention an entire collection of hand-painted Christmas cards that Winnicott had given to her, one of which adorns the cover of my 1996 Winnicott biography. To date, no other scholar has had access to this treasure trove of Winnicott material, and much of what I learned from Joyce and from her collection of papers has helped to inform both the content and the style of *Tea with Winnicott*. Joyce brought Winnicott back to life in a way that no amount of immersion in Winnicott's texts could ever hope to achieve.

In view of the warm association that I enjoyed with Mrs Coles during the final years of her life, I could not resist including her as a character in this posthumous interview. Her quiet, modest, unassuming, yet vital role in Winnicott's life belies the colourful vibrancy of her character. Without the constant protection and assistance that Mrs Coles offered – typing every one of Winnicott's essays and books multiple times, answering virtually every telephone call, preparing every patient bill, and so much more – Winnicott would not have enjoyed that particular facilitating environment which allowed him to develop the full fruits of his developmental psychology.

Of course, my "tea" with Winnicott remains my own construction, but one drawn from the thousands of hours that I have devoted to my study of this man's life and, I hope, his essence.

So, why did I invite Winnicott to a posthumous tea? I believe that I did so for two reasons in particular. First, having now authored or edited three books about various aspects of Winnicott's life and work, I have, over the years, received a number of invitations from various publishers to produce a short "student guide" to Winnicott. Hitherto, I have refrained from doing so, in part, because quite a number of colleagues have already done so. Thus, I thought it might be quite tedious to produce yet another little book of the "Donald-Winnicott-was-born-in-Plymouth-in–1896-and-he-was-very-good-with-children" variety. In the spirit of Winnicottianism, I hoped very much to find a creative way to bring Winnicott back to life in a more playful, more imaginative manner. The real Donald Winnicott adored the theatre, and he attended dramas, musicals, operettas, and concerts often throughout his life. By sculpting an interview in the form of a rudimentary play script, I hope that I have captured something of Winnicott's love of theatricality. I also thought that students might appreciate a more "chatty" introduction to Winnicott, rather than a stodgy, prosaic one. So many of the Winnicott primers prioritise the work and ignore the man, and this regrettable decontextualisation and dehistoricisation makes it harder for students to acquire a sense of the total Winnicott. Because Winnicott authored so many books, monographs, pamphlets, chapters, essays, articles, reviews, obituaries, short communications, and letters, it takes a quite a long time to grapple with the totality of his contributions and his experiences; thus, I hope that this short cup of tea might help students find a welcoming entry point into the study of Winnicott.

But I embarked upon this book not only as a means of helping fledgling mental health professionals to navigate the complexities of Donald Winnicott; I also wrote this book for a second reason. Since the publication of *D. W. Winnicott: A Biographical Portrait* in 1996, I have intensified my research in preparation for producing an even more extensive biography of Winnicott. As one might imagine, the mastery of such a behemoth collection of published writings, unpublished correspondence, and unpublished archival material and oral history interview material requires a great deal of synthesis and organisation. And by writing *Tea with Winnicott*, I set myself the challenge to see whether I could bring Winnicott – both the man and the work – alive in a satisfactory manner. Thus, I wrote this interview-script, in part, as an attempt to create a biographical arc and also to see whether I could successfully find Winnicott's "voice". The unpublished nuggets of Winnicott stories contained herein constitute less than one percent of the unpublished material which I hope will appear in the final biography, currently in preparation. And I must express my gratitude to readers for allowing me to use this fanciful interview as a means of helping me to organise my own thoughts, which, I trust, will continue to bear fruit for readers in subsequent publications.

I produced *Tea for Winnicott* not primarily for colleagues – although some fellow mental health professionals may find this volume of value – but, rather, for students. Tackling psychoanalysis nowadays proves to be such a minefield, as neophytes find themselves swimming in names such as Freud, Jung, Klein, Winnicott, Bowlby, Bion, Mahler, Erikson, Lacan, Mitchell, and so many more. The growing spate of psychoanalytic theories – whether classical psychoanalysis, interpersonal psychoanalysis, relational psychoanalysis, attachment-based psychoanalysis, modern psychoanalysis, neuropsychoanalysis, and so forth – often becomes confusing and, ultimately, indistinguishable. Students often flounder amid the morass of theories because they fail to grapple with these forefathers and foremothers of our field in a more intimate way.

Hopefully, *Tea with Winnicott* may provide a little oasis for trainees that will help to paint a sufficiently distinct picture of Donald Winnicott – one that will be useful in its own right, and one that might also inspire further study. I thank my readers for their willingness to engage with this more playful, more dramatical introduction to Winnicott and his world.

BIOGRAPHICAL REGISTER

For the benefit of those readers with more historical interests, I have written brief descriptions of all of the persons mentioned either in the Interview portion of *Tea with Winnicott* or in the Epilogue.

KARL ABRAHAM (1877–1925)   One of Professor Sigmund Freud's closest disciples, Dr Karl Abraham founded the psychoanalytic movement in Germany. His stirring clinical papers and his multiple contributions to theory, not least his detailed delineation of the stages and sub-stages of psychosexual development, have remained a source of inspiration to many contemporary psychological practitioners. Owing to Abraham's untimely death at the age of only 48 years, Winnicott had never met him, although he would have known various members of Abraham's family, who ultimately emigrated to London; furthermore, Winnicott would have absorbed many of Abraham's ideas through his supervision from Mrs Melanie Klein, one of Abraham's former patients.

MARY ADAMS (born 1924)   The daughter of Harold Stanley Ede, Winnicott's long-standing close personal friend, Mary Ede (later Mary Adams) spent a great deal of time with Donald Winnicott and Alice Winnicott during her childhood. She often stayed at Winnicott's home in Hampstead, in North London, only a short walk from the Ede house. Eventually, the Ede family moved to Tangier, in Morocco; both Winnicott and his wife went to visit them there. Mary Ede and her elder sister, Elisabeth Ede, became honorary daughters to Winnicott.

FRANZ ALEXANDER (1891–1964)   Born in Budapest, Hungary, Franz Alexander was the first person to graduate formally from a psychoanalytic training institute, and he soon became a highly respected disciple of Sigmund Freud. A "Renaissance Man" among psychoanalysts, Alexander made hugely important contributions in a multitude of fields, publishing studies on characterology, psychosomatic medicine, psychoanalytic criminology, the history of psychiatry and psychoanalysis, and much more. A consummate scientist, during the 1930s Alexander received considerable funding from the Rockefeller Foundation to investigate the unconscious psychosomatic origins of various illnesses, such as bronchial asthma and peptic ulcer. We have no knowledge that Winnicott and Alexander ever met, but they might well have overlapped at international psychoanalytic congresses. Certainly, Alexander's formulation of the psychoanalytic situation as a "corrective emotional experience" corresponds in many ways with aspects of Winnicott's own theorisation.

CHRISTOPHER ANDREWES (1896–1988)   Son of Dr Frederick Andrewes (later Sir Frederick Andrewes), a noted pathologist at St Bartholomew's Hospital in London, Christopher Andrewes followed in his father's footsteps and also became a Barts man; he was a contemporary of Winnicott. The two men worked together on the *St. Bartholomew's Hospital Journal* and also sang Gilbert and Sullivan songs to their patients. Andrewes became a lifelong friend to Winnicott. He went on to have a most distinguished career as a virologist, studying the causes of influenza, and he was eventually granted a knighthood for his services to medicine and health care.

ANTHONY ARMSTRONG-JONES (born 1930)   The grandson of Sir Robert Armstrong-Jones, Winnicott's first teacher in "mental diseases" at St Bartholomew's Hospital in London, Anthony Armstrong-Jones married Her Royal Highness The Princess Margaret, daughter of King George VI, and he became a noted photographer. Granted a peerage by his sister-in-law, Her Majesty Queen Elizabeth II, he assumed the title of The Right Honourable The Earl of Snowdon in 1961. We have no knowledge of any contact between Lord Snowdon and Dr Winnicott.

ROBERT ARMSTRONG-JONES (1857–1943)   Born plain Robert Jones to a modest Welsh family, Robert Armstrong-Jones became one of the most celebrated British psychiatrists in the late nineteenth and early twentieth centuries. In 1892, he became the first Medical Superintendent of the

Claybury Asylum, at Woodford Bridge, in Essex. While there, Armstrong-Jones recommended gardening and Turkish baths as therapeutic activities for his patients. He would also come to serve as President of the Royal Medico-Psychological Association. He not only received a knighthood for his psychiatric contributions, but he also became the Lord Chancellor's Visitor in Lunacy. A staunch critic of psychoanalysis, Sir Robert Armstrong-Jones, then Lecturer on Mental Diseases at the St Bartholomew's Hospital Medical School in London, taught Winnicott the rudiments of psychiatry.

ENID BALINT (1903–1994)   Born Enid Flora Albu, she later married the philologist Robert Eichholz and became known professionally as Mrs Enid Eichholz. In 1948 she helped to found the Family Discussion Bureau, which eventually became the Institute of Marital Studies, part of the Tavistock Institute of Medical Psychology, and which then became the Tavistock Centre for Couple Relationships, which remains to this day the centre of excellence in Great Britain for couple psychoanalysis and couple psychotherapy. Enid Eichholz underwent psychoanalytic treatment with Dr John Rickman, and then, after his untimely death, with Winnicott, eventually qualifying as a psychoanalyst in her own right. She and Winnicott developed a warm and convivial association which lasted over many years. In 1953, she married fellow psychoanalyst Dr Michael Balint, and together the two worked quite creatively to help introduce psychoanalytic ideas into medical settings.

MICHAEL BALINT (1896–1970)   Born Mihály Bergsmann in Budapest, Hungary, Dr Michael Balint, as he later became, underwent psychoanalytic training with Sigmund Freud's disciples Dr Hanns Sachs and Dr Sándor Ferenczi, before emigrating to Great Britain. A warm-hearted psychoanalytic practitioner renowned for his many creative contributions to the field, Balint specialised in work with regressed patients and in the application of psychological thinking to medical practice. He married three times, and all of his wives practised psychoanalysis! His third wife, Mrs Enid Flora Albu Eichholz Balint, underwent psychoanalytic treatment with Winnicott. Michael Balint enjoyed a most collegial relationship with Winnicott for over thirty years; and each held the other's clinical contributions in high regard.

BERNARD BARNETT (born 1933)   An English child psychologist, Dr Bernard Barnett trained subsequently as a psychoanalyst. And after years of work at the Child Guidance Training Centre, attached to the Tavistock

Clinic in London, he became a Training Analyst of the Institute of Psycho-Analysis. A popular teacher, writer, and clinical supervisor who knew Winnicott during his early professional years, Dr Barnett has also served as Director of the Squiggle Foundation, a national organisation devoted to furthering the study of Winnicott's work.

THE BEATLES – GEORGE HARRISON (1943–2001), JOHN LENNON (1940–1980), PAUL MCCARTNEY (born 1942), and RINGO STARR (born 1940)   Four of the most engaging performers in the history of entertainment, the Beatles defined the 1960s and created a revolution in music throughout the world. Although quite elderly at the time, the eternally puckish Winnicott adored their music and had enough open-mindedness to embrace the vibrant songs written by John Lennon and Paul McCartney. One of Winnicott's colleagues actually referred to him as the psychoanalytic equivalent of the Beatles – a supreme compliment at the time!

ISA BENZIE (1902–1988)   A noted radio producer who spent most of her career working for the British Broadcasting Corporation, Miss Isa Benzie (also known by her married name, Mrs Royston Morley) commissioned many of Winnicott's pioneering radio broadcasts during the 1940s and beyond. Winnicott credited Benzie for having recognised that his throwaway comment about mothers who devote themselves in an ordinary way to the care of their infants might be the basis of some important radio talks; consequently, she really deserves the credit for having helped to popularise the phrase "ordinary devoted mother".

SVETLANA BERIOSOVA (1932–1998)   A Lithuanian-born dancer who became a prima ballerina with the Royal Ballet in London, Svetlana Beriosova married Winnicott's patient Masud Khan and came to know virtually all of the leading psychoanalysts of the post-World-War II era. Sources differ as to what sort of relationship Beriosova had with Winnicott, some suggesting that she had analysis from Winnicott, others claiming she that she had met with him only for psychiatric consultations to help her with her marital difficulties and with her alcoholism. Certainly, Winnicott and his second wife, Clare Winnicott, socialised with Masud Khan and Svetlana Beriosova on many occasions, and Winnicott also enjoyed the privilege of watching her dance at the Royal Opera House in Covent Garden.

WILFRED BION (1897–1979)   Born to British Colonial parents in India, Wilfred Bion served as a tank commander during the First World War and received the Distinguished Service Order for his gallantry. Upon demobilisation, Bion studied history at the University of Oxford and then matriculated to University College London in the University of London, where he embarked upon his medical studies. After working at the Tavistock Clinic in London for many years, he entered psycho-analytic training, becoming a devoted disciple of Mrs Melanie Klein. Dr Wilfred Bion will be best remembered for his contributions to the study of group behaviour and for helping to develop the theory of group analysis. Similarly, he also remains well known for his work with psychotic patients and, most particularly, for his theory of thinking and of the ways in which primitive mental anxieties and mechanisms often attack thought processes. Winnicott and Bion had a tolerable collegial relationship, marked by a certain amount of mutual suspiciousness and perhaps rivalrousness. Their unpublished letters reveal a certain frisson of frostiness.

CHRISTOPHER BOLLAS (born 1944)   An American literary scholar, Dr Christopher Bollas came to England and trained as a psychoanalyst during the 1970s. Since that time, Bollas has become one of the most creative voices in the Independent School of psychoanalysis and has garnered worldwide acclaim for his many books on such diverse subjects as characterology, confidentiality, and "on demand" treatment. In addi-tion to his clinical contributions, Bollas has also written many compelling and engaging works of drama and fiction. A passionate enthusiast of the work of Winnicott, Bollas served on the Winnicott Publications Committee for many years and helped to prepare several volumes of Winnicottiana for publication.

BERTA BORNSTEIN (1899–1971)   A Polish-born woman who worked with handicapped children, Fräulein Berta Bornstein trained as a child psychoanalyst in Berlin, Germany, and became a close associate of Anna Freud. Like many Continental Jewish psychoanalysts of the period, Bornstein fled Nazi-infested Europe and emigrated to New York; eventually, she became one of the few non-medically trained Special Members of the New York Psychoanalytic Society, developing a reputation as a somewhat fierce teacher and supervisor. She had very little direct contact with Winnicott but would have known him from international psychoanalytic congresses. Winnicott cited Bornstein's work briefly in his paper on "Child Analysis" (later re-titled "Child Analysis in the Latency Period").

GEOFFREY BOURNE (1893–1970)   A contemporary of Winnicott's at St Bartholomew's Hospital, London, Dr Geoffrey Bourne became one of Great Britain's most celebrated cardiologists. He developed a strong pioneering interest in childhood cardiac disease and helped to develop the field that would, ultimately, become known as paediatric cardiology. During the 1940s, Bourne and Winnicott had private offices in the same building, and when Winnicott had a severe coronary in 1949, the timely intervention of Bourne may well have saved Winnicott's life.

ANTHONY BOWLBY (1855–1929)   One of the most pre-eminent surgeons of the twentieth century, Sir Anthony Bowlby taught for many years at St Bartholomew's Hospital in London, and his many students included Winnicott. Sir Anthony Bowlby made important contributions to the practice of trauma surgery, based on his experiences during both the Boer War and also the First World War. Additionally, he served as a surgeon in the Royal Households of both King Edward VII and King George V. His son, John Bowlby, followed his father by pursuing a medical career.

JOHN BOWLBY (1907–1990)   Undoubtedly one of the most potent thinkers and researchers in the history of human psychology, Dr John Bowlby is best known for his profound elucidation of what has come to be known as "attachment theory". Psychoanalysed by Joan Riviere, Bowlby moved beyond his colleagues' emphasis on the internal world and explored systematically the ways in which actual separations and losses during infancy and childhood contribute to the development of depression and other forms of psychopathology in later life. Although not a social intimate of Winnicott's, the two men held each other in deep regard, and one can detect many similarities in their ideas.

CONSTANTIN BRÂNCUȘI (1876–1957)   Born in Romania, Constantin Brâncuși became one of the most influential sculptors of the twentieth century, pioneering a modernist approach. Harold Stanley Ede, Winnicott's great friend from schooldays, became an art connoisseur and a curator, and he championed Brâncuși's work in Great Britain. Although Winnicott probably never met Brâncuși, he would have learned a great deal about modern approaches to art from his association with Ede and with Ede's glamorous literary and theatrical set. Such contacts might have contributed, one suspects, to the development of freshness and challenge that characterise so much of Winnicott's work.

MARJORIE BRIERLEY (1893–1984)   One of Winnicott's fellow students at the Institute of Psycho-Analysis, Dr Marjorie Brierley became a prominent figure in British psychoanalysis during the 1930s and 1940s. She will be remembered for her scholarly papers on a range of topics, including a key essay on feminine development, and also for her collaboration with Dr Edward Glover on a seminal survey of psychoanalytic technique. Known for her independence of mind, Brierley made many important contributions during the so-called "Controversial Discussions", which nearly divided the British Psycho-Analytical Society during the Second World War.

JAMES BRITTON (1908–1994)   The younger brother of Miss Clare Britton (later Mrs Clare Winnicott), James Britton distinguished himself as an academic in the field of educational studies. He taught for many years at the Institute of Education of the University of London and eventually became Goldsmiths Professor. Winnicott enjoyed a warm personal relationship with "Jimmy" Britton and once sent him a very intimate poem about Winnicott's own mother, entitled "The Tree".

HECTOR CAMERON (1878–1958)   A noted physician in children's medicine, Dr Hector Cameron developed a reputation for the treatment of youngsters suffering from nervous disorders. Based at Guy's Hospital in London for many years, Cameron objected to the use of psychoanalysis in the understanding of neuroses in children. Cameron and Winnicott came to represent very different ends of the spectrum in the treatment of psychological distress in children and families.

WINSTON CHURCHILL (1874–1965)   The most famous British politician of the twentieth century hardly requires a biographical entry, but Sir Winston Churchill does feature occasionally in Winnicott's writings, especially in a brief but important reference in an essay on "The Price of Disregarding Research Findings" (later republished as "The Price of Disregarding Psychoanalytic Research"). We have no evidence that Winnicott and Churchill had ever met.

ERIC CLYNE (1914–1987)   The son of Mrs Melanie Klein, he would eventually anglicise the spelling of his surname. Klein had sent her son to Winnicott for psychoanalytic treatment and had hoped to conduct the supervision of the case herself, but Winnicott refused this intrusive request. Clyne remained grateful to Winnicott, and the two men maintained a friendly relationship for some time. Quite apart from his involvement in the psychoanalytic movement, Eric Clyne has earned an important place in history as one of the liberators of the Nazi concentration camp Bergen-Belsen.

JOYCE COLES (1914–1997)   Miss Joyce Bird, later Mrs Joyce Coles, worked as secretary to Winnicott from 1948 until his death in 1971; thereafter, she assisted Winnicott's widow, Mrs Clare Winnicott, in a multitude of administrative tasks, not least preparing many of Winnicott's papers for publication. Mrs Coles devoted much of her adult life to Winnicott and to his legacy and functioned as a loyal and discreet clinical secretary. After Winnicott died in 1971, Clare Winnicott entrusted Coles to blacken out the names of Winnicott's patients in the many surviving letters and case files, suspecting – quite correctly, in fact – that these papers would one day become the subject of intensive scholarly scrutiny.

THOMAS CRANMER (1489–1556)   Undoubtedly one of the most influential clergymen in English history, Thomas Cranmer attended Jesus College at the University of Cambridge during the early sixteenth century. Winnicott would also attend Jesus College some four hundred years later. Cranmer became Archbishop of Canterbury under Henry VIII and helped to orchestrate the Reformation of the church. Although by no means a Lollard, like Winnicott, Archbishop Cranmer epitomised, nonetheless, the tradition of English Protestant religious dissent.

CHARLES DARWIN (1809–1882)   The most impactful of nineteenth-century British scientists, Charles Darwin is known throughout the world as the principal architect of evolutionary theory. Winnicott encountered the works of Darwin while still a schoolboy in Cambridge during the second decade of the twentieth century, and he came to describe Darwin as his "cup of tea". In many respects, Winnicott's theory of the natural, organic development of the infant into an adult through the provision of ordinary parental care mirrors Darwin's theory of the inexorable unfolding of evolution of the human species over time.

JOHN DAVIS (born 1923)   One of the foremost paediatricians of the twentieth century, Dr John Allen Davis had worked for Winnicott at the Paddington Green Children's Hospital as a young physician and became enamoured of his work. Davis eventually became Professor, first at the University of Manchester, and subsequently at the University of Cambridge, where he inaugurated the Winnicott Research Unit. His wife, Madeleine Davis, became one of the principal members of the Winnicott Publications Committee, helping to edit many of Winnicott's works for posthumous publication.

HENRY DICKS (1900–1977)   Born in Russia, Dr Henry Dicks became a noted British psychiatrist. He worked for many years at the Tavistock Clinic in London, during which time he helped to develop the psychoanalytically orientated treatment of marital couples. Dicks wrote a number of influential books on a range of topics, most especially his classic *Marital Tensions: Clinical Studies Towards a Psychological Theory of Interaction* (1967). He also became President of the Royal Medico-Psychological Association. Although he and Winnicott did not have a particularly close working relationship, the two men would certainly have known one another from their long-standing involvement in the Medical Section of the British Psychological Society.

HAROLD STANLEY EDE (1895–1990)   Born on 7 April 1895, exactly one year before Winnicott, Harold Stanley Ede, a fellow pupil at the Leys School in Cambridge, became Winnicott's best friend throughout life. A noted art historian and museum curator, Ede specialised in modern art, although he also had a deep scholarly knowledge of earlier periods as well. In his later years, Stanley Ede, known to friends as "Jim", transformed his home in Cambridge into a museum, Kettle's Yard, now part of the University of Cambridge, which exhibits the works of many of the artists whom he befriended during the 1920s and 1930s, such as Henry Moore, Ben Nicholson, and Christopher Wood, some (if not all) of whom Winnicott could have met at Ede's frequent Hampstead parties.

MILDRED EDE (c. 1873–1953)   Mother of Harold Stanley Ede, who became Winnicott's closest friend from childhood onwards, Mrs Mildred Mary Furley Blanch Ede knew Winnicott for many years. As a very young man, Winnicott had become engaged to Mildred Ede's daughter, Fiona Ede, a woman who eventually became the personal secretary to the opera diva Joan Sutherland.

EDWARD VIII (1894–1972)   Son of the future King George V and Queen Mary, His Highness Prince Edward of York ultimately became the Prince of Wales upon the death of his grandfather King Edward VII in 1910. The proverbial playboy prince, he received a welcome from Winnicott's father, Frederick Winnicott, the incumbent Mayor of Plymouth, in Devon, when he docked in Plymouth Harbour in 1922, having returned from a long sea voyage. Winnicott may well have attended the ceremony, although we cannot be certain. Upon the death of his father, the Prince of Wales became King Edward VIII. He reigned for a less than one year, abdicating in order to marry Mrs Wallis Simpson.

IRMI ELKAN (1918–2009)   After a very patchy career in the child welfare field, Miss Irmi Elkan sought guidance from Winnicott, who took her under his wing and helped to pay for her to have psychoanalytic treatment from his colleague, Mrs Marion Milner. With the support of Winnicott and Milner, Irmi Elkan succeeded in training as a psychoanalyst of both adults and children and eventually worked at the Hampstead Child-Therapy Clinic for Anna Freud. One of the few Anna Freudians who admired Winnicott deeply, she maintained a lifelong affection for both the man and his work.

BEATRICE ENSOR (1885–1974)   Born in Marseille, in France, Béatrice Nina Frédérica de Normann (later Beatrice Ensor) became a pioneering educationalist who emigrated to Great Britain and subsequently introduced and popularised many ideas on progressive education into British culture. Beatrice Ensor organised a landmark conference on the creativity of children in 1921, and she helped to inaugurate and promote the forward-thinking New Education Fellowship and its magazine, *The New Era in Home and School.* She invited many psychologists and psychoanalysts to contribute articles to her magazine, and Winnicott became one of its most fertile authors, reaching a wide audience.

ERIK ERIKSON (1902–1994)   Born in Germany and trained in Austria with Anna Freud, Professor Erik Homburger Erikson became one of the most distinguished psychoanalysts in the United States, publishing landmark books such as *Childhood and Society* (1950) and *Gandhi's Truth: On the Origins of Militant Nonviolence* (1969), which won the National Book Award. He elucidated a very rich developmental psychology, which encompassed the entire life cycle from infancy to senescence. Winnicott had told the American psychoanalytic historian, Dr Paul Roazen, that he greatly admired Erikson's contributions, which bear certain similarities to Winnicott's own work on dependency in early childhood.

SÁNDOR FERENCZI (1873–1933)   A Hungarian-born physician, Dr Sándor Ferenczi met Professor Sigmund Freud in 1908 and soon became one of his leading disciples, spearheading the development of the psychoanalytic movement in Budapest. A man of wide-ranging interests, Ferenczi made an enormous number of contributions to the psychoanalytic literature and is best remembered for his many clinical writings. In later life Ferenczi became increasingly preoccupied with technical experiments such as mutual analysis and physical contact with patients, which resulted in Freud's disapproval. In the wake of his untimely death from pernicious anaemia, Ferenczi became *persona non grata* within the psychoanalytic movement for many years, but in recent decades psychoanalysis has begun to reclaim him, and many contemporary practitioners have come to cherish Ferenczi's open-mindedness, his compassion, his Renaissance-like breadth of accomplishment, his recognition of the realities of child abuse, and his many other fine qualities. Although Winnicott rarely cited Ferenczi, he did own some of Ferenczi's writings, and he would have absorbed something of Ferenczi through his many contacts with Mrs Melanie Klein (who had had her first analysis with Ferenczi in Budapest). Numerous contemporary psychotherapeutic authors have come to regard Ferenczi as Winnicott's spiritual precursor in many respects.

JOHN FLÜGEL (1884–1955)   A psychologist and psychoanalyst of prodigious intelligence and creativity, Professor John Carl Flügel pioneered the development of both the psychological and the psychoanalytic professions in Great Britain, serving as a leading member of both the fledgling British Psychological Society and the British Psycho-Analytical Society. Winnicott knew Flügel and had studied with him during his early years as a candidate at the Institute of Psycho-Analysis. Flügel has earned an important position in the history of the mental health sciences, not only for having established connections between academic psychology and psychoanalysis and for having helped to introduce psychoanalysis into the university, but also for his landmark work on the application of psychoanalytic thinking to the understanding of the family, of marriage, and of culture at large.

MICHAEL FORDHAM (1905–1995)   One of the most seminal figures in the fields of child psychiatry and also Jungian analysis, Dr Michael Fordham first met Winnicott during the Second World War, while both men were working with youngsters evacuated and thus separated from their families. Although members of very different – and often noncommunicating – psychological communities, Fordham and Winnicott developed an affection for one another and became the first to cross the historical Jung–Freud divide in Great Britain. Winnicott shocked his psychoanalytic colleagues when he invited Michael Fordham to lecture to the British Psycho-Analytical Society.

DAVID FORSYTH (1877–1941)   An early member of the London Psycho-Analytical Society, Dr David Forsyth, a physician in children's medicine, became the first Englishman to travel to Vienna, Austria, after the First World War in order to undertake treatment with Professor Sigmund Freud. A founder member of the British Psycho-Analytical Society and author of a valuable textbook on *The Technique of Psycho-Analysis* (1922), which is still pertinent today, Forsyth anticipated Winnicott by embracing both children's medicine and psychoanalysis, although he did not develop the interrelationship between the two disciplines in the creative, expansive, and profound way in which Winnicott would come to do. Forsyth was already an elder statesman by the time Winnicott embarked upon training at the Institute of Psycho-Analysis, and the two men seem to have had very little intimate contact, although they certainly would have known each other from both paediatric and psychoanalytic circles.

FRANCIS FRASER (1885–1964)   Born in Edinburgh, Francis Fraser became one of Great Britain's most distinguished medical practitioners, researchers, and administrators. Fraser assumed the post of Professor of Medicine at St Bartholomew's Hospital Medical College, in which capacity he became an important early medical mentor to Winnicott and prepared him for his examinations. Fraser directed the Emergency Medical Service during the Second World War, for which he would receive a knighthood, and he also helped to establish the British Postgraduate Medical Federation. Winnicott remained in contact with Fraser until shortly before the latter's death.

ANNA FREUD (1895–1982)   The daughter of Professor Sigmund Freud, Fräulein Anna Freud became the only one of Freud's six children to follow her father into the practice of psychoanalysis. She pioneered the field of child psychoanalysis and also made an immense number of theoretical and clinical contributions to the field of adult psychoanalysis, most notably her elucidation of the mechanisms of defence. A refugee from the Nazis, Anna Freud accompanied her father to Great Britain in 1938 and nursed him during the final months of his life. After Freud's death, Anna Freud founded a war nursery in North London and created an intensive training programme in child psychoanalysis. Winnicott had great respect for Anna Freud, but he also harboured a certain wariness, as he practised child psychotherapy and child psychoanalysis in a somewhat different fashion. Although never a member of Anna Freud's inner circle, Winnicott earned her everlasting gratitude for his work on the Freud Statue Committee, raising money for the bronzing and erection of Oscar Nemon's statue of her father.

SIGMUND FREUD (1856–1939)   The founder of psychoanalysis requires little introduction to contemporary readers. Winnicott never met Professor Sigmund Freud personally, although he had come to visit the Freud family home in London to enquire about their wellbeing shortly after Freud and his entourage had emigrated from the Nazi menace. Prior to his own death, Winnicott worked laboriously to collect funds in order to have Oscar Nemon's statue of Freud bronzed and unveiled in Swiss Cottage, London. Today, Nemon's tribute to Freud stands outside the Tavistock Centre, headquarters of the Tavistock and Portman NHS Foundation Trust, in Belsize Park, North London.

ARCHIBALD GARROD (1857–1936)   A physician of tremendous vision, Dr Archibald Garrod enjoyed a long association with St Bartholomew's Hospital and helped to found the first children's outpatient department, laying the foundations for the burgeoning field of child health. Eventually, he became Director of the hospital's new Medical Unit and received a Professorship of Medicine in the University of London, as well as a knighthood. Winnicott worked for Professor Sir Archibald Garrod as a Ward Clerk, shortly after qualifying in medicine in 1920. Garrod succeeded Professor Sir William Osler as Regius Professor of Medicine at the University of Oxford and held a Fellowship at Christ Church.

HENRI GAUDIER-BRZESKA (1891–1915)   Born in Saint-Jean-de-Braye, not far from Orléans, in France, Henri Gaudier became a modernist sculptor and portraitist who died at the age of 23 years. After embarking upon a passionate and tortured love affair with a Polish writer, Sophie Brzeska, Henri Gaudier then hyphenated his surname, incorporating that of his lover. Winnicott had never made the acquaintance of Henri Gaudier-Brzeska, but he did know much about him from Harold Stanley Ede, Winnicott's great school friend, who became an art curator. He wrote a landmark book about Gaudier-Brzeska's life and work, *Savage*

Messiah, published in 1931, which rescued the artist from obscurity. Jim Ede's book became the basis of a 1972 film, also called *Savage Messiah*, directed by Ken Russell. A young Helen Mirren featured in the cast.

KING GEORGE V (1865–1936)   Son of the future King Edward VII and Queen Alexandra and grandson of Queen Victoria, His Royal Highness Prince George Frederick Ernest Albert of Wales would eventually succeed to the British throne in 1910 as King George V. Winnicott's father, Frederick Winnicott, received a knighthood from King George V for his long devotion to civil service in Plymouth, Devon. Winnicott never met George V, although as a devoted monarchist he would have followed the progress of the king and of the whole Royal Family as reported in the press; he did, however, write about King George V in his membership paper to the British Psycho-Analytical Society in 1935, theorising about the unconscious role of the monarch in psychological life.

KING GEORGE VI (1895–1952)   Son of the future King George V and Queen Mary, His Highness Prince Albert Frederick Arthur George of York should not, by right, have acceded to the throne; however, in 1936 his elder brother, King Edward VIII, abdicated, and consequently Prince Albert, then Duke of York, became King George VI. Although Winnicott had no formal contact with King George VI, he long nursed a fantasy that the Royal Family might summon him to psychoanalyse the king's daughters, Princess Elizabeth (later Her Majesty Queen Elizabeth II) and Princess Margaret Rose (later the Countess of Snowdon).

WILLIAM SCHWENCK GILBERT (1836–1911)   Undoubtedly the premier lyricist and librettist of English comic operetta, William Gilbert enjoyed an extraordinary collaboration with the composer Arthur Sullivan, creating some of the most important entertainments of the Victorian era. Winnicott grew up soaked in Gilbert and Sullivan operetta, and as a young medical student he used to sing highlights from their shows to his patients on the wards at St Bartholomew's Hospital in London. Gilbert received a knighthood for his contribution to the arts, as did Sullivan. He died from a heart attack, suffered while trying to save a seventeen-year-old girl who had lost her footing in a lake on the grounds of his North London home.

EDWARD GLOVER (1888–1972)   A Scot by birth, Dr Edward George Glover underwent a training analysis in Berlin, Germany, with Dr Karl

Abraham, and upon his return to Great Britain he became the amanuensis of Dr Ernest Jones and helped to develop psychoanalysis, both theoretically and also institutionally. Glover held many key positions over many years in the British Psycho-Analytical Society and the Institute of Psycho-Analysis, but ultimately he resigned in the wake of the "Controversial Discussions" during the 1940s, owing, in part, to his disagreements with Mrs Melanie Klein and to the odium that many younger members felt towards Glover's ostensible hunger for power within the institutional setting. Winnicott had extensive dealings with Glover from the time of his candidacy at the Institute of Psycho-Analysis, and the two men maintained reasonably cordial relationships for many years thereafter. Glover distinguished himself not only as the author of many vital books on psychoanalytic technique, but also because of his prescient contributions to the field of criminology.

ARTHUR GRAY (1852–1940)   A noted classicist and historian, Mr Arthur Gray served as Master of Jesus College at the University of Cambridge throughout Winnicott's undergraduate years. Author of numerous historical studies of Jesus College and of the city of Cambridge, Gray also wrote many ghost stories, set in the college, under the pseudonym "Ingulphus" (the name of a Saxon abbot from Lincolnshire). In all likelihood, Gray would have interviewed Winnicott for a student place at the University of Cambridge.

RALPH GREENSON (1911–1979)   The noted American psychoanalyst Dr Ralph Greenson made a large number of important clinical contributions to the study of psychoanalysis and wrote one of the most foundational textbooks in the field, the classic tome *The Technique and Practice of Psychoanalysis: Volume 1* (1967). Greenson and Winnicott shared similar views on many subjects, and they developed a warm relationship, having met often at international psychoanalytic conferences. Today, Greenson will best be remembered for having treated many celebrities, notably Frank Sinatra and, most especially, Marilyn Monroe (who, most controversially, lived with Greenson's family for a time).

PHYLLIS GROSSKURTH (1924–2015)   A prominent Canadian academic and professional biographer, Professor Phyllis Grosskurth will be remembered within the psychoanalytic community for her rich and skilful biography of Mrs Melanie Klein, published in 1986, which drew upon a great deal of unpublished documentation and interviews with eyewitnesses.

Grosskurth never met Winnicott personally, but she published several helpful anecdotes about Winnicott and his world, based on interviews with Mrs Clare Winnicott, one of Melanie Klein's last analysands.

Leonard Guthrie (1858–1918)   Trained at St Bartholomew's Hospital in London, Dr Leonard George Guthrie became a noted physician in the fledgling field of children's medicine and worked for many years at the Paddington Green Children's Hospital, rising to the rank of Senior Physician, specialising in the treatment of nervous diseases in youngsters. A President of the Society for the Study of Disease in Children and a medical historian of some note, Guthrie came to specialise in his own pre-Freudian version of psychological approaches to children's medical symptoms, having taken a particular interest in enuresis and *pavor nocturnus* [night terror]. In his landmark book, *Functional Nervous Disorders in Childhood*, published in 1907, Guthrie critiqued some of the more punitive treatments meted out to children who struggled with psychological symptoms. Although the two men had never met, Winnicott derived much encouragement from Guthrie's book. In fact, Winnicott owned at least two copies of Guthrie's groundbreaking work.

Herman Hardenberg (1911–1967)   A physician, psychiatrist, and psychoanalyst, Dr Herman Edward William Hardenberg had worked as a junior to Winnicott at the Paddington Green Children's Hospital in West London for many years. Hardenberg proved a loyal disciple to Winnicott, supporting his critique of psychosurgical treatments in the pages of the *British Medical Journal*. He established a successful private psychoanalytic practice, first on Welbeck Street, and then on Upper Wimpole Street, in Central London, where his patients included the celebrated choreographer Kenneth Macmillan. Hardenberg's wife, Dr Janet Hardenberg, edited two of Winnicott's most successful books.

Janet Hardenberg (1913–2004)   Born Janet Agnes Walker, she married Dr Herman Hardenberg. A physician in her own right, Dr Hardenberg worked very diligently, assisting Winnicott by editing his first two full-length psychoanalytic books, *The Child and the Family: First Relationships*, and *The Child and the Outside World: Studies in Developing Relationships*. Winnicott had worked with a number of people before he had engaged the services of Dr Hardenberg. Whereas her predecessors had failed to complete the task, Hardenberg succeeded admirably in the preparation of an elegant text of his many radio broadcasts. The two volumes became among the most influential of Winnicott's publications and served as the basis for an even more popular omnibus edition, *The Child, the Family, and the Outside World*.

DORA HARTMANN (1902–1974)   Born in Hinterbrühl bei Mödling, south of Vienna, in Austria, Dora Karplus (later known as Dora Hartmann) trained as a physician and ultimately as a psychoanalyst, specialising in child analysis. The wife of the distinguished Viennese psychoanalyst Dr Heinz Hartmann, she emigrated with her husband and children to New York City in the wake of the Nazi infestation of Austria. Dr Dora Hartmann inspired many as a teacher of child psychoanalysis, although she wrote few papers on the subject. Winnicott knew Dr Dora Hartmann from international congresses and held both her as well as her husband in some regard. Their sons became eminent psychiatrists: Professor Ernest Hartmann would come to specialise in the study of dreams, and Professor Lawrence Hartmann would serve as President of the American Psychiatric Association.

HENRY VIII (1491–1547)   Arguably the most compelling and complex of English kings, Henry VIII has a relevance to the life of Winnicott, owing to his reformation of the church. In an unprecedented assault on papal authority, Henry VIII, once a staunch Catholic and *fidei defensor* [defender of the faith], came to establish himself as Supreme Head of the Church of England and later launched the infamous looting and dissolution of numerous Catholic monasteries. His subjugation of Catholicism laid the groundwork for the development of various branches of Protestantism, including, centuries later, Wesleyan Methodism, which became a bedrock of Winnicott's philosophy.

HIPPOCRATES (c. 460 BCE–c. 370 BCE)   An ancient Greek physician often referred to as the father of modern medicine, Hippocrates will best be remembered for the oath that bears his name, although it remains unclear whether he himself actually authored the Hippocratic oath to which all physicians subscribe. Although Winnicott never undertook the formal study of ancient medicine, he did maintain a passing interest in ancient philosophy and may, at some point, have glanced at the works of Hippocrates. Winnicott did, however, endeavour to practise medicine according to the basic Hippocratic principle of avoiding harm to patients, although he did not always manage to do so.

JULIET HOPKINS (born 1934)   The niece of Dr John Bowlby, Miss Juliet Phelps Brown (later Dr Juliet Hopkins) became a psychologist, child psychotherapist, and adult psychotherapist who spent most of her professional career working in the Child and Family Department at the Tavistock Clinic in London, where she became a seminal teacher and supervisor. During her training, Juliet Hopkins underwent clinical supervision with Winnicott. In later years, when the Tavistock Clinic training became dominated by Kleinian practitioners, Hopkins remained an exemplar of independent thinking, in part by teaching the work of Winnicott and of her uncle, John Bowlby.

THOMAS HORDER (1871–1955) Of humble origins, the son of a draper in Shaftesbury, in Dorset, Thomas Horder became one of the most illustrious British physicians of all time, serving no fewer than five monarchs in succession: King Edward VII, King George V, King Edward VIII, King George VI, and Queen Elizabeth II. A long-standing physician at St Bartholomew's Hospital, Horder developed a reputation as a thorough – indeed superb – diagnostician, and as one of the few physicians of the era to discuss the nature of the doctor–patient relationship. Although we have no archival evidence that Winnicott worked closely with Horder at St Bartholomew's Hospital, as various writers have suspected, Winnicott certainly would have encountered Horder and would have benefited from his frequent publications in the *St. Bartholomew's Hospital Journal*. In addition to his institutional work, Horder had arguably the most successful private medical practice in the early twentieth century and treated a large number of aristocrats. He received first a knighthood and then a baronetcy for his services to medicine, becoming Lord Horder, 1st Baron Horder of Ashford.

HERMINE HUG-HELLMUTH (1871–1924) Born in Vienna, Hermine Wilhelmina Ludovika Hug von Hugenstein, later known as Hermine Hug-Hellmuth or as Hermine von Hug-Hellmuth, received a doctoral degree in physics from the Universität zu Wien and then subsequently joined the psychoanalytic movement and became the first person to practise child psychoanalysis. Tragically, her nephew, Rudolf Hug, strangled her to death. Apparently, she had endeavoured to psychoanalyse him. It seems unlikely that Winnicott had ever read her writings, most of which had not appeared in English translation during Winnicott's lifetime.

SUSAN ISAACS (1885–1948) Susan Sutherland Fairhurst grew up in a Wesleyan Methodist family, hailing from Turton, Lancashire, in the north of England. A supporter of liberal causes such as women's suffrage and Fabianism, she trained as a research psychologist at the University of Manchester and also at the University of Cambridge, specialising in developmental psychology. As Dr Susan Isaacs, she became a pioneer of progressive education for children and served as Principal of the Malting House School in Cambridge. She also trained in psychoanalysis at the Institute of Psycho-Analysis and became a close friend to Winnicott. After Isaacs assumed the directorship of the Department of Child Development at the Institute of Education, part of the University of London, she invited Winnicott to teach her students, which he continued to do for more than thirty years.

ERNEST JONES (1879–1958)   With the exception of Professor Sigmund Freud, no one did more to develop psychoanalysis as an international, administrative movement than Dr Ernest Jones. A Welshman by birth, Jones trained as a physician and discovered psychoanalysis quite early in his career. He survived both a scandal and an arrest for sexual impropriety with disabled children to become the founder, in 1913, of the London Psycho-Analytical Society and subsequently, in 1919, of the British Psycho-Analytical Society. He also spearheaded the creation of the Institute of Psycho-Analysis, the London Clinic of Psycho-Analysis, and *The International Journal of Psycho-Analysis*, and he also served as President of the International Psycho-Analytical Association. Jones is best remembered, perhaps, for his tendentious, but nevertheless highly valuable, well-written three-volume biography of Freud. A controversial figure who made many enemies, Jones did, however, take a great liking to Winnicott.

KATHERINE JONES (1892–1983)   Born in Vienna, Austria, Fräulein Katherine Jokl, a relation of Professor Sigmund Freud's close disciple Dr Hanns Sachs, came to marry the young British psychoanalyst Dr Ernest Jones. Apparently the neurotic symptoms displayed by Katherine Jones and by her children compelled Ernest Jones to arrange for Frau Melanie Klein to emigrate permanently from Germany to Great Britain in order to treat them, thus changing the course of psychoanalytic history. Katherine Jones, known to her familiars as "Kitty", maintained a long-standing interest in psychoanalysis as a highly informed and well-placed layperson, and she certainly entertained Winnicott in her home.

CARL GUSTAV JUNG (1875–1961)   Born in Kesswil, in the canton of Thurgau, in Switzerland, Dr Carl Gustav Jung became arguably the most influential theoretician of depth psychology apart from Professor Sigmund Freud. Jung began his career at the Burghölzli asylum, working for Professor Eugen Bleuler, where he developed an extensive body of knowledge about the psychology of schizophrenia. After meeting Freud, Jung soon became his anointed successor and assumed the post as President of the Internationale Psychoanalytische Vereinigung [International Psycho-Analytical Association]. But owing to Jung's growing independence of mind and to certain theoretical disputes about the role of sexuality in the aetiology of the neuroses, Jung and Freud parted company. Jung then devoted the rest of his life to the development of his own version of dynamic psychology, which has become known as analytical psychology. Winnicott became one of the first British Freudian psychoanalysts to engage seriously with the Jungian corpus of writings, and he not only read some of Jung's works, but also invited the Jungian analyst Dr Michael Fordham to lecture at the British Psycho-Analytical Society.

HARRY KARNAC (1919–2014)   Founder of H. Karnac (Books), Harry Karnac began his career as a generalist bookseller. But with encouragement from Dr Clifford Scott, as well as from Winnicott, he began to specialise in psychoanalytic titles; eventually, his establishment on London's Gloucester Road became the first bookshop dedicated almost entirely to publications on mental health. Winnicott visited Harry Karnac frequently, and the two men enjoyed a pleasant relationship. Winnicott often borrowed biographies from the shop and then returned them, having read only the chapters on the subject's early childhood, telling Karnac that he lost interest in the biographies of the protagonists after they had grown up! Towards the end of his time working in the bookshop, Harry Karnac launched a publishing arm. Today, Karnac Books produces approximately one hundred new psychoanalytic titles every year.

JOHN MAYNARD KEYNES (1883–1946)   The distinguished English economist John Maynard Keynes enjoyed a long association with Winnicott's first psychoanalyst, James Strachey. Keynes and Strachey had met as students at the University of Cambridge and became sexual partners over many years. Both men subsequently married women. Keynes and Strachey also shared a house in Bloomsbury in which Strachey practised psychoanalysis. Winnicott certainly recalled seeing both Keynes and his wife, the Russian ballerina Lydia Lopokova, when he attended for sessions with Strachey. A long-standing consultant to British politicians, Keynes helped to advise the government on the country's economic crises during and after both the First World War and the Second World War. Eventually, he received a baronetcy for his contributions to the study of economics.

MASUD KHAN (1924–1989)   Undoubtedly one of the most controversial figures in the history of psychoanalysis, Masud Khan made enormous clinical, theoretical, and administrative contributions to the field, garnering international recognition. But during the last two decades of his life he began deteriorating both physically and psychologically, treating patients in a deeply unethical manner. His many infractions resulted in his eventual expulsion from membership in both the British Psycho-Analytical Society and the British Association of Psychotherapists. Inextricably linked with Winnicott, who served as his clinical supervisor, as well as his personal psychoanalyst, and as his colleague, Khan's behaviour in later years has since brought both men into disrepute, evoking much criticism from contemporary writers, in large measure as a result of the complex, overlapping personal and professional relationships in which both men participated.

TAHIR KHAN (1923–1982)   We know very little about Mohammed Tahir Raza Khan, the elder brother of Winnicott's sometime patient and disciple Mohammed Masud Raza Khan. Tragically, he suffered from alcoholism and from bipolar illness during adulthood. We also have little knowledge about the extent of Winnicott's contact with Tahir Khan. But we do know that Masud Khan's brother took the photograph of Winnicott that appears on the dust jacket of Winnicott's 1958 book, *Collected Papers: Through Paediatrics to Psycho-Analysis*. He died from a heart attack aged only 58 years.

PEARL KING (1918–2015)   One of the most beloved figures in British psychoanalysis, Miss Pearl King began her career as an industrial psychologist and then trained as a psychoanalyst of both adults and children, undergoing supervision with Winnicott. A tireless worker, she served alongside Winnicott in a number of administrative capacities, notably as Secretary of the committee established by the International Psycho-Analytical Association to accredit the fledgling psychoanalytic society in Finland; and she also held the post of Deputy President of the British Psycho-Analytical Society during Winnicott's second term as President. She eventually became President herself years later, the first non-physician to occupy this role. A noted psychoanalytic historian, Pearl King created the archives at the British Psycho-Analytical Society and lovingly preserved thousands of unpublished documents.

TRUBY KING (1858–1938)   Born in New Plymouth, in New Zealand, Frederic Truby King trained as a physician and attended the lectures of Professeur Jean-Martin Charcot, the noted French neurologist, as did the young Dr Sigmund Freud. Dr Truby King came to special-ise in the care of infants, and he became a fervent spokesperson for strict regimentation in the feeding, toileting, and sleeping of infants. A prominent physician in his homeland, Dr King served as Director of Child Welfare in New Zealand's Department of Health, and he eventually received a knighthood and, ultimately, a state funeral. We have no knowledge of any encounter between Winnicott and King, but Winnicott certainly rejected King's overly restrictive approach to the handling of the child.

MELANIE KLEIN (1882–1960)   Born in Vienna, Austria, Melanie Reizes endured an unhappy marriage to Arthur Klein but bore him three chil-dren. Dissatisfied with domestic life, Klein travelled first to Budapest, Hungary, to undergo psychoanalysis with Dr Sándor Ferenczi, and then to Berlin, Germany, for further psychoanalytic treatment from Dr Karl Abraham, all the while developing her burgeoning interest in working with children. A deeply creative woman, Klein became aware of the most primitive and aggressive underpinnings of the human personality and devised a style of interpreting this aspect of the patient's mind. In 1926, Klein emigrated to England permanently, at the request of Dr Ernest Jones, and began to write her magnum opus, *Die Psychoanalyse des Kindes* [*The Psycho-Analysis of Children*], published in 1932, which had a huge influence on Winnicott, who read the work in English translation, and who became Klein's supervisee and student. Although Winnicott admired Klein greatly, he eventually began to develop his own original ideas, much to her displeasure. Klein continued to produce an unabated stream of books and articles throughout her long and productive career, but her seminal work on envy, published shortly before her death, alien-ated not only Winnicott, but also Dr John Bowlby, and quite a few other members of the Middle Group of British psychoanalysts.

ERNST KRIS (1900–1957)   Born in Vienna, Austria, Ernst Kris became a noted art historian who specialised in the Renaissance and who held a curatorship at the Kunsthistorisches Museum. After his marriage to Dr Marianne Rie (the daughter of one of Professor Sigmund Freud's closest friends), Ernst Kris became a member of the inner circle of the psychoanalytic movement and eventually began practising psychoanalysis himself. Dr Ernst Kris and his family emigrated to England in 1938, and both Kris and his wife became members of the British Psycho-Analytical Society. Winnicott certainly knew Ernst Kris during his time in London; however, before long, he and his family relocated once again, settling permanently in the United States, where Kris became one of the principal architects of ego psychology.

MARIANNE KRIS (1900–1980)   Marianne Rie grew up at the heart of the Viennese psychoanalytic community. Her father, the children's physician Dr Oskar Rie, enjoyed a close personal friendship with Dr Sigmund Freud for many decades; her mother, Frau Melanie Rie (*née* Bondy) had a sister, Fräulein Ida Bondy, who married Freud's one-time confidante Dr Wilhelm Fliess. Marianne Rie's own sister, Margarethe Rie, married the Viennese psychoanalyst Dr Hermann Nunberg. Marianne Rie trained as a physician and then, in 1927, married the young art historian Dr Ernst Kris. Soon Marianne Kris, long interested in children's medicine, became one of the seminal figures in the burgeoning field of child analysis, stimulated, in part, by her lifelong association with Fräulein Anna Freud. After taking flight from the Nazis, Marianne Kris lived in Great Britain for a short while before emigrating permanently to the United States. She became a celebrated psychoanalyst of children and adults and served as the founding President of The American Association for Child Psychoanalysis. Winnicott knew Marianne Kris from her time in London and maintained a cordial relationship with her through their periodic meetings at international congresses of psychoanalysis. Both of Kris's children became psychoanalysts themselves – Dr Anna Kris Wolff and Dr Anton Kris.

JACQUES LACAN (1901–1981)   A highly provocative and controversial psychoanalyst, Dr Jacques Lacan became one of the most celebrated and revered figures in French cultural life during the 1960s. Winnicott met Lacan on many occasions and even dined with him in Paris, and appreciated his company. But ultimately Winnicott joined a team appointed by the International Psycho-Analytical Association to investigate Lacan's competency as a clinician, owing to rumours that he conducted shortened sessions with his growing coterie of patients. As a result of the deliberations of the committee, Lacan lost his membership in the International Psycho-Analytical Association; consequently, he had to create his own psychoanalytic organisation.

RONALD LAING (1927–1989)   The Scottish-born psychiatrist Dr Ronald David Laing became a *cause célèbre* in Great Britain during the 1960s and 1970s, spearheading what became known as the anti-psychiatry movement. Though trained at the Institute of Psycho-Analysis in London, Laing disliked most of his teachers and found them stuffy and uncreative, with the exception of Winnicott and those close to Winnicott such as Mrs Marion Milner, one of Laing's supervisors. Laing had sent some of his writings to Winnicott, who offered warm encouragement.

LYDIA LOPOKOVA (1892–1981)   Born in St Petersburg, in Tsarist Russia, daughter of a former serf, Lidia Vasilyevna Lopukhova – better known as Lydia Lopokova – became a celebrated ballerina, best known for her work with Sergei Diaghilev's Ballets Russes. In 1925 she married the English economist and Bloomsbury Group stalwart John Maynard Keynes and, for a time, shared a house with James Strachey and Alix Strachey in Gordon Square, in Central London. Winnicott sometimes saw Lopokova in her tutu when visiting Gordon Square for his psychoanalytic sessions with James Strachey. In 1942, with her husband's ennoblement to the peerage as Baron Keynes of Tilton, in the County of Sussex, she became Baroness Keynes.

EDWARD MACDOWELL (1860–1908)   A native New Yorker, Edward Mac-Dowell trained in Paris, France, and in Frankfurt, Germany; and in time he became a highly accomplished pianist and composer. Encouraged at an early age by Franz Liszt, MacDowell began to write many piano pieces, often quite Romantic in style, and these compositions gradually brought him recognition. MacDowell's works included a number of piano suites, notably the *New England Idyls* (sometimes spelled *New England Idylls*). As a schoolboy, Winnicott performed some of MacDowell's music in a concert at the Leys School in Cambridge.

RONALD MACKEITH (1908–1977)   Educated at the University of Oxford and at St Mary's Hospital Medical School in the University of London, Dr Ronald MacKeith became one of Great Britain's most distinguished paediatricians, specialising in the study of cerebral palsy and other illnesses. A children's doctor with a strong interest in the nascent field of child psychiatry, MacKeith used to attend Winnicott's private seminars for paediatricians, and he became a fervid admirer. Along with Dr John Davis, Dr Peter Tizard, and other young paediatricians, MacKeith helped to bring Winnicott's writings to the attention of medical practitioners.

MARGARET MAHLER (1897–1985)   Born in Sopron, Hungary, Margaret Schönberger trained as a physician, specialising in children's medicine, before undertaking her psychoanalytic training in Vienna, Austria. After her marriage to a Dr Paul Mahler, a chemist, Dr Margaret Mahler emigrated first to Great Britain, in flight from the Nazis, before settling permanently in New York City. Mahler worked extensively with psychotic children as well as with the handicapped and disabled. Subsequently, she embarked upon a detailed elaboration of her own very particular psychoanalytic theory of developmental psychology, tracing the infant's trajectory from a state of autistic preoccupation, through to symbiosis with the maternal caregiver, and then, eventually, to the complex stage of separation–individuation, in which the infant gradually emerges as a person in his or her own right. Winnicott and Mahler certainly knew one another from international psychoanalytic congresses, but they did not collaborate or develop a friendship, in part, one suspects, because of the enormous similarities between their work, albeit written in very different accents.

PRINCESS MARGARET (1930–2002)   The younger daughter of Albert, the Duke of York (later King George VI) and sister to the future Queen Elizabeth II, Her Royal Highness The Princess Margaret Rose married Anthony Armstrong-Jones, grandson of Winnicott's lecturer in mental diseases, Sir Robert Armstrong-Jones. Winnicott probably never met Princess Margaret, although he had always hoped that the Royal Family would either reward him with a knighthood (as they had done for his father Sir Frederick Winnicott), or that they would summon him to treat a member of their inner circle.

MARY, QUEEN OF SCOTS (1542–1587)   Mary Stuart, daughter of King James V of Scotland and Marie de Guise, inherited her father's throne at the age of only six days. Like many child monarchs, denied a suitable apprenticeship, her life became more than unusually fraught with challenges, and she would ultimately be imprisoned by her cousin, Queen Elizabeth I of England, and then beheaded at 44 years of age. Winnicott loved history, and he particularly enjoyed monarchical history, so it seems likely, although not certain, that he would have read

Lady Antonia Fraser's much-acclaimed biography of the Scottish ruler, *Mary Queen of Scots*, which appeared in 1969 and became a much-discussed bestseller.

DONALD MELTZER (1922–2004)   Born in the United States, Dr Donald Meltzer, a psychiatrist, came to Great Britain in order to undergo psychoanalytic treatment and training. The last of Mrs Melanie Klein's analysands, Meltzer became a very powerful force in the development of Kleinian and post-Kleinian thinking, authoring many seminal works that illuminate the often more sinister side of human psychology, most especially *The Claustrum: An Investigation of Claustrophobic Phenomena*, published in 1992. Winnicott admired Meltzer's willingness to work with psychotic patients, and thus he referred patients to this younger colleague. But Winnicott objected to Meltzer's use of lengthy Kleinite verbal interpretations in psychoanalytic sessions, which he found excessive. Meltzer eventually ceased to hold membership in the British Psycho-Analytical Society, giving rise to conjecture as to the cause.

ISABEL MENZIES LYTH (1917–2008)   Born in Dysart, Fife, in Scotland, Isabel Menzies studied economics and experimental psychology at the University of St Andrews. During the Second World War, she took up a post at the War Office Selection Board, where she met many psychoanalysts. Miss Menzies eventually began to work at the Tavistock Institute of Human Relations and trained as a psychoanalyst of adults and children at the Institute of Psycho-Analysis. Best known for her work as a pioneer of psychoanalytic organisational consultancy, Isabel Menzies undertook a number of projects in which she explored the role of anxiety within institutions, examining the ways in which both conscious and unconscious fears inhibited enjoyment and creativity in the workplace. Late in life, she married fellow psychoanalyst Dr Oliver Lyth and lived with him in Oxford. The University of East London awarded her an honorary doctorate in 1997, at which time she became known as Dr Isabel Menzies Lyth. Winnicott knew her through their membership in the British Psycho-Analytical Society, and Menzies had the unenviable task of informing Winnicott that he had become too old to serve as a Training Analyst to new candidates, following his nearly fatal heart attack in 1968.

ARTHUR MILLER (1915–2005)   Son of Polish immigrants, Arthur Asher Miller grew up in Harlem, in the north of New York City, and rose to become one America's most celebrated playwrights. In 1956, Arthur Miller received worldwide attention by marrying the Hollywood screen legend Marilyn Monroe. Winnicott had an interest in Arthur Miller, not only because of his long-standing acquaintance with Dr Marianne Kris, one of Marilyn Monroe's psychoanalysts, but also because of Miller's book, *Jane's Blanket*, an illustrated children's book first published in 1963, inspired by the author's baby daughter Jane Miller and her relationship to her blanket. Winnicott had the temerity to write to Arthur Miller, enquiring whether Miller had actually based *Jane's Blanket* on Winnicott's own work on the transitional object.

EMANUEL MILLER (1892–1970)   One of Great Britain's first child psychiatrists, Emanuel Miller grew up in London, the son of a fur trader. He received his preclinical education at St John's College at the University of Cambridge and then completed his medical studies at the London Hospital, before specialising in psychological work with children. A pioneer of the child guidance movement, Miller worked at the Tavistock Clinic, at the Maudsley Hospital, and at many other institutions. A psychodynamically orientated psychiatrist who never allied himself exclusively with one particular school of thought, Dr Miller helped to integrate the child and adolescent mental health professions by founding both the Association of Child Psychology and Psychiatry and its periodical, the *Journal of Child Psychology and Psychiatry and Allied Disciplines*. Though never close friends with Winnicott, the two men held each other in high regard over the course of many years. After his death, an Emanuel Miller Centre (subsequently renamed The Child and Adolescent Mental Health Services Emanuel Miller Centre East Sector) opened in Dr Miller's honour, to provide psychological services for children and families in East London. His *alma mater*, St John's College at the University of Cambridge, eventually came to sponsor an Emanuel Miller Prize in his honour.

MARION MILNER (1900–1998)   Marion Blackett grew up in London. After her marriage to Dennis Milner, a man with a plethora of medical and psychological difficulties, she trained first as a psychologist and later as a psychoanalyst of both adults and children. Marion Milner and Winnicott had a very complicated relationship over many years. Letters reveal that Milner certainly harboured a deep sexual attraction to Winnicott, who also psychoanalysed both Marion Milner and her husband and even treated Mrs Milner in her own home. After Winnicott's death, Milner became one of Winnicott's greatest champions, and during her eighties and nineties she attended meetings of the Squiggle Foundation – an organisation devoted to the elucidation of Winnicott's work – with admirable regularity. She is best remembered for her own unique contributions to psychoanalysis, which range from her treatment of "Susan", a severely psychologically ill woman who lived in Winnicott's house, to her studies of the importance of playfulness and spontaneity. She also wrote beautifully about the joys of relishing perception, and she published some of her most evocative findings under the pseudonym of "Joanna Field".

STEPHEN MITCHELL (1946–2000)   The American psychologist and psychoanalyst Professor Stephen Mitchell pioneered the field of "relational psychoanalysis", and in 1991 he helped to found its notable journal, *Psychoanalytic Dialogues: A Journal of Relational Perspectives*, since renamed as *Psychoanalytic Dialogues: The International Journal of Relational Perspectives*. Although Winnicott died before Mitchell reached professional maturity and the two men never met, one senses that Winnicott would have enjoyed Mitchell's conceptualisation of psychoanalysis as a truly interactional enterprise, a philosophy that derived much inspiration, in fact, from Winnicott's own work in this respect. Mitchell died from a heart attack at the age of 54 years.

MARILYN MONROE (1926–1962)   Born in Los Angeles, California, Norma Jeane Mortenson survived a traumatic childhood marred by parental neglect and parental mental illness and grew up to become one of the most sexually charismatic film stars of all time. Marilyn Monroe underwent a great deal of psychiatric and psychoanalytic treatment during her short lifetime, including intensive psychoanalyses from both Dr Marianne Kris and Dr Ralph Greenson. Although Winnicott never met Marilyn Monroe, he certainly knew something about her psychoanalytic experiences through the professional grapevine, and he even wrote about this to Arthur Miller, Monroe's *quondam* husband. Monies from her estate eventually helped to fund various child mental health projects in London, including the Day Unit at the Tavistock Clinic, which would no doubt have pleased Winnicott.

OSCAR NEMON (1906–1985)   Born in Osijek, Croatia, Oscar Nemon became a sculptor of great repute, who, at the behest of the early Viennese psychoanalyst Dr Paul Federn, made a statue of Professor Sigmund Freud, which remained unbronzed for many decades. Winnicott established a Freud Statue Committee for the express purpose of raising money from psychoanalysts around the world in order to pay Nemon for the expensive bronzing process and for the erection of the statue in a public location. After years of painstaking fundraising, Winnicott and his colleagues succeeded in their efforts and funded Nemon. With tremendous practical assistance from Joyce Coles, the Freud Statue Committee arranged for the unveiling of Nemon's newly bronzed sculpture in a special ceremony held on 2 October 1970, only weeks before Winnicott's death. The statue stood for many years outside the library in Swiss Cottage, in North London, but has since found a new home outside the Tavistock Centre (formerly the Tavistock Clinic), in Belsize Park, not far from its original location. Nemon will be remembered not only for his statue of Freud, but also for his many statues of Winston Churchill and other well-known personalities, including Queen Elizabeth II and Queen Elizabeth the Queen Mother.

ISAAC NEWTON (1642–1727) Undoubtedly one of the world's most influential scientists, the Englishman Isaac Newton will best be remembered for his work on the theory of gravity. Although Winnicott seems never to have studied Newton's work in any detail, if at all, the two men both enjoyed membership of the University of Cambridge, albeit centuries apart.

SYLVIA PAYNE (1880–1976) Born Sylvia May Moore, in London, this highly dedicated and hugely competent woman became one of the first female physicians in Great Britain, qualifying in medicine in 1906. Trained in psychoanalysis in Berlin, Germany, under the auspices of Dr Hanns Sachs, Sylvia Payne returned to England and became an early member of the British Psycho-Analytical Society. In 1944 she succeeded Dr Ernest Jones, becoming the second President of the organisation since its inception in 1919. A deeply gracious person, beloved by many, Dr Payne took Winnicott very much under wing and helped him greatly throughout his career. The two of them developed a warm association, which lasted until Winnicott's death. One of her sons, Kenneth Payne, became a champion rower and, at the age of 19 years, competed in the Summer Olympics of 1932, in Los Angeles, California.

OSKAR PFISTER (1873–1956) A Swiss pastor from Wiedikon, in Zurich, Pfarrer Oskar Pfister became one of the first Gentiles to join the psychoanalytic movement; and in spite of his devotion to formal religion, he succeeded in maintaining a warm and cordial lifelong relationship with the atheistic Professor Sigmund Freud. Although Freud often struggled to tolerate divergent ideas from his epigones, he nevertheless harboured unusual respect for Pfister and for his spirituality. Winnicott had read the British edition of Pfister's textbook on psychoanalysis while a young man, and this stirred his interest in the field.

THE PIGGLE (born 1961)   The daughter of two psychologically minded parents, "The Piggle" first met Winnicott in 1964, in order to have occasional "on demand" psychotherapeutic consultations to help her to deal with the arrival of a younger sister. As the family lived outside London, regular child psychoanalysis proved impossible; but Winnicott, who knew the family, sensed that intensive treatment might be neither desirable nor necessary. Winnicott's account of his work with "The Piggle" appeared in print several years after his death. "The Piggle", now a grown woman, has become a very substantial personality, working creatively and successfully in the mental health field.

OTTO RANK (1884–1939)   Born Otto Rosenfeld in Vienna, Austria, he changed his surname, as did many Jews of the period, in the hope of avoiding anti-Semitic assaults. A long-standing devotee of Professor Sigmund Freud, the young Rank worked tirelessly to promote psychoanalysis through his many writings and through his work as Freud's personal secretary. As Rank matured, he began to develop his own ideas and no longer concentrated solely on the slavish elucidation of Freud's concepts. After Rank published his book on birth trauma, which implied that anxiety and neurosis might result not simply from the strains of the Oedipus complex, he and Freud became estranged from one another. Although Winnicott never met Rank, he deeply admired Rank's work on the birth trauma, which inspired his own contributions in this area.

JOHN RICKMAN (1891–1951)   A physician and a Quaker, Dr John Rickman became one of the earliest and one of the most deeply committed members of the British Psycho-Analytical Society. Analysed first by Professor Sigmund Freud in Vienna, Austria, and then by Dr Sándor Ferenczi in Budapest, Hungary, and ultimately, by Mrs Melanie Klein in London, Rickman developed a reputation not only as a clinician and scholar, but also as a man of great independence of mind. Consequently, Winnicott came to value Rickman as a sort of older brother-figure who took him under his wing. The two men remained deeply fond of one another throughout. During his distinguished psychoanalytic career, Rickman served as Editor of *The International Journal of Psycho-Analysis* and as President of the British Psycho-Analytical Society. He will also be remembered greatly for his work as an army psychiatrist during the Second World War, applying psychoanalytic ideas to the task of officer selection.

JOAN RIVIERE (1883–1962)   The daughter of a solicitor from Brighton, in Sussex, Joan Hodgson Verrall married Evelyn Riviere, a successful barrister. As a young woman, she attended meetings of the Society for Psychical Research, where she discovered the work of Professor Sigmund Freud; subsequently, she underwent treatment with Dr Ernest Jones, who diagnosed her as a case of hysteria. Riviere developed a highly eroticised transference towards Jones, who no doubt fuelled – or instigated – the situation by lending his house to her! Subsequently, she enjoyed a much more satisfactory analysis in Vienna with Freud himself, and this experience gave her greater grounding and solidity and allowed her to sublimate her often uncontrollable passions into the more sober work of translating many of Freud's works from German into English. An early member of the British Psycho-Analytical Society, Riviere became one of the most fervent champions of Frau Melanie Klein; she even helped Klein to master the English language after she arrived in Great Britain. Winnicott undertook his second analysis with Joan Riviere and had a tempestuous – partly appreciative and partly infuriating – relationship with her. Her detractors from within the Middle Group of psychoanalysts experienced her as a bully, and even her sympathisers from the Kleinian group found her slightly terrifying. Some of her psychoanalytic papers, such as "Womanliness as a Masquerade" (1929) and "A Contribution to the Analysis of the Negative Therapeutic Reaction" (1936), remain classics to this day.

PAUL ROAZEN (1936–2005)   The American political theorist, historian, and biographer Professor Paul Roazen pioneered the field of the history of psychoanalysis with landmark biographies of Professor Sigmund Freud – especially *Freud and His Followers* (1975), based, uniquely, on a series of face-to-face interviews conducted throughout the 1960s with dozens of Freud's surviving patients and students. Roazen interviewed Winnicott in London in 1965, and the transcript of this encounter appeared in a book of essays written by various authors, entitled *The Legacy of Winnicott: Essays on Infant and Child Mental Health*, published in 2002.

JAMES ROBERTSON (1911–1988) Born into a family of very modest means in Rutherglen, Scotland, James Robertson worked for a time as handyman at Anna Freud's wartime nurseries in London, and then trained as a social worker at the London School of Economics and Political Science in the University of London, before proceeding to psychoanalytic training at the Institute of Psycho-Analysis. Supported by Dr John Bowlby at the Tavistock Clinic, James Robertson and his wife, Joyce Robertson, made a series of landmark films about the impact of hospitalisation upon young children, documenting, in an undeniable way, the painful consequences of the separation of young people from their caretakers. The work of the Robertsons influenced paediatric hospital practice in Great Britain and elsewhere and resulted in extended visiting hours for the parents of sick children. Winnicott championed the Robertsons' work, and he arranged for a screening of their film at the Royal Society of Medicine.

JOYCE ROBERTSON (1919–2013) Born in London, Joyce User studied at the Workers' Education Association in Birmingham, where she met her future husband, James Robertson. During the Second World War, she went to work at Anna Freud's nurseries in Hampstead, North London, and then joined her husband in making pioneering films about the impact of separation on young children, especially in medical settings. Joyce Robertson played a vital role in these educational film projects and collaborated closely both with her husband and with Dr John Bowlby in order to explore the effects of early separation between children and parents. After retiring from the Tavistock Clinic, the couple set up the Robertson Centre in order to promote their work and to rent out their films. Joyce Robertson became an Honorary Member of the Association of Child Psychotherapists.

HERBERT ROSENFELD (1910–1986) Born in Nuremberg, Germany, Dr Herbert Rosenfeld emigrated to Great Britain in 1935 in order to flee from the growing incursion of Nazism. Rosenfeld studied first at the Tavistock Clinic in London and later at the Maudsley Hospital. He undertook his psychoanalytic training at the Institute of Psycho-Analysis, having chosen Mrs Melanie Klein as his Training Analyst. A devoted Kleinian, Rosenfeld made many contributions to the treatment of schizophrenia and borderline states. Although he and Winnicott endeavoured to be collegial with one another, and although Rosenfeld entertained Winnicott in his home, the unpublished correspondence between the two men reveals considerable discomfort. Rosenfeld came to regard Winnicott as an attacker of Melanie Klein, and Winnicott harboured certain reservations about Rosenfeld's approach to psychoanalysis.

WILLIAM SARGANT (1907–1988)   Educated at the Leys School in Cambridge, albeit some years after Winnicott had matriculated to this Methodist institution, William Sargant became undoubtedly the most prominent biologically orientated British psychiatrist of his generation. A virulent critic of psychoanalysis, Sargant advocated electrical shock treatment and leucotomy (psychosurgery) for patients suffering from severe mental illnesses. Winnicott's letters of protest to Dr William Sargant – mostly unpublished – remain among his finest pieces of writing. A masterful diplomat, Winnicott managed to excoriate Dr Sargant while finding a way to remain both respectful of Sargant's position in psychiatry and considerate of his views, even though he regarded Sargant's somatic treatments as essentially quite cruel. Sargant's seminal textbook, *An Introduction to Physical Methods of Treatment of Psychiatry* (1944), co-authored by Dr Eliot Slater, became the *locus classicus* for an entire generation of British doctors.

MELITTA SCHMIDEBERG (1904–1983)   Born Melitta Klein, the only daughter of Frau Melanie Klein, she trained first as a physician and then as a psychoanalyst. She married Walter Schmideberg, an Austrian psychoanalyst who had come to settle in Berlin, Germany. She underwent several periods of psychoanalysis, first with Dr Karen Horney in Germany, and then with Dr Edward Glover in England. Various sources have suggested that her mother had also psychoanalysed her, thus contributing to the deep bitterness that developed between the two women. Although she was never close to Winnicott, the two psychoanalysts had an admiration for one another, and Dr Schmideberg had even supervised Winnicott's work early in his career. In her later years, Melitta Schmideberg emigrated to the United States and helped to pioneer psychoanalytic treatment for offender patients. She ultimately resigned from the British Psycho-Analytical Society, unimpressed by many of her former colleagues.

CLIFFORD SCOTT (1903–1997)   A Canadian by birth, Dr Clifford Scott trained alongside Winnicott at the Institute of Psycho-Analysis, qualifying in record time. A convivial and creative man with a great deal of clinical psychiatric and psychoanalytic experience to his credit, he analysed not only Winnicott's first wife, Mrs Alice Buxton Taylor Winnicott, but also Miss Clare Britton, who became the second Mrs Winnicott. Scott served as President of the British Psycho-Analytical Society. He eventually returned to his native Canada and helped to establish the Canadian Psychoanalytic Society.

NINA SEARL (c. 1882–1955)   A pioneer of child psychoanalysis in Great Britain, Miss Nina Searl supervised many of the early trainees in the field, including Winnicott and also Dr John Bowlby and Dr Clifford Scott. A one-time favoured colleague of Mrs Melanie Klein, many fellow clinicians gradually turned against Nina Searl because of her strong interest in spiritual healing. According to one report, Searl would fraternise with people who believed themselves reincarnated from ancient Egypt. She became increasingly alienated from the psychoanalytic community, and when she eventually resigned from membership in the British Psycho-Analytical Society, Nina Searl's one-time clinical colleagues expressed great relief at her departure.

HANNA SEGAL (1918–2011)   Born in Poland during the Great War, Hanna Poznanska emigrated first to France, and then to Great Britain, where she trained as a psychoanalyst. After her marriage she became known as Dr Hanna Segal. She worked predominantly in private practice for most of her career. Segal developed a long-standing antagonism towards Winnicott and became, instead, the leading disciple of Mrs Melanie Klein. Few people realise that she had once worked for Winnicott at the Paddington Green Children's Hospital and had expressed great disappointment during the 1940s when he refused to psychoanalyse her. A clinician of deep intelligence and clinical perspicacity, Segal devoted much of her work to the elucidation and elaboration of Klein's theories.

ELLA FREEMAN SHARPE (1875–1947)   One of the founding mothers of the psychoanalytic movement in Great Britain, Miss Ella Freeman Sharpe served as one of Winnicott's early clinical supervisors during his training at the Institute of Psycho-Analysis, and they remained convivial throughout her life. A highly literate woman and a one-time teacher, Miss Sharpe will be remembered above all for her seminal textbook, *Dream Analysis: A Practical Handbook for Psycho-Analysts* (1937), and for her impressive, posthumously published volume, *Collected Papers on Psycho-Analysis* (1950).

HELEN SHEEHAN-DARE (1885– date unknown)   Formerly the Organising Headmistress of the Abbey School in Battle, in the county of Sussex,

Miss Helen Sheehan-Dare became a factory welfare worker during the First World War and later gravitated towards psychoanalysis. She and Winnicott had trained side by side in child psychoanalysis, joined later by Mrs Susan Isaacs. Miss Sheehan-Dare came ultimately to specialise in child psychoanalysis, and during the Second World War Winnicott engaged her services to provide psychotherapy for some of the evacuated children living in special hostels in Oxfordshire for whom he held medical and psychiatric responsibility.

WALLIS WARFIELD SIMPSON (1896–1986)   Born in a hotel in Blue Ridge Summit, Pennsylvania, only days after the birth of Winnicott, Bessie Wallis Warfield became first the lover, and then the wife, of His Royal Highness Prince Edward, The Prince of Wales, later His Majesty King Edward VIII. Famously, King Edward abdicated the throne in order to marry this American woman, notorious for being both a commoner and for having divorced two husbands, first the naval pilot Earl Winfield Spencer, Jr., and later the shipping executive Ernest Aldrich Simpson. Although it seems unlikely that Winnicott had ever met her, his father, Frederick Winnicott, had certainly greeted the young Prince of Wales on a visit to Plymouth. After Mrs Simpson's marriage to the former monarch, she became the Duchess of Windsor, although her new brother-in-law, His Majesty King George VI, refused to grant her the prefix "Her Royal Highness", an act regarded by many as a petty, hostile snub.

ADRIAN STEPHEN (1883–1948)   The younger brother of Virginia Woolf (the former Virginia Stephen), Dr Adrian Stephen, with his wife, Dr Karin Stephen, trained as a psychoanalyst alongside Winnicott. He became a leading instigator in the overthrow of Dr Ernest Jones and Dr Edward Glover during the "Controversial Discussions" in the British Psycho-Analytical Society. He published only one book – not a psychoanalytic text but, rather, an account of a prank, known as the "Dreadnought Hoax", in which he, as a young man, along with his sister and some friends, had boarded a Royal Navy battleship, impersonating members of the entourage of an Abyssinian prince.

ALIX STRACHEY (1892–1973)   The American-born Alix Sargant-Florence moved to England as a girl and received her education at the Bedales School, the Slade School of Fine Art, and the University of Cambridge. A member of the Bloomsbury set, she married James Strachey in 1920; shortly thereafter, the newlyweds set off for Vienna, Austria, where each underwent a brief period of analysis with Professor

Sigmund Freud. Mrs Strachey practised psychoanalysis for a limited period of time, but ultimately she devoted the bulk of her energies to assisting her husband in the preparation of the 24-volume collected works of Freud. Winnicott kept in touch with her after James Strachey's death, and he represented her at the German Embassy when, in 1967, her husband received the Schlegel-Tieck Prize for translation, presented posthumously.

JAMES STRACHEY (1887–1967)   The youngest son of a distinguished family whose members included the increasingly prominent and outrageous writer Lytton Strachey, James Strachey struggled to find a calling until he discovered psychoanalysis. Having had a training analysis from Professor Sigmund Freud, Strachey became a deep admirer, and he devoted nearly half a century to the translation of Freud's works from German into English. Though often criticised – sometimes in a carping, gratuitous manner – Strachey's translations still remain the gold standard of Freud texts. Strachey wrote very few papers of his own, concentrating, instead, predominantly on his translation work; however, his 1934 essay on "The Nature of the Therapeutic Action of Psycho-Analysis", which focused on the importance of the transference interpretation as a mutative agent and on the role of the psychoanalyst as an auxiliary superego to the patient, has become a classic. Winnicott underwent a decade-long analysis with Strachey, which, in spite of certain shortcomings, he found deeply helpful and which permitted him to develop his own voice as a world leader in the field of child psychology.

LYTTON STRACHEY (1880–1932)   One of the most colourful figures in British life after the First World War, Lytton Strachey, the elder brother of James Strachey, became renowned as a provocative, controversial, and often subversive writer. His hugely popular biographical quadtych, *Eminent Victorians: Cardinal Manning – Florence Nightingale – Dr Arnold – General Gordon*, published in 1918, attacked the stuffiness of nineteenth-century sensibilities and helped to usher in a new era of progressivism. A biographer, novelist, reviewer, and *littérateur* of unflagging energy and productivity, Lytton Strachey even corresponded with Professor Sigmund Freud. We do not know whether Winnicott had ever met Lytton Strachey personally, although he may have done through his daily visits to Bloomsbury for psychoanalytic sessions with James Strachey. Winnicott did, however, have a certain sensitivity to the fact that he, like Lytton Strachey and James Strachey, had an extremely high-pitched speaking voice.

ARTHUR SULLIVAN (1842–1900) Undoubtedly the most versatile, inventive, and playful musical composer of the Victorian era, Arthur Sullivan authored numerous deftly satirical and highly comic operettas with his writing partner, William Schwenck Gilbert. Winnicott grew up singing the songs of Gilbert and Sullivan, and he knew virtually the whole of the repertoire by heart, affording him much pleasure throughout life. Sullivan's classic operettas, co-authored by W. S. Gilbert, include *H.M.S. Pinafore; or, The Lass That Loved a Sailor, The Pirates of Penzance; or, The Slave of Duty*, and of course, *The Mikado; or, The Town of Titipu*. He received a knighthood in 1883.

ELISABETH SWAN (born 1921) The daughter of Harold Stanley Ede and his wife Helen Ede, Elisabeth Ede knew Winnicott quite well throughout her childhood. Indeed, she and her younger sister often stayed at the home of Winnicott in Hampstead while her parents travelled. Winnicott had even hoped to adopt her, but her parents refused this request. She ultimately qualified in medicine and married Dr Harold Swan, who became a haematologist and also a noted medical historian at the University of Sheffield, South Yorkshire. In later years, Dr Elisabeth Swan retired to Edinburgh, Scotland.

SYBIL THORNDIKE (1882–1976) One of the most distinguished British classical theatre actresses of the twentieth century, Sybil Thorndike had a great interest in mental health causes and in left-wing politics more generally. In 1934 she served as a guest of honour at a luncheon held to raise awareness for the work of the Tavistock Clinic in London. Winnicott did not attend this luncheon, and, to the best of our knowledge, he never met Dame Sybil Thorndike; but he would certainly have known of her work. An avid theatre-goer for many decades, Winnicott would, in all likelihood, have seen Sybil Thorndike on stage at some point.

PETER TIZARD (1916–1993) Son of a distinguished scientist, Peter Tizard became a paediatrician of great repute. He and Winnicott met at least as early as 1949, when Tizard received an appointment to the Paddington Green Children's Hospital. A specialist in neonatology, with a long-standing interest in infant psychology (stimulated by Winnicott),

Tizard became the first Professor of Paediatrics at the University of Oxford and President of the British Paediatric Association. He received a knighthood for his services to children's medicine. Tizard maintained a long professional friendship with Winnicott and delivered an oration at Winnicott's funeral service.

QUEEN VICTORIA (1819–1901)   Her Imperial Majesty, Victoria, Queen of the United Kingdom of Great Britain and Ireland, and Empress of India, sat upon the throne for 63 years. The epitome of moral rectitude and sexual conservatism, Queen Victoria abhorred the sight of pregnant women and, in spite of her own private lustiness, insisted that all displays of affection be banished from public view. Winnicott certainly never met Queen Victoria, but throughout his career he would have had to counteract the impact of Victorian child-rearing practices, especially among the gentry, who farmed out their babies to nurses and governesses.

PEGGY VOLKOV (1899–1973)   A student of child welfare, child psychology, and progressive education, Peggy Volkov succeeded Beatrice Ensor as the editor of *The New Era in Home and School*, a vital publication that helped to spread psychoanalytic ideas to the general public, especially during the 1940s. A deep admirer of Winnicott and of his work, Volkov encouraged Winnicott to publish his radio broadcasts.

JOHN WESLEY (1703–1791)   Son of an Anglican clergyman, John Wesley and his younger brother, Charles Wesley, became the founders of English Methodism, subsequently known as Wesleyan Methodism, a branch of Protestantism characterised by a commitment to good works and civic consciousness. John Wesley also preached widely and educated untold numbers of people with his evangelical speeches and sermons. Unlike the Calvinists, who believed in predestination (either salvation or damnation), Wesley espoused the more hopeful possibility of universal redemption. Winnicott grew up steeped in Wesleyan Methodism, a theology that became an indispensable backdrop to his entire philosophy of care and concern for others.

ALICE WINNICOTT (1891–1969)   Born Alice Buxton Taylor, daughter of a prominent gynaecological surgeon, she attended Newnham College for women in the University of Cambridge, where she studied natural sciences. She married Winnicott in 1923, and during their years together she developed her work as a ceramicist and painter. Often dismissed as Winnicott's "mad" first wife – a gross underestimation of her charms and capabilities – she created, in fact, a successful pottery business and sold many of her pieces to some of London's top shops. She and Donald Winnicott divorced in 1951, and she never remarried. Her private correspondence reveals that she endured a very lonely old age.

CLARE WINNICOTT (1906–1984)   Born Elsie Clare Nimmo Britton, she became a psychiatric social worker, based in Oxfordshire during the Second World War. Employed to oversee a series of hostels for disturbed, evacuated children, Clare Britton met Winnicott, who served as the psychiatric consultant. During the Second World War, Winnicott and Britton developed a deep and growing passion; eventually, in 1951, Winnicott divorced his long-standing wife Alice Winnicott and married Miss Britton. As Mrs Clare Winnicott, she became a devoted spouse and colleague, and eventually underwent a training analysis with Mrs Melanie Klein, qualifying as a psychoanalyst in her own right. She made a deep impact as a tutor of child care students and social work students at the London School of Economics and Political Science in the University of London, and she also took up an important position in the Home Office, helping to improve standards of social work training. After her husband's death, Clare Winnicott continued to work as a psychoanalyst. During her later years, she wrote a small number of book chapters and papers, but she devoted most of her literary efforts to the preservation of her husband's legacy.

DONALD WINNICOTT (1896–1971)   Born in Plymouth, in Devon, son of the merchant Frederick Winnicott and the chemist's daughter Elizabeth Martha Woods Winnicott, Donald Winnicott attended the Leys School in Cambridge, followed by undergraduate studies at Jesus College, University of Cambridge, and by medical studies at the St Bartholomew's Hospital Medical College, part of the University of London. Winnicott worked as a physician in children's medicine and then trained as a psychoanalyst, becoming the first man in Great Britain to qualify as a child psychoanalyst. Throughout a long and creative lifetime, Winnicott produced many books on all aspects of psychoanalytic theory and practice. He served his profession ably as President of the British Psycho-Analytical Society and of many other organisations as well. And he pioneered the field of mental health broadcasting during the Second World War and thereafter. His many published contributions in the fields of psychoanalysis and child psychiatry remain a testament to his lifetime of devoted clinical labours.

ELIZABETH WINNICOTT (1862–1925)   Winnicott's mother grew up in Plymouth, Devon, the daughter of a chemist (pharmacist). Although suspected of having suffered from depression, Elizabeth Winnicott (later Lady Winnicott) devoted herself greatly to charitable works. Among her many activities, she founded a support group for impoverished Plymouth mothers and their babies. Lady Winnicott died at a relatively young age, having suffered from a catarrhal pulmonary congestion and syncope.

FREDERICK WINNICOTT (1855–1948)   Winnicott's father, John Frederick Winnicott, grew up in Plymouth, Devon, and eventually succeeded to the directorship of Winnicott Brothers, a firm of tinsmiths and ironmongers that also sold fancy goods. Frederick Winnicott ran this business with his elder brother, Richard Winnicott. A much-loved and kind-hearted man, he spent much of his time engaged in voluntary work and served as Mayor of Plymouth for two terms. Frederick Winnicott received a knighthood for his unceasing contributions to civic life in Plymouth, and he lived until the age of 93 years. A dedicated and proud father, he supported his son not only emotionally, but also financially, for a great many years.

KATHLEEN WINNICOTT (1891–1979)   The younger of Winnicott's two sisters, Kathleen Winnicott maintained a lifelong devotion to her baby brother. She participated greatly in Plymouth life through her religious works, through her charitable activities, and through philanthropy. During the Second World War, Kathleen Winnicott and her sister, Violet Winnicott, helped the city of Plymouth in many ways and even survived an air raid in the process.

RICHARD WINNICOTT (1853–1929)   The elder brother of Frederick Winnicott, Richard Winnicott served as co-owner of Winnicott Brothers in Plymouth, Devon. Like his younger brother, he, too, became a Mayor of Plymouth, and he made a huge contribution to Plymouth life. Richard Winnicott and his family lived in a house called "Hyperion", directly adjacent to Frederick Winnicott's family home, "Rockville".

VIOLET WINNICOTT (1889–1984)   The elder of Winnicott's two sisters, Violet Winnicott remained a lifelong spinster and devoted herself to charitable works, like all the members of her family. A passionate musician and animal-lover, Miss Winnicott survived her younger brother by more than a decade. Her death marked the extinction of the Winnicott family line.

VIRGINIA WOOLF (1882–1941) Born Virginia Stephen, daughter of the great Victorian *littérateur* Leslie Stephen, she became one of the most significant novelists of the twentieth century. Married to Leonard Woolf, the publisher and co-founder of the Hogarth Press, Virginia Woolf flourished at the heart of the Bloomsbury community, whose members included many early British psychoanalysts, including her brother, Dr Adrian Stephen, and his wife, Dr Karin Stephen, as well as James Strachey and Alix Strachey. Woolf lived near James Strachey's home, and it seems highly possible that Winnicott would have bumped into her from time to time, having gone to Strachey's consulting room in Gordon Square six times a week over a period of ten years. Regrettably, Virginia Woolf never pursued psychoanalytic treatment, and she eventually drowned herself.

RECOMMENDED READINGS

Donald Winnicott produced an extraordinary number of books, monographs, pamphlets, chapters, articles, essays, commentaries, reviews, obituaries, reports, memoranda, letters, case reports, case notes, doggerel, sketches, and squiggles during his lifetime, some of which have never appeared in published form. A serious student of Winnicott's work would require at least a decade or more to read everything that he wrote, and I suspect it might take longer than ten years to absorb the material in a meaningful way.

Fortunately, one need not immerse oneself in the *entire* corpus of Winnicott's writings. One can certainly acquire a reasonably good grasp of Winnicottian ideas by studying a selection of his books.

For those who have never read a word of Winnicott's texts, I would suggest that one might begin with the slim, but nonetheless meaty, volume *Babies and Their Mothers*, published in 1987. And for those who have already embarked on careers in the mental health field, or for those who have already accumulated quite a lot of clinical experience, I heartily recommend the foundational essays in *Collected Papers: Through Paediatrics to Psycho-Analysis*, published in 1958, followed by those contained in *The Maturational Processes and the Facilitating Environment: Studies in the Theory of Emotional Development*, published in 1965.

Of course, Winnicott offered himself to the world as an object to be *used*. And just like the baby who must find his or her own transitional object, so too must each student of psychology find his or her own way through the heaving mass of Winnicottiana. Certainly, I began my own study of Winnicott (more than thirty years ago) in a very unstructured, free-associative manner, simply by leafing through his essays and pausing from time to time to read something that captured my attention.

But whether one reads Winnicott in a systematic, chronological, scholarly fashion, or whether one dips into his world in a more creative, playful, meandering way, one will always find oneself in the presence of a truly magnificent thinker who provides endless engagement and inspiration. Each Winnicott essay will lead one happily to another, and if one devotes a bit of time and attention to Winnicott's work, one soon comes to recognise the *fil conducteur* that runs through his many writings, linking clinical vignettes with developmental theory, often peppered with witty observations about important aspects of human existence.

Winnicott's writings have, of course, spawned an enormous secondary literature, with a growing number of books and articles written by contemporary practitioners. Most of the commentary about Winnicott pales in comparison to his original writings. I would, therefore, encourage novices to begin their journey into the world of Winnicott by investigating the primary texts themselves. *Tea with Winnicott*, the volume in hand, should serve merely to whet the appetite.

Below, I provide a sample of Winnicott's "greatest hits". I have divided these publications into three sections: first, a bibliography of the books and pamphlets published during his lifetime; second, a list of books published posthumously; and, third, a selection of book chapters, journal articles, and short communications that I have found to be particularly helpful. In all instances, I have provided the original bibliographical citation, although many of the books and essays have appeared subsequently in other formats.

BOOKS AND PAMPHLETS
PUBLISHED IN WINNICOTT'S LIFETIME

1931   *Clinical Notes on Disorders of Childhood.* London: William Heinemann (Medical Books).

1945   *Getting to Know Your Baby.* London: William Heinemann (Medical Books).

1949   *The Ordinary Devoted Mother and Her Baby: Nine Broadcast Talks. (Autumn 1949.)* London: C.A. Brock and Company.

1957   *The Child and the Family: First Relationships.* Janet Hardenberg (Ed.). London: Tavistock Publications.

1957   *The Child and the Outside World: Studies in Developing Relationships.* Janet Hardenberg (Ed.). London: Tavistock Publications.

1958   *Collected Papers: Through Paediatrics to Psycho-Analysis.* London: Tavistock Publications.

1964   *The Child, the Family, and the Outside World.* Harmondsworth, Middlesex: Penguin Books.

1965   *The Family and Individual Development.* London: Tavistock Publications.

1965   *The Maturational Processes and the Facilitating Environment: Studies in the Theory of Emotional Development.* London: Hogarth Press and the Institute of Psycho-Analysis.

BOOKS PUBLISHED POSTHUMOUSLY

1971   *Playing and Reality.* London: Tavistock Publications.

1971   *Therapeutic Consultations in Child Psychiatry.* London: Hogarth Press and the Institute of Psycho-Analysis.

1977   *The Piggle: An Account of the Psychoanalytic Treatment of a Little Girl.* Ishak Ramzy (Ed.). New York: International Universities Press.

1984   *Deprivation and Delinquency.* Clare Winnicott, Ray Shepherd, and Madeleine Davis (Eds.). London: Tavistock Publications.

1986   *Holding and Interpretation: Fragment of an Analysis.* London: Hogarth Press and the Institute of Psycho-Analysis.

1986   *Home Is Where We Start From: Essays by a Psychoanalyst.* Clare Winnicott, Ray Shepherd, and Madeleine Davis (Eds.). New York: W. W. Norton & Company.

1987   *Babies and Their Mothers.* Clare Winnicott, Ray Shepherd, and Madeleine Davis (Eds.). Reading, Massachusetts: Addison-Wesley Publishing Company.

1987 *The Spontaneous Gesture: Selected Letters of D.W. Winnicott.* F. Robert Rodman (Ed.). Cambridge, Massachusetts: Harvard University Press.

1988 *Human Nature.* Christopher Bollas, Madeleine Davis, and Ray Shepherd (Eds.). London: Free Association Books.

1989 *Psycho-Analytic Explorations.* Clare Winnicott, Ray Shepherd, and Madeleine Davis (Eds.). London: H. Karnac (Books).

1993 *Talking to Parents.* Clare Winnicott, Christopher Bollas, Madeleine Davis, and Ray Shepherd (Eds.). Reading, Massachusetts: Addison-Wesley Publishing Company.

1996 *Thinking About Children.* Ray Shepherd, Jennifer Johns, and Helen Taylor Robinson (Eds.). London: H. Karnac (Books).

SELECTED CHAPTERS, ARTICLES, AND ESSAYS

1928 The Only Child. In Eva Isaacs, Viscountess Erleigh (Ed.). *The Mind of the Growing Child: A Series of Lectures*, pp. 47–64. London: Scientific Press/ Faber and Gwyer.

1930 Enuresis. *Proceedings of the Royal Society of Medicine, 23*, 255.

1933 Short Communication on Enuresis. *British Journal of Children's Diseases, 30*, 41–42.

1933 Pathological Sleeping. *British Journal of Children's Diseases, 30*, 205–206.

1935 The Manic Defence. In Donald W. Winnicott (1958). *Collected Papers: Through Paediatrics to Psycho-Analysis*, pp. 129–144. London: Tavistock Publications.

1936 Appetite and Emotional Disorder. In Donald W. Winnicott (1958). *Collected Papers: Through Paediatrics to Psycho-Analysis*, pp. 33–51. London: Tavistock Publications.

1941 The Observation of Infants in a Set Situation. *International Journal of Psycho-Analysis, 22*, 229–249.

1942 Child Department Consultations. *International Journal of Psycho-Analysis, 23*, 139–146.

1943 Prefrontal Leucotomy. *The Lancet* (10 April), 475.

1943 Shock Treatment of Mental Disorder. *British Medical Journal* (25 December), 829–830.

1943 Treatment of Mental Disease by Induction of Fits. In Donald W. Winnicott (1989). *Psycho-Analytic Explorations.* Clare Winnicott, Ray Shepherd, and Madeleine Davis (Eds.), pp. 516–521. London: H. Karnac (Books).

1944 Shock Therapy. *British Medical Journal* (12 February), 234–235.

1944 Introduction to a Symposium on the Psycho-Analytic Contribution to the Theory of Shock Therapy. In Donald W. Winnicott (1989). *Psycho-Analytic Explorations*. Clare Winnicott, Ray Shepherd, and Madeleine Davis (Eds.), pp. 525–528. London: H. Karnac (Books).

1944 Kinds of Psychological Effect of Shock Therapy. In Donald W. Winnicott (1989). *Psycho-Analytic Explorations*. Clare Winnicott, Ray Shepherd, and Madeleine Davis (Eds.), pp. 529–533. London: H. Karnac (Books).

1945 Primitive Emotional Development. *International Journal of Psycho-Analysis*, *26*, 137–143.

1945 Physical Therapy in Mental Disorder. *British Medical Journal* (22 December), 901–902.

1947 Physical Therapy of Mental Disorder. *British Medical Journal* (17 May), 688–689.

1947 Battle Neurosis Treated with Leucotomy. *British Medical Journal* (13 December), 974.

1948 Children's Hostels in War and Peace: A Contribution to the Symposium on "Lessons for Child Psychiatry". Given at a Meeting of the Medical Section of the British Psychological Society, 27 February 1946. *British Journal of Medical Psychology*, *21*, 175–180.

1948 Pediatrics and Psychiatry. *British Journal of Medical Psychology*, *21*, 229–240.

1949 Hate in the Counter-Transference. *International Journal of Psycho-Analysis*, *30*, 69–74.

1949 Birth Memories, Birth Trauma, and Anxiety. In Donald W. Winnicott (1958). *Collected Papers: Through Paediatrics to Psycho-Analysis*, pp. 174–193. London: Tavistock Publications.

1950 Some Thoughts on the Meaning of the Word Democracy. *Human Relations*, *3*, 175–186.

1950 Knowing and Learning. In Donald W. Winnicott (1957). *The Child and the Family: First Relationships*. Janet Hardenberg (Ed.), pp. 69–73. London: Tavistock Publications.

1950 Instincts and Normal Difficulties. In Donald W. Winnicott (1957). *The Child and the Family: First Relationships*. Janet Hardenberg (Ed.), pp. 74–79. London: Tavistock Publications.

1950 "Yes, But How Do We Know It's True?". In Donald W. Winnicott (1996). *Thinking About Children*. Ray Shepherd, Jennifer Johns, and Helen Taylor Robinson (Eds.), pp. 13–18. London: H. Karnac (Books).

1951 Notes on the General Implications of Leucotomy. In Donald W. Winnicott (1989). *Psycho-Analytic Explorations*. Clare Winnicott, Ray Shepherd, and Madeleine Davis (Eds.), pp. 548–552. London: H. Karnac (Books).

1953 Transitional Objects and Transitional Phenomena: A Study of the First Not-Me Possession. *International Journal of Psycho-Analysis*, *34*, 89–97.

1953 Psychoses and Child Care. *British Journal of Medical Psychology, 26,* 68–74.

1953 Symptom Tolerance in Paediatrics: President's Address. *Proceedings of the Royal Society of Medicine, 46,* 675–684.

1954 Play in the Analytic Situation. In Donald W. Winnicott (1989). *Psycho-Analytic Explorations.* Clare Winnicott, Ray Shepherd, and Madeleine Davis (Eds.), pp. 28–29. London: H. Karnac (Books).

1954 Mind and Its Relation to the Psyche-Soma. *British Journal of Medical Psychology, 27,* 201–209.

1955 Metapsychological and Clinical Aspects of Regression within the Psycho-Analytical Set-Up. *International Journal of Psycho-Analysis, 36,* 16–26.

1955 Adopted Children in Adolescence. In *Report of the Residential Conference Held at Roehampton: July 13th–15th, 1955,* pp. 33–39. London: Standing Conference of Societies Registered for Adoption.

1956 On Transference. *International Journal of Psycho-Analysis, 37,* 386–388.

1956 Primary Maternal Preoccupation. In Donald W. Winnicott (1958). *Collected Papers: Through Paediatrics to Psycho-Analysis,* pp. 300–305. London: Tavistock Publications.

1956 The Antisocial Tendency. In Donald W. Winnicott (1958). *Collected Papers: Through Paediatrics to Psycho-Analysis,* pp. 306–315. London: Tavistock Publications.

1956 Prefrontal Leucotomy. *British Medical Journal* (28 January), pp. 229–230.

1958 The Capacity to Be Alone. *International Journal of Psycho-Analysis, 39,* 416–420.

1958 Psychogenesis of a Beating Fantasy. In Donald W. Winnicott (1989). *Psycho-Analytic Explorations.* Clare Winnicott, Ray Shepherd, and Madeleine Davis (Eds.), pp. 45–48. London: H. Karnac (Books).

1960 String. *Journal of Child Psychology and Psychiatry and Allied Disciplines, 1,* 49–52.

1960 The Theory of the Parent–Infant Relationship. *International Journal of Psycho-Analysis, 41,* 585–595.

1960 Ego Distortion in Terms of True and False Self. In Donald W. Winnicott (1965). *The Maturational Processes and the Facilitating Environment: Studies in the Theory of Emotional Development,* pp. 140–152. London: Hogarth Press and the Institute of Psycho-Analysis.

1960 The Relationship of a Mother to Her Baby at the Beginning. In Donald W. Winnicott (1965). *The Family and Individual Development,* pp. 15–20. London: Tavistock Publications.

1961 The Effect of Psychotic Parents on the Emotional Development of the Child. *British Journal of Psychiatric Social Work, 6,* 13–20.

1962 The Aims of Psycho-Analytical Treatment. In Donald W. Winnicott (1965). *The Maturational Processes and the Facilitating Environment: Studies in the*

Theory of Emotional Development, pp. 166–170. London: Hogarth Press and the Institute of Psycho-Analysis.

1962 A Personal View of the Kleinian Contribution. In Donald W. Winnicott (1965). *The Maturational Processes and the Facilitating Environment: Studies in the Theory of Emotional Development*, pp. 171–178. London: Hogarth Press and the Institute of Psycho-Analysis.

1963 The Mentally Ill in Your Case Load. In Joan F. S. King (Ed.). *New Thinking for Changing Needs*, pp. 50–66. London: Education Sub-Committee, Association of Social Workers.

1963 The Young Child at Home and at School. In William Roy Niblett (Ed.). *Moral Education in a Changing Society*, pp. 96–111. London: Faber & Faber.

1963 Dependence in Infant Care, in Child Care, and in the Psycho-Analytic Setting. *International Journal of Psycho-Analysis*, *44*, 339–344.

1963 Regression as Therapy Illustrated by the Case of a Boy Whose Pathological Dependence was Adequately Met by the Parents. *British Journal of Medical Psychology*, *36*, 1–12.

1963 The Development of the Capacity for Concern. *Bulletin of the Menninger Clinic*, *27*, 167–176.

1963 Symposium: Training for Child Psychiatry. *Journal of Child Psychology and Psychiatry and Allied Disciplines*, *4*, 85–91.

1963 Communicating and Not Communicating Leading to a Study of Certain Opposites. In Donald W. Winnicott (1965). *The Maturational Processes and the Facilitating Environment: Studies in the Theory of Emotional Development*, pp. 179–192. London: Hogarth Press and the Institute of Psycho-Analysis.

1963 Psychiatric Disorder in Terms of Infantile Maturational Processes. In Donald W. Winnicott (1965). *The Maturational Processes and the Facilitating Environment: Studies in the Theory of Emotional Development*, pp. 230–241. London: Hogarth Press and the Institute of Psycho-Analysis.

1963 Struggling Through the Doldrums. *New Society*. 25th April, pp. 8–11.

1964 The Value of Depression. *British Journal of Psychiatric Social Work*, *7*, 123–127.

1964 The Neonate and His Mother. *Acta Paediatrica Latina*, *17* (Supplement), 747–758.

1964 This Feminism. In Donald W. Winnicott (1986). *Home Is Where We Start From: Essays by a Psychoanalyst*. Clare Winnicott, Ray Shepherd, and Madeleine Davis (Eds.), pp. 183–194. New York: W. W. Norton & Company.

1965 The Price of Disregarding Research Findings. In *The Price of Mental Health*, pp. 34–41. London: National Association for Mental Health.

1966 A Psychoanalytic View of the Antisocial Tendency. In Ralph Slovenko (Ed.). *Crime, Law and Corrections*, pp. 102–130. Springfield, Illinois: Charles C Thomas, Publisher.

1966   The Ordinary Devoted Mother. In Donald W. Winnicott (1987). *Babies and Their Mothers*. Clare Winnicott, Ray Shepherd, and Madeleine Davis (Eds.), pp. 3–14. Reading, Massachusetts: Addison-Wesley Publishing Company.

1967   D.W.W. on D.W.W. In Donald W. Winnicott (1989). *Psycho-Analytic Explorations*. Clare Winnicott, Ray Shepherd, and Madeleine Davis (Eds.), pp. 569–582. London: H. Karnac (Books).

1967   The Aetiology of Infantile Schizophrenia in Terms of Adaptive Failure. In Donald W. Winnicott (1996). *Thinking About Children*. Ray Shepherd, Jennifer Johns, and Helen Taylor Robinson (Eds.), pp. 218–223. London: H. Karnac (Books).

1968   The Squiggle Game. *Voices: The Art and Science of Psychotherapy*, 4, 98–112.

1968   Sleep Refusal in Children. *Paediatrics*, July, pp. 8–9.

1968   Infant Feeding and Emotional Development. *Maternal and Child Care*, 4 (Number 33), 7–9.

1968   Delinquency as a Sign of Hope. *Prison Service Journal*, 7 (Number 27), 2–7.

1969   The Use of an Object. *International Journal of Psycho-Analysis*, 50, 711–716.

1971   The Concept of a Healthy Individual. In John D. Sutherland (Ed.). *Towards Community Mental Health*, pp. 1–15. London: Tavistock Publications.

1974   Fear of Breakdown. *International Review of Psycho-Analysis*, 1, 103–107.

ACKNOWLEDGEMENTS

A number of very dear colleagues commented upon the type-script of *Tea with Winnicott* and not only offered much-cherished encouragement about this project, but also provided me with hugely helpful and insightful reflections. Dr Susie Orbach, a truly wonder-ful writer, read the very first incarnation of this interview, and she responded with characteristic generosity, for which I thank her deeply. Her appreciation of both the seriousness and the whimsy of this experiment in posthumous historical writing certainly gave me the confidence to finish this little work.

Soon thereafter, I had the great benefit of sharing the first draft of the book with two remarkable men – both psychoanalysts, and both gentlemen – Dr Abrahão Brafman and Dr Bernard Barnett. Having had the privilege of studying and supervising with each of these distinguished senior clinicians, I value their insights and their acuity of thought very deeply. Abe Brafman, a brilliant child psy-chiatrist and psychoanalyst who has extended Winnicott's squiggle technique in his own novel ways, exemplified in his rich legacy of publications, offered me a meticulous line-by-line commentary that surpassed all expectations, and I have incorporated many of his sug-gestions with gratitude and with delight. And Bernie Barnett, quon-dam Director of the Squiggle Foundation – an organisation devoted to the furtherance of the work of Winnicott – and author of a deeply compassionate textbook on the superego, provided me with much warm and generous encouragement of this project. Both Dr Brafman and Dr Barnett have the added advantage of being among the last surviving members of the psychoanalytic community to have known Donald Winnicott personally, having met him and having studied with him more than forty years ago; hence, I particularly wished to have their blessing and their confirmation that I had managed to capture Winnicott's voice and spirit with what I hope to be a high degree of accuracy. When Abe and Bernie told me that they recognised Winnicott in these pages, I felt emboldened to proceed further.

I also benefited from having had a detailed reading of the type-script from one other very special person who knew the real Donald Winnicott – namely, Winnicott's celebrated child patient, known to us as "The Piggle". I first met this young woman back in 1996, while undertaking a series of interviews with members of Winnicott's circle, in preparation for writing a full-scale biography. And since our first supper together "The Piggle" and I have become friendly, and we have remained in contact since that time. "The Piggle", now an adult in her fifties, has become a warm-hearted, accomplished, and gracious person, and a talented professional in her own right. She very kindly took the time to read a draft of *Tea with Winnicott* and offered extensive thoughts, reflections, recommendations, and above all, a confirmation that although she had known Winnicott only as a child, long ago, I had succeeded in capturing the essence of the man she remembered from personal contact and from many conversations at home with her parents (who knew Winnicott rather better). I thank "The Piggle" from the bottom of my heart for her tremendous generosity and support for this project.

A number of other friends and colleagues shared very help-ful suggestions, most especially Professor Peter Rudnytsky, a fellow clinician–historian, who, like Dr Abe Brafman, offered a meticulous line-by-line reading of the entire text. His capacity for playful enjoyment and rigorous scholarly attention to detail always inspires me, and I have learned, and continue to learn, an enormous amount from our conversations, for which I remain extremely grateful. With similar generosity, Dr Valerie Sinason, a psychoanalyst and poet blessed with remarkable clinical and literary sensitivities, read the typescript of this book not once, but twice, and provided me with characteristically incisive observations and recommendations which proved extremely helpful, for which I offer my deepest appreciation. A great friend and mentor over nearly thirty years, Dr Sinason has taught me more about the spirit of Winnicott through her remarkable capacity to integrate love, work, and play in such a creative and organic manner.

I must also thank the many hundreds of people whom I interviewed between 1982 and 2014 who had known Donald Winnicott personally. Some of this material has appeared already in print, and much more will, I hope, become incorporated into a series of forthcoming scholarly works. But certainly, I could not have written this more playful book without having spent literally decades absorbing the many reminiscences of a large number of Winnicott's relatives, social friends, colleagues, patients, consultees, students, godchildren, and, even, enemies. Although I remain loath to single out any one person (and many of these men and women will be acknowledged more fully in a subsequent volume), I must, of course pay my deepest thanks to the late Mrs Joyce Coles, who features in *Tea with Winnicott*, albeit in a dramatised – though still, I hope accurate – guise. Without my numerous conversations with Joyce, and without the aid of her priceless archive of papers that she bequeathed to me, I doubt that I would have persevered with my research over such a long period of time.

Mrs Diana Brimblecombe, the granddaughter of Melanie Klein, graciously responded to a research query for me, kindly facilitated through Ms Mary Block and Dr Michael Feldman of the Melanie Klein Trust.

I must also thank the many historians, librarians, and archivists who have assisted me in so many ways over the years, especially in relation to my researches on Donald Winnicott. I must begin by offering deepest gratitude to Professor Lesley Caldwell, former Chair of the Winnicott Trust, and to her predecessor, Dr Jennifer Johns, for the kind permission to consult Winnicott's unpublished letters and manuscripts, housed partly in the Archives and Manuscripts of the Wellcome Library, at the Wellcome Collection, in London, and also in the Archives of Psychiatry in The Oskar Diethelem Library at The DeWitt Wallace Institute for the History of Psychiatry, Department of Psychiatry, at the Joan and Sanford I. Weill Medical College, at Cornell University, in New York City. Dr Lesley Hall and Dr Jennifer Haynes and their team have helped me greatly at the Wellcome Library on innumerable occasions, as have Professor George Makari and his predecessor, the late Professor Eric Carlson, as well as the former librarian Ms Diane Richardson at Cornell University, for which I take pleasure in expressing my grateful appreciation. I must also thank the many librarians, archivists, and research staff at various other institutions, including, *inter alia*, those at the Library of Congress in Washington, DC, as well as those at the Members' Library of the Royal Society of Medicine in London (especially Mr Robert Greenwood and Ms Grace Sweetman), and at the Manuscripts Collection of the British Library, and also at the Bodleian Library of the University of Oxford, and at the London Library, too.

I take pleasure in offering a special tribute to the late Miss Pearl King, founder of the Archives of the British Psychoanalytical Society, who, over the course of many years, took me under wing and taught me most generously, steering me through the holdings first at Mansfield House in Central London, and later at Byron House in West London. Furthermore, she shared her many personal memories of Donald Winnicott in the most unstinting way, as well as her reminiscences of large numbers of the persons mentioned in this book. And with unparalleled generosity she gave me unrestricted access to her professional and personal papers in her own home, which ranged from original letters written by Sándor Ferenczi to minutes of committee meetings that one could find nowhere else. It will be some time before historians of mental health come to realise the true profundity of Miss King's contributions to the field.

I first conceived the idea of *Tea with Winnicott* over a cup of tea – quite literally – with my favourite publisher, Mr Oliver Rathbone, Director and Publisher, of Karnac Books. He responded with enthusiasm to the idea, and his encouragement helped to bring this project to life, offering many helpful and creative ideas throughout. Oliver convinced me that a work such as this – what we have come to regard as "imaginative non-fiction" – could be of value as a tool for introducing great psychological thinkers to students and to young practitioners. As ever, Oliver has proved the most reliable and most honest of friends and colleagues, and I thank him, and the entire staff of Karnac Books, most especially Ms Cecily Blench, Ms Constance Govindin, Mr Alex Massey, Ms Kate Pearce, and Dr Rod Tweedy.

Mr Eric King and Mrs Klara Majthényi King created the beautiful art deco design and undertook the meticulous copy-editing of this book.

And Ms Alison Bechdel, a star-quality artist and a Winnicott scholar in her own right, has provided the most wonderful illustrations for this book, for which I remain eternally grateful.

Even closer to home, I thank my dedicatees for years of very special friendship. And, of course, I embrace the members of my family, several of whom read the manuscript at a fledgling stage and offered many important suggestions, observations, requests for clarification, and so much more.

REFERENCES

The following list provides full bibliographical citations to very particular works mentioned directly, or alluded to, in the course of the interview or in the surrounding editorial apparatus.

Abraham, Karl (1924). A Short Study of the Development of the Libido, Viewed in the Light of Mental Disorders. In Karl Abraham (1927). *Selected Papers of Karl Abraham M.D.* Douglas Bryan and Alix Strachey (Transls.), pp. 418–501. London: Leonard and Virginia Woolf at the Hogarth Press.

Alexander, Franz (1926). Neurosis and the Whole Personality. *International Journal of Psycho-Analysis*, 7, 340–352.

Alexander, Franz (1927). *Psychoanalyse der Gesamtpersönlichkeit: Neun Vorlesungen über die Anwendung von Freuds Ichtheorie auf die Neurosenlehre.* Vienna: Internationaler Psychoanalytischer Verlag.

Alexander, Franz (1946). The Principle of Corrective Emotional Experience. In Franz Alexander, Thomas Morton French, Catherine Lillie Bacon, Therese Benedek, Rudolf A. Fuerst, Margaret Wilson Gerard, Roy Richard Grinker, Martin Grotjahn, Adelaide McFadyen Johnson, Helen Vincent McLean, and Edoardo Weiss. *Psychoanalytic Therapy: Principles and Application*, pp. 66–70. New York: Ronald Press Company.

Alexander, Franz (1957). Psychosomatische Wechselbeziehungen. In Alexander Mitscherlich (Ed.). *Freud in der Gegenwart: Ein Vortragszyklus der Universitäten Frankfurt und Heidelberg zum hundertsten Geburtstag*, pp. 279–306. Frankfurt am Main: Europäische Verlagsanstalt.

Alexander, Franz; Eisenstein, Samuel, and Grotjahn, Martin (Eds.). (1966). *Psychoanalytic Pioneers*. New York: Basic Books.

Alexander, Franz; French, Thomas M., and Pollock, George H. (Eds.). (1968). *Psychosomatic Specificity: Volume 1. Experimental Study and Results*. Chicago, Illinois: University of Chicago Press.

Alexander, Franz G., and Selesnick, Sheldon T. (1966). *The History of Psychiatry: An Evaluation of Psychiatric Thought and Practice from Prehistoric Times to the Present*. New York: Harper & Row, Publishers.

Alexander, Franz, and Staub, Hugo (1929). *Der Verbrecher und seine Richter: Ein psychoanalytischer Einblick in die Welt der Paragraphen*. Vienna: Internationaler Psychoanalytischer Verlag.

Alexander, Franz, and Szasz, Thomas S. (1952). The Psychosomatic Approach in Medicine. In Franz Alexander and Helen Ross (Eds.). *Dynamic Psychiatry*, pp. 369–400. Chicago, Illinois: University of Chicago Press.

Armstrong-Jones, Robert (1920). Consciousness: The Unconscious Mind and Psycho-Analysis. *St. Bartholomew's Hospital Journal*, *28*, 19–20.

Barnett, Bernard (2007). *"You Ought To!": A Psychoanalytic Study of the Superego and Conscience*. London: Karnac Books.

Bion, Wilfred R. (1956). Development of Schizophrenic Thought. *International Journal of Psycho-Analysis*, *37*, 344–346.

Bion, Wilfred R. (1961). *Experiences in Groups and Other Papers*. London: Tavistock Publications.

Bion, Wilfred R. (1962). *Learning from Experience*. London: William Heinemann Medical Books.

Bion, Wilfred R. (1962). The Psycho-Analytic Study of Thinking: II. A Theory of Thinking. *International Journal of Psycho-Analysis*, *43*, 306–310.

Bion, Wilfred R. (1970). *Attention and Interpretation: A Scientific Approach to Insight in Psycho-Analysis and Groups*. London: Tavistock Publications.

Bollas, Christopher (1987). *The Shadow of the Object: Psychoanalysis of the Unthought Known*. London: Free Association Books.

Bollas, Christopher, and Bollas, Sacha (2013). *Catch Them Before They Fall: The Psychoanalysis of Breakdown*. Hove, East Sussex: Routledge/Taylor & Francis Group.

Bollas, Christopher, and Sundelson, David (1995). *The New Informants: The Betrayal of Confidentiality in Psychoanalysis and Psychotherapy*. London: H. Karnac (Books).

Bornstein, Berta (1951). On Latency. *Psychoanalytic Study of the Child*, *6*, 279–285. New York: International Universities Press.

Bowlby, John (1969). *Attachment and Loss: Volume I. Attachment*. London: Hogarth Press and the Institute of Psycho-Analysis.

Bowlby, John (1973). *Attachment and Loss: Volume II. Separation. Anxiety and Anger*. London: Hogarth Press and the Institute of Psycho-Analysis.

Bowlby, John (1980). *Attachment and Loss: Volume III. Loss. Sadness and Depression*. London: Hogarth Press and the Institute of Psycho-Analysis.

Bowlby, John; Miller, Emanuel, and Winnicott, Donald W. (1939). Evacuation of Small Children. *British Medical Journal*, 16th December, 1202–1203.

Bowlby, John, and Robertson, James (1953). A Two-Year-Old Goes to Hospital. *Proceedings of the Royal Society of Medicine*, 46, 425–426.

Brafman, Abrahão H. (1978). The Family, the Child and the Psychiatrist: A Psychoanalyst's View of Therapy. In John Connolly (Ed.). *Therapy Options in Psychiatry*, pp. 208–226. Tunbridge Wells, Kent: Pitman Medical Publishing Company.

Brafman, Abrahão H. (1988). Infant Observation. *International Review of Psycho-Analysis*, 15, 45–59.

Brafman, Abrahão H. (1997). Winnicott's *Therapeutic Consultations* Revisited. *International Journal of Psycho-Analysis*, 78, 773–787.

Brafman, Abrahão H. (2000). The Child is Still Ill – How Are the Parents? *Psychoanalytic Psychotherapy*, 14, 153–162.

Brafman, Abrahão H. (2001). *Untying the Knot: Working with Children and Parents*. London: H. Karnac (Books)/Other Press.

Brafman, Abrahão H. (2004). *Can You Help Me?: A Guide for Parents*. London: H. Karnac (Books).

Brafman, Abrahão H. (2011). *Fostering Independence: Helping and Caring in Psychodynamic Therapies*. London: Karnac Books.

Brafman, Abrahão H. (2012). *The Language of Drawings: A New Finding in Psychodynamic Work*. London: Karnac Books.

Brierley, Marjorie (1936). Specific Determinants in Feminine Development. *International Journal of Psycho-Analysis*, 17, 163–180.

Brierley, Marjorie (1937). Affects in Theory and Practice. *International Journal of Psycho-Analysis*, 18, 256–268.

Brierley, Marjorie (1939). A Prefatory Note on 'Internalized Objects' and Depression. *International Journal of Psycho-Analysis*, 20, 241–245.

Brierley, Marjorie (1942). 'Internal Objects' and Theory. *International Journal of Psycho-Analysis*, 23, 107–112.

Brierley, Marjorie (1943). Theory, Practice and Public Relations. *International Journal of Psycho-Analysis*, 24, 119–125.

Brierley, Marjorie (1947). Notes on Psycho-Analysis and Integrative Living. *International Journal of Psycho-Analysis*, 28, 57–105.

Brierley, Marjorie (1951). *Trends in Psycho-Analysis*. London: Hogarth Press and the Institute of Psycho-Analysis.

Brierley, Marjorie (1969). 'Hardy Perennials' and Psychoanalysis. *International Journal of Psycho-Analysis*, *50*, 447–452.

Cameron, Hector Charles (1919). *The Nervous Child*. London: Henry Frowde/ Oxford University Press, and Hodder and Stoughton.

Darwin, Charles. (1859). *On the Origin of Species by Means of Natural Selection, or the Preservation of Favoured Races in the Struggle for Life*. London: John Murray.

Darwin, Charles (1872). *The Expression of the Emotions in Man and Animals*. London: John Murray.

Dicks, Henry V. (1967). *Marital Tensions: Clinical Studies Towards a Psychological Theory of Interaction*. London: Routledge & Kegan Paul.

Dicks, Henry V. (1968). Experiences with Marital Tensions Seen in the Psychological Clinic. In John G. Howells (Ed.). *Theory and Practice of Family Psychiatry*, pp. 267–287. Edinburgh: Oliver and Boyd.

Dicks, Henry V. (1970). *Fifty Years of the Tavistock Clinic*. London: Routledge & Kegan Paul.

Ede, Harold S. (1931). *Savage Messiah*. London: William Heinemann.

Erikson, Erik H. (1950). *Childhood and Society*. New York: W. W. Norton & Company.

Erikson, Erik H. (1969). *Gandhi's Truth: On the Origins of Militant Nonviolence*. New York: W. W. Norton & Company.

Ferenczi, Sándor (1910). *Introjektion und Übertragung: Eine psychoanalytische Studie*. Vienna: Franz Deuticke.

Ferenczi, Sándor (1919). *Hysterie und Pathoneurosen*. Vienna: Internationaler Psychoanalytischer Verlag.

Ferenczi, Sándor (1919). Die Psychoanalyse der Kriegsneurosen. In Sigmund Freud, Sándor Ferenczi, Karl Abraham, Ernst Simmel, and Ernest Jones. *Zur Psychoanalyse der Kriegsneurosen*, pp. 9–30. Vienna: Internationaler Psychoanalytischer Verlag.

Ferenczi, Sándor (1920). The Further Development of an Active Therapy in Psycho-Analysis. In Sándor Ferenczi (1926). *Further Contributions to the Theory and Technique of Psycho-Analysis*. John Rickman (Ed.). Jane Isabel Suttie (Transl.), pp. 198–216. London: Hogarth Press and the Institute of Psycho-Analysis.

Ferenczi, Sándor (1921). Weiterer Ausbau der "aktiven Technik" in der Psychoanalyse. *Internationale Zeitschrift für Psychoanalyse*, *7*, 233–251.

Ferenczi, Sándor (1922). *Populäre Vorträge über Psychoanalyse*. Vienna: Internationaler Psychoanalytischer Verlag.

Ferenczi, Sándor (1988). *Ohne Sympathie keine Heilung: Das klinische Tagebuch von 1932*. Judith Dupont (Ed.). Frankfurt am Main: S. Fischer/S. Fischer Verlag.

Ferenczi, Sándor, and Rank, Otto (1924). *Entwicklungsziele der Psychoanalyse: Zur Wechselbeziehung von Theorie und Praxis.* Vienna: Internationaler Psychoanalytischer Verlag.

Field, Joanna (1934). *A Life of One's Own.* London: Chatto & Windus.

Field, Joanna (1937). *An Experiment in Leisure.* London: Chatto & Windus.

Field, Joanna (1950). *On Not Being Able to Paint.* London: William Heinemann.

Flügel, John C. (1921). *The Psycho-Analytic Study of the Family.* London: International Psycho-Analytical Press.

Forsyth, David (1922). *The Technique of Psycho-Analysis.* London: Kegan Paul, Trench, Trubner and Company.

Fraser, Antonia (1969). *Mary Queen of Scots.* London: Weidenfeld & Nicolson.

Freud, Anna (1936). *Das Ich und die Abwehrmechanismen.* Vienna: Internationaler Psychoanalystischer Verlag.

Freud, Sigmund (1912). Ratschläge für den Arzt bei der psychoanalytischen Behandlung. *Zentralblatt für Psychoanalyse, 2,* 483–489.

Freud, Sigmund (1912). Recommendations for Physicians on the Psycho-Analytic Method of Treatment. In Sigmund Freud (1924). *Collected Papers: Vol. II.* Joan Riviere (Transl.), pp. 323–333. London: Leonard and Virginia Woolf at the Hogarth Press, and the Institute of Psycho-Analysis.

Freud, Sigmund (1912). Recommendations to Physicians Practising Psycho-Analysis. Joan Riviere and James Strachey (Transls.). In Sigmund Freud (1958). *The Standard Edition of the Complete Psychological Works of Sigmund Freud: Volume XII. (1911–1913). The Case of Schreber. Papers on Technique and Other Works.* James Strachey, Anna Freud, Alix Strachey, and Alan Tyson (Eds. and Transls.), pp. 111–120. London: Hogarth Press and the Institute of Psycho-Analysis.

Glover, Edward (1928). *The Technique of Psycho-Analysis.* London: Institute of Psycho-Analysis/Baillière, Tindall and Cox.

Glover, Edward (1955). *The Technique of Psycho-Analysis.* London: Baillière, Tindall and Cox.

Glover, Edward (1960). *Selected Papers on Psycho-Analysis: Volume II. The Roots of Crime.* London: Imago Publishing Company.

Glover, Edward, and Brierley, Marjorie (Eds.). (1940). *An Investigation of the Technique of Psycho-Analysis.* London: Baillière, Tindall and Cox.

Glover, Edward; Mannheim, Hermann, and Miller, Emanuel (1951). Editorial. In Edward Glover, Hermann Mannheim, and Emanuel Miller (Eds.). *Papers on Psychopathy,* pp. 77-83. London: Institute for the Study and Treatment of Delinquency/Baillière Tindall and Cox.

Gray, Arthur (1902). *Jesus College.* London: F. E. Robinson and Company.

Gray, Arthur (1912). *Cambridge and Its Story.* London: Methuen and Company.

Gray, Arthur (1925). *The Town of Cambridge: A History*. Cambridge: Heffer and Sons.

Gray, Arthur (1933). *The Master's Lodge of Jesus College, Cambridge*. Cambridge: Heffer and Sons.

Gray, Arthur, and Brittain, Frederick (1960). *A History of Jesus College Cambridge*. London: William Heinemann.

Greenson, Ralph R. (1967). *The Technique and Practice of Psychoanalysis: Volume 1*. New York: International Universities Press.

Grosskurth, Phyllis (1986). *Melanie Klein: Her World and Her Work*. New York: Alfred A. Knopf.

Guthrie, Leonard G. (1907). *Functional Nervous Disorders in Childhood*. London: Henry Frowde/Oxford University Press, and Hodder and Stoughton.

Hardenberg, Herman E. W. (1956). Prefrontal Leucotomy. *British Medical Journal* (11th February), 350.

Hardenberg, Herman E. W. (1956). Prefrontal Leucotomy. *British Medical Journal* (31st March), 746.

Hartmann, Dora (1969). A Study of Drug-Taking Adolescents. *Psychoanalytic Study of the Child*, 24, 384–398. New York: International Universities Press.

Hopkins, Juliet (2002). From Baby Games to Let's Pretend: The Achievement of Playing. In Brett Kahr (Ed.). *The Legacy of Winnicott: Essays on Infant and Child Mental Health*, pp. 91–99. London: H. Karnac (Books).

Horder, Thomas (1918). Medical Notes. *St. Bartholomew's Hospital Journal*, 25, 83–84.

Horder, Thomas (1918). Medical Notes. *St. Bartholomew's Hospital Journal*, 25, 93–94.

Horder, Thomas (1918). Medical Notes. *St. Bartholomew's Hospital Journal*, 25, 104–105.

Horder, Thomas (1918). Medical Notes. *St. Bartholomew's Hospital Journal*, 26, 3–5.

Horder, Thomas (1918). Medical Notes. *St. Bartholomew's Hospital Journal*, 26, 14–15.

Horder, Thomas (1918). Medical Notes. *St. Bartholomew's Hospital Journal*, 26, 26.

Horder, Thomas (1919). Medical Notes. *St. Bartholomew's Hospital Journal*, 26, 53–54.

Horder, Thomas (1919). Medical Notes. *St. Bartholomew's Hospital Journal*, 26, 61–62.

Horder, Thomas (1919). Medical Notes. *St. Bartholomew's Hospital Journal*, 26, 103–104.

Horder, Thomas (1919). Medical Notes. *St. Bartholomew's Hospital Journal*, 26, 115–116.

Horder, Thomas (1919). Medical Notes. *St. Bartholomew's Hospital Journal*, 27, 6.

Horder, Thomas (1919). Medical Notes. *St. Bartholomew's Hospital Journal*, 27, 36–37.

Horder, Thomas (1920). Medical Notes. *St. Bartholomew's Hospital Journal*, 27, 55–56.

Horder, Thomas (1920). Medical Notes. *St. Bartholomew's Hospital Journal*, 27, 96–97.

Horder, Thomas (1920). The Future of Medicine. *St. Bartholomew's Hospital Journal*, 27, 143–145.

Hug-Hellmuth, Hermine von (1914). Kinderpsychologie, Pädagogik. *Jahrbuch der Psychoanalyse*, 6, 393–404.

Hug-Hellmuth, Hermine (Ed.). (1919). *Tagebuch eines halbwüchsigen Mädchens*. Vienna: Internationaler Psychoanalytischer Verlag.

Hug-Hellmuth, Hermine (1922). Correspondence. *British Journal of Psychology: Medical Section*, 2, 257.

"Ingulphus" [Arthur Gray] (1919). *Tedious Brief Tales of Granta and Gramarye*. Cambridge: W. Heffer and Sons, and London: Simpkin, Marshall, Hamilton, Kent, and Company.

James, Colin (1971). Letter to Clare Winnicott, 26th January. PP/DWW/G/6/1. Folder 1. Donald Woods Winnicott Collection. Archives and Manuscripts, Rare Materials Room, Wellcome Library, Wellcome Collection, The Wellcome Building, London.

Jones, Ernest (1937). Letter to Sigmund Freud. 23rd February. In Sigmund Freud and Ernest Jones (1993). *The Complete Correspondence of Sigmund Freud and Ernest Jones: 1908–1939*. R. Andrew Paskauskas (Ed.), pp. 755–756. Cambridge, Massachusetts: Belknap Press of Harvard University Press.

Jones, Ernest (1953). *The Life and Work of Sigmund Freud: Volume 1. The Formative Years and the Great Discoveries. 1856–1900*. New York: Basic Books.

Jones, Ernest (1955). *The Life and Work of Sigmund Freud: Volume 2. Years of Maturity. 1901–1919*. New York: Basic Books.

Jones, Ernest (1957). *The Life and Work of Sigmund Freud: Volume 3. The Last Phase. 1919–1939*. New York: Basic Books.

Kahr, Brett (1996). *D.W. Winnicott: A Biographical Portrait*. London: H. Karnac (Books).

Kahr, Brett (Ed.). (2002). *The Legacy of Winnicott: Essays on Infant and Child Mental Health*. London: H. Karnac (Books).

Khan, M. Masud R. (1988). *When Spring Comes: Awakenings in Clinical Psycho-analysis*. London: Chatto & Windus.

King, Pearl (1965). *Report of the Sponsoring Committee of the Finnish Study Group to the Council of the I.PA.* PP/DWW/M.2/2. Donald Woods Winnicott Collection. Archives and Manuscripts, Rare Materials Room, Wellcome Library, Wellcome Collection, The Wellcome Building, London.

King, Pearl (1979). The Contributions of Ernest Jones to the British Psycho-Analytical Society. *International Journal of Psycho-Analysis*, *60*, 280–284.

King, Pearl H.M. (1984). Clare Winnicott's Funeral: (Golders Green). Unpublished Typescript.

King, Pearl (1989). Activities of British Psychoanalysts During the Second World War and the Influence of Their Inter-Disciplinary Collaboration on the Development of Psychoanalysis in Great Britain. *International Review of Psycho-Analysis*, *16*, 15–33.

King, Pearl (1991). Biographical Notes on the Main Participants in the Freud–Klein Controversies in the British Psycho-Analytical Society, 1941–45. In Pearl King and Riccardo Steiner (Eds.). *The Freud–Klein Controversies: 1941–45*, pp. ix–xxv. London: Tavistock/Routledge.

King, Pearl (1991). Background and Development of the Freud–Klein Controversies in the British Psycho-Analytical Society. In Pearl King and Riccardo Steiner (Eds.). *The Freud–Klein Controversies: 1941–45*, pp. 9–36. London: Tavistock/Routledge.

King, Pearl (1997). Talk on Sept. 5, 1987 on the Twentieth Anniversary of the Founding of the Finnish Psycho-Analytical Society. In Aira Laine, Helena Parland, and Esa Roos (Eds.). *Psykoanalyysin uranuurtajat Suomessa*, pp. 161–168. Kemijärvi: LPT Lapin Painotuote Oy.

King, Pearl (2003). (Ed.). *No Ordinary Psychoanalyst: The Exceptional Contributions of John Rickman*. London: H. Karnac (Books).

King, Pearl (2003). Introduction: The Rediscovery of John Rickman and His Work. In Pearl King (Ed.). *No Ordinary Psychoanalyst: The Exceptional Contributions of John Rickman*, pp. 1–68. London: H. Karnac (Books).

King, Pearl (2005). *Time Present and Time Past: Selected Papers of Pearl King*. London: Karnac Books.

King, Pearl (2005). Foreword. In Roger Willoughby. *Masud Khan: The Myth and the Reality*, pp. x–xix. London: Free Association Books.

King, Pearl, and Steiner, Riccardo (Eds.). (1991). *The Freud–Klein Controversies: 1941–45*. London: Tavistock/Routledge.

Klein, Melanie (1932). *Die Psychoanalyse des Kindes*. Vienna: Internationaler Psychoanalytischer Verlag.

Klein, Melanie (1932). *The Psycho-Analysis of Children*. Alix Strachey (Transl.). London: Hogarth Press and the Institute of Psycho-Analysis.

Klein, Melanie (1935). A Contribution to the Psychogenesis of Manic-Depressive States. *International Journal of Psycho-Analysis, 16*, 145–174.

Klein, Melanie (1937). Love, Guilt and Reparation. In Melanie Klein and Joan Riviere. *Love, Hate and Reparation: Two Lectures*, pp. 57–119. London: Leonard and Virginia Woolf at the Hogarth Press, and the Institute of Psycho-Analysis.

Klein, Melanie (1946). Notes on Schizoid Mechanisms. *International Journal of Psycho-Analysis, 27*, 99–110.

Klein, Melanie (1948). *Contributions to Psycho-Analysis: 1921–1945*. London: Hogarth Press and the Institute of Psycho-Analysis.

Klein, Melanie (1950). On the Criteria for the Termination of a Psycho-Analysis. *International Journal of Psycho-Analysis, 31*, 78–80.

Klein, Melanie (1957). *Envy and Gratitude: A Study of Unconscious Sources*. London: Tavistock Publications.

Klein, Melanie (1959). Our Adult World and Its Roots in Infancy. *Human Relations, 12*, 291–303.

Klein, Melanie (1961). *Narrative of a Child Analysis: The Conduct of the Psycho-Analysis of Children as Seen in the Treatment of a Ten Year Old Boy*. London: Hogarth Press and the Institute of Psycho-Analysis.

Laing, Ronald D. (1960). *The Divided Self: A Study of Sanity and Madness*. London: Tavistock Publications.

Mahler, Margaret S. (1979). *The Selected Papers of Margaret S. Mahler, M.D.: Volume 1. Infantile Psychosis and Early Contributions*. New York: Jason Aronson.

Mahler, Margaret S. (1979). *The Selected Papers of Margaret S. Mahler, M.D.: Volume 2. Separation-Individuation*. New York: Jason Aronson.

Mahler, Margaret S., Pine, Fred, and Bergman, Anni (1975). *The Psychological Birth of the Human Infant: Symbiosis and Individuation*. New York: Basic Books.

Meltzer, Donald (1973). *Sexual States of Mind*. Ballinluig, Perthshire: Clunie Press.

Meltzer, Donald (1978). *The Kleinian Development: Part I. Freud's Clinical Development. Part II. Richard Week-by-Week. Part III. The Clinical Significance of the Work of Bion*. Strath Tay, Perthshire: Clunie Press.

Meltzer, Donald (1992). *The Claustrum: An Investigation of Claustrophobic Phenomena*. Oxford: Clunie Press.

Meltzer, Donald (1994). *Sincerity and Other Works: Collected Papers of Donald Meltzer*. Alberto Hahn (Ed.). London: H. Karnac (Books).

Miller, Arthur (1963). *Jane's Blanket*. New York: Crowell-Collier Press, and London: Collier-Macmillan.

Milner, Marion (1938). *The Human Problem in Schools: A Psychological Study Carried Out on Behalf of the Girls' Public Day School Trust*. London: Methuen and Company.

Milner, Marion (1952). Aspects of Symbolism in Comprehension of the Not-Self. *International Journal of Psycho-Analysis, 33*, 181–195.

Milner, Marion (1956). The Communication of Primary Sensual Experience: (The Yell of Joy). *International Journal of Psycho-Analysis, 37*, 278–281.

Milner, Marion (1969). *The Hands of the Living God: An Account of a Psychoanalytic Treatment*. London: Hogarth Press and the Institute of Psycho-Analysis.

Milner, Marion (1987). *Eternity's Sunrise: A Way of Keeping a Diary*. London: Virago Press.

Milner, Marion (1987). *The Suppressed Madness of Sane Men: Forty-Four Years of Exploring Psychoanalysis*. London: Tavistock Publications.

Pfister, Oskar (1913). *Die psychanalytische Methode: Eine erfahrungswissenschaftlich-systematische Darstellung*. Leipzig: Julius Klinkhardt.

Pfister, Oskar (1917). *The Psychoanalytic Method*. Charles Rockwell Payne (Transl.). London: Kegan Paul, Trench, Trubner and Company.

Rank, Otto (1924). *Das Trauma der Geburt und seine Bedeutung für die Psychoanalyse*. Vienna: Internationaler Psychoanalytischer Verlag.

Rank, Otto (1929). *The Trauma of Birth*. London: Kegan Paul, Trench, Trubner and Company, and New York: Harcourt, Brace and Company.

Rickman, John (Ed.). (1940). *Children in War-Time: The Uprooted Child, the Problem of the Young Child, the Deprived Mother, Foster-Parents, Visiting, the Teacher's Problems, Homes for Difficult Children*. London: New Education Fellowship.

Rickman, John (1957). *Selected Contributions to Psycho-Analysis*. W. Clifford M. Scott (Ed.). London: Hogarth Press and the Institute of Psycho-Analysis.

Riviere, Joan (1929). Womanliness as a Masquerade. *International Journal of Psycho-Analysis, 10*, 303–313.

Riviere, Joan (1936). A Contribution to the Analysis of the Negative Therapeutic Reaction. *International Journal of Psycho-Analysis, 17*, 304–320.

Roazen, Paul (1969). *Brother Animal: The Story of Freud and Tausk*. New York: Alfred A. Knopf.

Roazen, Paul (1975). *Freud and His Followers*. New York: Alfred A. Knopf.

Roazen, Paul (1985). *Helene Deutsch: A Psychoanalyst's Life*. Garden City, New York: Anchor Press/Doubleday.

Roazen, Paul (1993). *Meeting Freud's Family*. Amherst, Massachusetts: University of Massachusetts Press.

Roazen, Paul (1995). *How Freud Worked: First-Hand Accounts of Patients*. Northvale, New Jersey: Jason Aronson.

Roazen, Paul (Ed.). (1995). Oral History of Sandor Rado. In Paul Roazen and Bluma Swerdloff. *Heresy: Sandor Rado and the Psychoanalytic Movement*, pp. 19–174. Northvale, New Jersey: Jason Aronson.

Roazen, Paul (2000). *Oedipus in Britain: Edward Glover and the Struggle Over Klein*. New York: Other Press.

Roazen, Paul (2001). *The Historiography of Psychoanalysis*. New Brunswick, New Jersey: Transaction Publishers.

Roazen, Paul (2002). A Meeting with Donald Winnicott in 1965. In Brett Kahr (Ed.). *The Legacy of Winnicott: Essays on Infant and Child Mental Health*, pp. 23–35. London: H. Karnac (Books).

Roazen, Paul (2005). *Edoardo Weiss: The House That Freud Built*. New Brunswick, New Jersey: Transaction Publishers.

Roazen, Paul, and Swerdloff, Bluma (Eds.). (1995). *Heresy: Sandor Rado and the Psychoanalytic Movement*. Northvale, New Jersey: Jason Aronson.

Sargant, William, and Slater, Eliot (1944). *An Introduction to Physical Methods of Treatment in Psychiatry*. Edinburgh: E. and S. Livingstone.

Sharpe, Ella Freeman (1937). *Dream Analysis: A Practical Handbook for Psycho-Analysts*. London: Leonard and Virginia Woolf at the Hogarth Press, and the Institute of Psycho-Analysis.

Sharpe, Ella Freeman (1950). *Collected Papers on Psycho-Analysis*. Marjorie Brierley (Ed.). London: Hogarth Press and the Institute of Psycho-Analysis.

Stephen, Adrian (1936). *The "Dreadnought" Hoax*. London: Leonard and Virginia Woolf at the Hogarth Press.

Strachey, James (1934). The Nature of the Therapeutic Action of Psycho-Analysis. *International Journal of Psycho-Analysis, 15*, 127–159.

Strachey, Lytton (1918). *Eminent Victorians: Cardinal Manning – Florence Nightingale – Dr. Arnold – General Gordon*. London: Chatto & Windus.

Wesley, John (1747). *Primitive Phyfick or, an Eafy and Natural Method of Curing Moft Difeafes*. Holborn, London: Thomas Trye.

Winnicott, Clare (1963). Face to Face with Children. In Joan F. S. King (Ed.). *New Thinking for Changing Needs*, pp. 28–50. London: Education Sub-Committee, Association of Social Workers.

Winnicott, Clare (1964). Development Towards Self Awareness. In Frederick G. Lennhoff (Ed.). *Challenges, Frustrations, Rewards for Those Who Work with People in Need*, pp. 3–10. Harmer Hill, Shrewsbury, Shropshire: Shotton Hall Publication.

Winnicott, Clare (1978). D.W.W.: A Reflection. In Simon A. Grolnick, Leonard Barkin, and Werner Muensterberger (Eds.). *Between Reality and Fantasy: Transitional Objects and Phenomena*, pp. 17–33. New York: Jason Aronson.

Winnicott, Clare (1980). Fear of Breakdown: A Clinical Example. *International Journal of Psycho-Analysis*, *61*, 351–357.

Winnicott, Clare (1984). Introduction. In Donald W. Winnicott. *Deprivation and Delinquency*. Clare Winnicott, Ray Shepherd, and Madeleine Davis (Eds.), pp. 1–5. London: Tavistock Publications.

Winnicott, Clare (1988). Preface. In Donald W. Winnicott. *Human Nature*. Christopher Bollas, Madeleine Davis, and Ray Shepherd (Eds.), p. ix. London: Free Association Books.

Winnicott, Clare (2004). *Face to Face with Children: The Life and Work of Clare Winnicott*. Joel Kanter (Ed.). London: H. Karnac (Books).

Winnicott, Donald W. (1931). *Clinical Notes on Disorders of Childhood*. London: William Heinemann (Medical Books).

Winnicott, Donald W. (1935). The Manic Defence. In Donald W. Winnicott (1958). *Collected Papers: Through Paediatrics to Psycho-Analysis*, pp. 129–144. London: Tavistock Publications.

Winnicott, Donald W. (1945). *Getting to Know Your Baby*. London: William Heinemann (Medical Books).

Winnicott, Donald W. (1945). Primitive Emotional Development. *International Journal of Psycho-Analysis*, *26*, 137–143.

Winnicott, Donald W. (1949). *The Ordinary Devoted Mother and Her Baby: Nine Broadcast Talks. (Autumn 1949.)* London: C.A. Brock and Company.

Winnicott, Donald W. (1949). Hate in the Counter-Transference. *International Journal of Psycho-Analysis*, *30*, 69–74.

Winnicott, Donald W. (1949). Birth Memories, Birth Trauma, and Anxiety. In Donald W. Winnicott (1958). *Collected Papers: Through Paediatrics to Psycho-Analysis*, pp. 174–193. London: Tavistock Publications.

Winnicott, Donald W. (1953). Transitional Objects and Transitional Phenomena: A Study of the First Not-Me Possession. *International Journal of Psycho-Analysis*, *34*, 89–97.

Winnicott, Donald W. (1953). Psychoses and Child Care. *British Journal of Medical Psychology*, *26*, 68–74.

Winnicott, Donald W. (1956). Primary Maternal Preoccupation. In Donald W. Winnicott (1958). *Collected Papers: Through Paediatrics to Psycho-Analysis*, pp. 300–305. London: Tavistock Publications.

Winnicott, Donald W. (1957). *The Child and the Family: First Relationships*. Janet Hardenberg (Ed.). London: Tavistock Publications.

Winnicott, Donald W. (1957). *The Child and the Outside World: Studies in*

Developing Relationships. Janet Hardenberg (Ed.). London: Tavistock Publications.

Winnicott, Donald W. (1958). *Collected Papers: Through Paediatrics to Psycho-Analysis.* London: Tavistock Publications.

Winnicott, Donald W. (1958). The Capacity to Be Alone. *International Journal of Psycho-Analysis, 39,* 416–420.

Winnicott, Donald W. (1958). Child Analysis. *A Criança Portuguesa, 17,* 219–229.

Winnicott, Donald W. (1958). Child Analysis in the Latency Period. In Donald W. Winnicott (1965). *The Maturational Processes and the Facilitating Environment: Studies in the Theory of Emotional Development,* pp. 115–123. London: Hogarth Press and the Institute of Psycho-Analysis.

Winnicott, Donald W. (1960). The Theory of the Parent–Infant Relationship. *International Journal of Psycho-Analysis, 41,* 585–595.

Winnicott, Donald W. (1960). Ego Distortion in Terms of True and False Self. In Donald W. Winnicott (1965). *The Maturational Processes and the Facilitating Environment: Studies in the Theory of Emotional Development,* pp. 140–152. London: Hogarth Press and the Institute of Psycho-Analysis.

Winnicott, Donald W. (1962). Ego Integration in Child Development. In Donald W. Winnicott (1965). *The Maturational Processes and the Facilitating Environment: Studies in the Theory of Emotional Development,* pp. 56–63. London: Hogarth Press and the Institute of Psycho-Analysis.

Winnicott, Donald W. (1962). The Aims of Psycho-Analytical Treatment. In Donald W. Winnicott (1965). *The Maturational Processes and the Facilitating Environment: Studies in the Theory of Emotional Development,* pp. 166–170. London: Hogarth Press and the Institute of Psycho-Analysis.

Winnicott, Donald W. (1963). Dependence in Infant Care, in Child Care, and in the Psycho-Analytic Setting. *International Journal of Psycho-Analysis, 44,* 339–344.

Winnicott, Donald W. (1963). Communicating and Not Communicating Leading to a Study of Certain Opposites. In Donald W. Winnicott (1965). *The Maturational Processes and the Facilitating Environment: Studies in the Theory of Emotional Development,* pp. 179–192. London: Hogarth Press and the Institute of Psycho-Analysis.

Winnicott, Donald W. (1964). *The Child, the Family, and the Outside World.* Harmondsworth, Middlesex: Penguin Books.

Winnicott, Donald W. (1964). The Concept of the False Self. In Donald W. Winnicott (1986). *Home Is Where We Start From: Essays by a Psychoanalyst.* Clare Winnicott, Ray Shepherd, and Madeleine Davis (Eds.), pp. 65–70. New York: W. W. Norton & Company.

Winnicott, Donald W. (1965). The Price of Disregarding Research Findings. In *The Price of Mental Health*, pp. 34–41. London: National Association for Mental Health.

Winnicott, Donald W. (1965). The Price of Disregarding Psychoanalytic Research. In Donald W. Winnicott (1986). *Home Is Where We Start From: Essays by a Psychoanalyst.* Clare Winnicott, Ray Shepherd, and Madeleine Davis (Eds.), pp. 172–182. New York: W. W. Norton & Company.

Winnicott, Donald W. (1966). The Location of Cultural Experience. *Scientific Bulletin: The British Psycho-Analytical Society and the Institute of Psycho-Analysis, 9*, 1–8.

Winnicott, Donald W. (1967). The Location of Cultural Experience. *International Journal of Psycho-Analysis, 48*, 368–372.

Winnicott, Donald W. (1969). James Strachey: 1887–1967. *International Journal of Psycho-Analysis, 50*, 129–131.

Winnicott, Donald W. (1969). The Use of an Object. *International Journal of Psycho-Analysis, 50*, 711–716.

Winnicott, Donald W. (1971). *Playing and Reality.* London: Tavistock Publications.

Winnicott, Donald W. (1977). *The Piggle: An Account of the Psychoanalytic Treatment of a Little Girl.* Ishak Ramzy (Ed.). New York: International Universities Press.

Winnicott, Donald W. (1988). *Human Nature.* Christopher Bollas, Madeleine Davis, and Ray Shepherd (Eds.). London: Free Association Books.

Winnicott, Donald W. (1993). *Talking to Parents.* Clare Winnicott, Christopher Bollas, Madeleine Davis, and Ray Shepherd (Eds.). Reading, Massachusetts: Addison-Wesley Publishing Company.

INDEX